The Gen X Series

ENGLISH OLYMPIAD 10

Useful for English Olympiads Conducted at School, National & International Levels

Author
Sahil Gupta

Peer Reviewer
P. Shyamla

Strictly According to the Latest Syllabus of English Olympiad

V&S PUBLISHERS

Published by:

F-2/16, Ansari road, Daryaganj, New Delhi-110002
☎ 23240026, 23240027 • *Fax:* 011-23240028
✉ info@vspublishers.com • 🌐 www.vspublishers.com

Online Brandstore: amazon.in/vspublishers

Regional Office : Hyderabad
5-1-707/1, Brij Bhawan (Beside Central Bank of India Lane)
Bank Street, Koti, Hyderabad - 500 095
☎ 040-24737290
✉ vspublishershyd@gmail.com

Follow us on:

BUY OUR BOOKS FROM: | AMAZON | | FLIPKART |

© Copyright: *V&S PUBLISHERS*
ISBN 978-93-579407-8-8
New Edition

DISCLAIMER

While every attempt has been made to provide accurate and timely information in this book, neither the author nor the publisher assumes any responsibility for errors, unintended omissions or commissions detected therein. The author and publisher makes no representation or warranty with respect to the comprehensiveness or completeness of the contents provided.

All matters included have been simplified under professional guidance for general information only, without any warranty for applicability on an individual. Any mention of an organization or a website in the book, by way of citation or as a source of additional information, doesn't imply the endorsement of the content either by the author or the publisher. It is possible that websites cited may have changed or removed between the time of editing and publishing the book.

Results from using the expert opinion in this book will be totally dependent on individual circumstances and factors beyond the control of the author and the publisher.

It makes sense to elicit advice from well informed sources before implementing the ideas given in the book. The reader assumes full responsibility for the consequences arising out from reading this book.

For proper guidance, it is advisable to read the book under the watchful eyes of parents/guardian. The buyer of this book assumes all responsibility for the use of given materials and information.

The copyright of the entire content of this book rests with the author/publisher. Any infringement/transmission of the cover design, text or illustrations, in any form, by any means, by any entity will invite legal action and be responsible for consequences thereon.

Publisher's Note

General Trade and Mass Appeal books across various genres have helped **V&S Publishers** to gain widespread popularity. In a short span of 10 years, we have successfully published more than 1000 titles across 9 languages in our 50 subject categories. Being into the publishing business for about 40 years, we have always been a dynamic publishing house, with a massive distribution network, across India; including E-commerce platforms.

Understanding the need of inculcating knowledge and developing a spirit of healthy competition amongst students to make them ready for the world outside schools and colleges; we created Olympiad Series under the **GEN X SERIES Imprint** which, owning to its rich content and unique representation became popular amongst students, in no time. The motivation is not to improve marks in terms of numbers, but is to make sure that the students are already prepared to face competitive environment with respect to college admissions and cracking various entrance examinations, while ensuring their conceptual clarity.

Published for classes 1-10 across subjects English, Mathematics, Science, Computers, General Knowledge, the books are unlike any other in the market and are written in a guidebook pattern and exhaustively include examples and Multiple-Choice Questions.

Here, we present the latest Edition of **ENGLISH OLYMPIAD CLASS 10.**

Unique Features of the book are as follows:
- Authored by Subject Matter Experts' and Peer reviewed by School Principals and HOD's for the respective subjects
- Books based on principles of Applied Psychology and Bloom's Taxonomy
- Suited for Olympiad Examinations held at School level, National level & International Level irrespective of organizing body.
- The only Olympiad Book in India written in Guidebook Pattern with Concise Theory, images and illustrations.
- Exhaustively include Examples, MCQs, Subjective Questions, and HOTS with Answer Keys & Solutions.
- Multiple Model Papers for thorough practice also given inside the book with solutions.
- OMR sheets appended at the end of the book for simulating exam environment.

Besides, we are also planning to launch an App very soon for the Olympiad preparation which further testifies our constant endeavor to keep up with student demands. We have made sure to closely follow syllabus patterns of not only Olympiad conducting bodies but also education boards & organizations like CBSE and NCERT, to make sure that our books prove useful to students; helping them to boost their academic performance in schools as well.

P.S. While every care has been taken to ensure the correctness of the content, if you come across any error, howsoever minor, do not hesitate to discuss with teachers while pointing that out to us in no uncertain terms.

We wish you All the Best!

DISTINCTIVE

WHY OLYMPIADS?
Olympiads are just like competitive exams; conducted by various bodies at national and international levels. The aim is to experience a competitive examination at the school level and also to help students to discover their interest acrss subjects like English, Mathematics, Science and General Knowledge.

WHY V&S OLYMPIADS?
We at V&S Publishers aim to build an avid-reading student audience. Hence, our resolve is to follow an innovative pedagogic pattern which would help students to navigate through the book with utmost ease and comfort. Crisp theory practical examples and illustrations keep our book interactive and comprehensive.

01 LEARNING OBJECTIVES
They list the whole chapter as subtopics, helping the teachers to guide children in a step-by-step manner.

02 DID YOU KNOW
Enhance your knowledge by getting acquainted with some amazing facts across various subjects like science, Mathematics and English.

03 MULTIPLE CHOICE QUESTIONS
MCQs act as an excellent learning aid, helping you to understand and work on your mistakes.

04 THINGS TO REMEMBER
A quick recap of the chapter in a summarized format helps in faster revision along with conceptual clarity.

05 HOTS
The High Order Thinking Questions aim to help the student to solve Application-based questions and gain practical understanding of the subject.

FEATURES

06 SUBJECTIVE QUESTIONS
Help to place the knowledge gained in orderly fashion by using **"WH"** questions, mostly in the form of bullet points.

07 ACHIEVER'S SECTION
Offers a quick revision of the book along with some new facts for the students to discover.

08 A SET OF OMR SHEETS
To allow the student to practice question in an exam-like format which would help them to get the "feel" of how Olympiad exams take place.

09 MODEL TEST PAPERS
Two model test papers are provided at the end of each book, which help the student to test the knowledge which they have gained after thorough reading of all chapters.

10 ANSWER KEY & SOLUTION
Detailed Answer Key along with explanations aid the pupil to indentify, understand the mistakes they make during the course of Olympiad preparation.

COMPLEMENT SCHOOL SYLLABI

The syllabi across all Olympiad examination closely follow the pattern of academic books. Hence, they not only provide a competitive examination experience, but also help to revise topics for school examinations as well, while strengthening conceptual precision.

ENHANCEMENT OF ANALYTICAL & LOGICAL REASONING

Practicing analytical ability questions, not only helps in developing intellectual ability but also plays a vital role in building critical thinking ability which helps an individual to think about a question or a crisis like situation in day to day life; from all aspects and directions.

Note to Parents

Dear Parents,

Olympiad examinations come with a plethora of advantages. First and foremost among such advantages is the application of knowledge studied, in the form of multiple-choice questions. It helps the child not only to step away from rote learning, but also helps them to exhibit their competencies across various subjects.

In addition to this, Olympiads help the student to understand the importance of revision and practice, and to imbibe upon these practices; which also prove useful in academic performance of the child.

The Olympiads are conducted across multiple subjects, and help the child to recognize their field of interest, thereby encouraging the students to make a career in the field where they can excel the most.

However, cognitive development of a child is not just limited to the four walls of classroom. Following steps can be encouraged by you, to ensure their ward is able to grasp various concepts with ease or lesser difficulty:

- **Eat a balanced diet:** Ensure intake of vitamins and minerals to keep you active. Include fruits and super foods like millet in your diet to ensure healthy functioning of organs. Huge intake of junk food should be avoided.
- **Indulge in outdoor activities:** Outdoor games break the monotony of life. Play your heart out in greenery to keep yourself alert, active and fit.
- **Sleep well:** A sound sleep of 7-8 hours refreshes the brain and makes it ready to understand new topics with more clarity. A sleep derived person faces difficulty in doing even the simplest tasks of day to day life.
- **Reduce your Screen time:** More screen time leads to not only weakening of eyesight but decreases concentration span. Regulated Screen time should be encouraged
- **Do not hesitate to raise a hand:** Having a doubt in class? Do not hesitate to ask your parents or teachers. This ensures more Conceptual Clarity and hence leads to Application based understanding of various subjects and topics.
- **Teach and Learn:** No need to do rote-learning. Once you understand a topic teach or explain it to your friends, siblings and parents. It brings clarity and ensures the child does his revision this way.
- **Keep smiling:** A positive attitude promotes a growth mindset and encourages the child to be more inquisitive and try to learn something new, everyday!

HAPPY LEARNING!

Contents

SECTION 1: WORD AND STRUCTURE KNOWLEDGE

1. Noun — 9
2. Adjective — 14
3. Articles and Prepositions — 21
4. Verbs, Adverbs, Phrasal Verbs and Modals — 31
5. Conjunction — 63
6. Punctuations — 70
7. Tenses — 84
8. Conditionals — 103
9. Voice and Narration — 110
10. Spelling, Analogy and Collocations — 122
11. Synonyms, Antonyms, Homophones and Homonyms — 132
12. One Word — 144
13. Idioms — 151
14. Question Tags — 159

SECTION 2: READING COMPREHENSION

Comprehension — 64

SECTION 3: SPOKEN AND WRITTEN EXPRESSIONS

Giving and Accepting Compliments — 173

SECTION 4: ACHIEVERS' SECTION

Some Thoughtful Questions — 176
Subjective Section — 181
Model Test Paper–1 — 194
Model Test Paper–2 — 196

ANSWER KEYS (Access Content online on Dropbox) — 198
Appendix — 213

SECTION 1
WORD AND STRUCTURE KNOWLEDGE

Noun

Learning Objectives : In this chapter, students will learn about:
- Types of Noun
- Uses of Noun

CHAPTER SUMMARY

A noun is the name of a person, place, thing, or idea. Whatever we see, can be named, and that name is a noun. A proper noun, is the name of a specific person, place, or thing. (Carlos, Middle East, Jerusalem, Malaysia, God, Spanish, Buddhism, the Republican Party). It is generally capitalized. A proper noun used as an addressed person's name is called a noun of address. Common nouns name everything else, things that usually are not capitalized.

Types of Noun
There are two main types of noun.
(i) Common Noun
(ii) Proper Noun

Common Noun
Name of a common or a non-specific thing, place, or person is called common noun.

Common noun refers to a non-specific or non-particular thing, place or person in class or group.

Example:
book, pen, room, gardener, girl, road, camera, month, day, chair, school, boy and car are common nouns because each of these nouns refers to a common thing, place or person. It is never capitalized unless it is the beginning of a sentence.

Proper Noun
Name of a particular or a specific thing, place or person is called proper noun.

Example:
BMW car, April, Monday, Oxford University, New York, America, John, Newton, Einstein and R.H Stephen are proper nouns because each of these nouns refers to a particular thing, place or person.

If a common noun is specified, it becomes a proper noun.

Example:
"Day" is a common noun but if it is specified like Monday or Friday, it becomes proper noun. Similarly, car is a common noun but if it is specified like BMW car, it becomes proper noun.

Use of Capital Letter for Proper Noun
The first letter of a proper noun is always written in capital letter.

Example:
(a) He lives in Paris.
(b) She studies in Oxford University.
(c) The author of this book is John Stephen.
(d) The laws of motion were presented by Newton.
(e) The richest person of the world is Bill Gates.

Uses of 'The' for Proper Noun
☞ The article 'the' is used before some proper nouns. Here are some rules for the use of article 'the' before proper nouns.

☞ Article 'the' is not used before the name of countries, cities.
Example:
New York, Mexico, Canada, Toronto, London, Paris, America. But, if the name of country or city or place expresses group of places or lands or states, then article 'the' will be used before it.
The Philippines, the Netherlands, the United States.

☞ Article 'the' is not used before the name of universities.
Example:
Oxford University, Yale University, or Columbia University. But if the name of university is written in an order that it includes the word 'of' then article 'the' will be used before it.
The University of British Colombia, the university of Oxford, the University of Toronto.

☞ Article 'the' is used before names composed of both common noun and proper noun.
Example:
The New York city, the Dominion of Canada, the River Nile.

☞ 'The' is used before the names of laws, principles, theories or devices.
Example:
The Pythagorean Theorem, the Fahrenheit Scale, the Law of Newton, the Allais effect. But, if the proper noun is used in possessive form, no article will be used.
Newton's Laws of Motion, Hooke's Law of Elasticity, Dalton's Law of Partial Pressures.

☞ 'The' is used before the name of ocean, sea, river, desert or forest (except lakes and fall)
Example:
The Pacific Ocean, the Mediterranean Sea, the Sahara, the Black Forests.

☞ 'The' is used before the names of buildings, hotels, libraries having particular names.
Example:
The Brunel Hotel, the Lahore Museum, the Library of Congress.

☞ 'The' is used before the name of a geographical region and point on globe.
Example:
The Middle East, the West, the Equator, the North Pole.

☞ 'The' is usually used before the names of organizations.
Example:
The Association of Chartered Accountants, the World Health Organization.

Countable and Uncountable Nouns

Countable Nouns

A noun which can be counted is called countable noun.

Pen is a countable noun because we can count it and can say one pen, two pens, three pens or more pens. Pen, chair, cup, room, man, baby, bottle, dog, and cat are examples of countable nouns.

TRIVIA

"Rhythms" is the longest English word without the normal vowels, a, e, i, o, or u.

Singular and Plural Noun (Countable Noun)

Singular Noun (Countable Noun): A countable noun can be singular as well as plural. Article 'a' or 'an' is used before singular noun but not before plural noun.

If a singular noun starts with consonant letter then 'a' is used before it, i.e. a book, a cat, a pen. If a singular noun starts with a vowel letter or with consonant which sounds like vowel in that word, 'an' is used before it i.e. an apple, an umbrella, an onion, an hour.

Plural Noun (Countable Noun): Plural noun means more than one person, place or thing. The word 'chair' is a singular noun but the word 'chairs' is a plural noun.

Plurals are usually formed by adding –s or –es to singular nouns, for example: book–books, cat–cats, box–boxes, tax–taxes. If a word ends with 'y', the 'y' is changed to 'i' then –es is added to make it plural.

Example:
baby–babies, lady–ladies. There may be some exceptions.

Some plurals are formed in different ways, for example: man–men, child–children, leaf–leaves, wife–wives, foot–feet, toot–teeth, datum–data, basis–bases. Such plurals are called irregular plural forms.

Some nouns have same plural and singular forms.

Example:
sheep–sheep, deer–deer, swine–swine.

Uncountable Nouns
Uncountable noun refers to things which cannot be counted. For example, water is an uncountable noun because we cannot count it. We cannot say, one water or two water. Such substances, which cannot be counted in terms of numbers, are called uncountable nouns.

Example:
Water, milk, bread, honey, rain, furniture, news, information, pleasure, honesty, courage, weather, music, preparation, warmth, wheat. They are all examples of uncountable nouns.

Uses of Uncountable Nouns
- Uncountable nouns are usually treated as singular nouns for auxiliary verbs in sentence and articles "a or an" are usually not used before uncountable nouns.
  Example:
  (a) Water maintains its level.
  (b) Necessity is the mother of invention.
  (c) His preparation was not good.
  (d) The weather is very pleasant today.
  (e) This information is very helpful in solving the problem.
  (f) The warmth of sun causes evaporation of water.
- Uncountable nouns may be used as countable nouns when they refer to an individual thing.
  Example:

Life is an uncountable noun but it is used as a countable noun if it refers to individual or lives.

It was feared that two lives had been lost.
- We can also use words like, some, any, no, little, more, etc., before uncountable nouns, if needed, in a sentence.
  Example:
  They have no information about the accused.
  There is little milk in the glass.

Changing Uncountable Nouns into Countable Nouns
We can change an uncountable noun into a countable noun if we specify a unit or measuring standard for it. For example water is an uncountable noun but we can make it countable by saying 'one glass of water' or 'two glasses of water,' etc. In this example, we selected a unit that is glass. We can also say 'one litre of water' or 'one cup of water,' etc. By selecting such units or measuring standards, we can change an uncountable noun into a countable, which can be counted in terms of numbers.

Example:
Uncountable – countable
Bread – a piece of bread
Wheat – a grain of wheat
Milk – a glass of milk
Information – a piece of information

Eight uses of a Noun
- **Subject of the Sentence:** The subject is the person, place, thing, or idea that the sentence is about.
  Example:
  The book was heavy.
- **Predicate Noun:** A predicate noun comes after the verb to be or a linking verb that replaces or means the same thing as the subject of the sentence.
  Example:
  My brother is the clown.

- **Appositive:** An appositive is a word or phrase that comes after another word. It explains, identifies, or gives information about that word. The appositive is set off from the sentence by one or two commas.
  Example:
  Our teacher, Mr. Ford, taught us English.
- **Direct Object of a Verb:** The direct object is the person, place, thing, or idea that receives the action of the verb.
  Example:
  Jack slammed the door.
- **Indirect Object of a Verb:** The indirect object receives the action of the verb indirectly.
  Our teacher gave us a gift.
- **Object of the Preposition:** A preposition is a word that shows location, movement, or direction. Common ones are in, on, with, under for, and by. A preposition is always followed by a noun or pronoun that is called the object of the preposition. Together, they form a prepositional phrase.
  Example:
  over the house
  under the highway
- **Object Complement:** An object complement is a word that completes the meaning of a direct object. It is used when the direct object would not make complete sense by itself.
  Example:
  I named my cat Garfield.
- **To show Possession:** A possessive noun tells who or what owns something.
  Example:
  Hawaii's volcanoes are still active.

MUST REMEMBER

→ Whatever we see, can be named, and that name is a noun.
→ A proper noun used as an addressed person's name is called a noun of address.
→ Common noun refers to a non-specific or non-particular thing, place or person in class or group.
→ Name of a particular or a specific thing, place or person is called proper noun.

PRACTICE EXERCISE

I. Identify whether the underlined nouns are common or proper.
1. My <u>sister</u> is a doctor.
2. A <u>teacher</u> must have patience.
3. The first game of basketball was played in <u>Massachusetts</u>.
4. I didn't believe the <u>girl's</u> story.
5. He worked at the <u>YMCA Training School</u>.
6. Not all cricketers in this team are <u>Indians</u>.
7. James is a bright <u>student</u>.
8. He went to a college in <u>Seattle</u>.
9. <u>Solomon</u> was famous for his wisdom.
10. A <u>player</u> must not run with the ball.

II. Write whether the underlined nouns are countable or uncountable.
1. I drink <u>milk</u> twice a day.
2. My mother puts <u>butter</u> on my bread slices.
3. Today traffic <u>policemen</u> are organizing a traffic awareness event.
4. Can you give me some <u>juice</u> please?
5. I have finished my <u>exercises</u>.
6. I have already filled up five <u>buckets</u> with water.
7. In summers, you should drink lots of <u>water</u> to avoid dehydration.
8. Only qualified <u>candidates</u> are allowed to attend this seminar.
9. My mother prepares delicious <u>bread</u>.
10. There's a hike in the price of <u>oil</u>.

HOTS

Fill in the blanks with the noun form of the words provided.
1. Please take the teacher's _____ (permit) to participate in NCC.
2. It is my firm _____ (believe) that you will win the match.
3. Her English is very bad. She must make _____ (improve)
4. The witness can provide lot of _____ (inform) about the incident.
5. I find _____ (happy) in small things of life.

Adjective **2**

Learning Objectives : In this chapter, students will learn about:
- Basic concept of Adjectives
- Types of Adjectives

CHAPTER SUMMARY

Adjectives is a word that qualifies a noun or a pronoun. They describe nouns. They are also called noun-helpers.

Adjectives are a large class of words (for example, good, bad, new, accurate, careful) which define more precisely the reference of a noun or pronoun. An adjective gives more distinct meaning to a noun or a pronoun by describing or limiting it.

All adjectives answer three specific questions about the nouns or pronouns they are qualifying.

Example:
(i) What kind? _____ strong, cheerful, red
(ii) Which one(s)? _____ this, that, these, those
(iii) How many? _____ few, some, three, several

How to Spell Adjectives?

Adjectives have different suffixes. Many adjectives are created simply by adding certain suffixes to words that were previously nouns or verbs.

☞ Some adjectives end with suffix -'ful'. These adjectives describe noun or pronouns that are full of something or have a lot of something.
Example:
Joyful: a joyful smile
Beautiful: a beautiful face
Careful: a careful student
Cheerful: a cheerful baby
Powerful: a powerful machine
Wonderful: a wonderful time
Colourful: colourful clothes
Useful: a useful book
Skilful: a skilful player

☞ Some adjectives end in suffix '-ous'.
Example:
Mountainous: a mountainous area
Famous: a famous writer
Dangerous: a dangerous job
Poisonous: a poisonous snake
Humorous: a humorous film
Generous: a generous gift

☞ Some adjectives end with the letter 'y'.
Example:
Sunny: a sunny day
Noisy: a noisy car
Dirty: dirty hands
Easy: an easy test
Cloudy: a cloudy sky
Stormy: stormy weather

☞ Some adjectives end with the suffix 'less'. These adjectives describe a person or thing that does not have something.
Example:
Meaningless: a meaningless word
Sleeveless: a sleeveless dress
Fearless: a fearless fighter
Careless: a careless driver
Cloudless: a cloudless sky
Seedless: seedless grapes

☞ Some adjectives end with the suffix '-al'.
Example:
Actual: the actual story
Final: final victory
General: general health
Mental: mental health
Physical: physical education
Special: special treatment

☞ Here are some adjectives that end with '-ic', '-ish', '-ible', '-able', '-ive' and '-ly'.
Example:
Enthusiastic: enthusiastic shout
Comfortable: comfortable clothes
Expensive: expensive jewellery
Selfish: a selfish act
Likeable: a likeable child
Friendly: friendly teachers
Fantastic: a fantastic singer
Visible: visible footprints
Imaginative: an imaginative story

☞ Many adjectives end with the suffix '-ing'.
Example:
Smiling: a smiling face
Outstanding: an outstanding swimmer
Chattering: chattering monkeys
Loving: loving parents
Disappointing: a disappointing result
Caring: a caring nurse

☞ Many adjectives end with the suffix '-ed'.
Example:
Boiled: boiled eggs
Satisfied: satisfied customers
Wasted: wasted time
Excited: excited students
Reduced: reduced prices
Invited: invited guests

☞ Many adjectives end in -ar.
Example:
Familiar: familiar face
Particular: particular car
Popular: popular singer

Types of Adjectives

There are different types of adjectives based upon their effect on a noun and what they tell about the noun. There are five categories of adjectives:

I. Adjectives of Quality – Descriptive Adjectives

These adjectives are used to describe the nature of a noun. These adjectives show the kind, quality, color, shape, size of nouns or pronouns.

Example:
Honest, Kind, Large, Bulky, Beautiful, Ugly, etc.

New Delhi is a large city with many historical monuments.

Sheila is a beautiful woman.

II. Adjectives of Quantity – Quantitative Adjectives

These adjectives help to show the amount or the approximate amount of the noun or pronoun. These adjectives do not provide exact numbers; rather they tell us the amount of the noun in relative or whole terms.

Example:
All, Half, Many, Few, Little, No, Enough, Great, etc.

They have finished most of the rice.

Many people came to visit the fair.

III. Adjectives of Number

These adjectives are used to show the number of nouns and their place in an order. There are three different sections within adjectives of number; they are:

(a) **Definite Numeral Adjective**
Those which clearly denote an exact number of nouns or the order of the noun.
One, Two, Twenty, Thirty-Three, etc. also known as Cardinals.
First, Second, Third, Seventh, etc. also known as Ordinals.

(b) **Indefinite Numeral Adjective**
Those adjectives that do not give an exact numerical amount but just give a general idea of the amount.
Some, Many, Few, Any, Several, All, etc.
Example:
There were many people present at the meeting.

(c) **Distributive Numeral Adjective**
Those adjectives that are used to refer to individual nouns within the whole amount.
Either, Neither, Each, Another, Other, etc.
Example:
Taxes have to be paid by every employed citizen.

IV. Demonstrative Adjectives
These adjectives are used to point out or indicate a particular noun or pronoun using the adjectives - This, That, These and Those.
Example:
That bag belongs to Neil.
Try using this paintbrush in art class.
I really like those shoes.
These flowers are lovely.

Note:
When this, that, these, and those are followed by a noun, they are adjectives. When they appear without a noun following them, they are pronouns.
Example:
This house is for sale.
(Here, This is an adjective.)
This is for sale.
(Here, This is a pronoun.)

V. Interrogative Adjectives
These adjectives are used to ask questions about nouns or in relation to nouns; they are: Where, What, Which and Whose.
Example:
Where did he say he was going?
What assignment did I miss out on?
Which is your favourite author?
Whose pen is this?

VI. Possessive adjectives:-
Possessive adjectives express the state of possession of nouns and are placed before nouns and show possession. For example 'my', 'your', 'his', 'her', 'its', 'our', 'their etc are possessive adjectives.
Example:
1. My cottage is amidst the hills.
2. We most do our duty.

Forms of Adjectives: Degrees of Comparison
Adjectives come in three forms, also called degrees. An adjective in its normal or usual form is called a positive degree adjective. There are also the comparative and superlative degrees, which are used for comparison, as in the following examples:

Positive	Comparative	Superlative
Sweet	Sweeter	Sweetest
Bad	Worse	Worst
Efficient	More efficient	Most efficient

Degrees of Comparison are used when we compare one person or a thing with another.
Let us look at all the three Degrees of Comparison one by one.

Positive Degree
When we speak about only one person or thing, we use the Positive degree.
Example: This house is big.
☞ In this sentence, only one noun "This house" is being talked about.

Example:

He is a tall student. This flower is beautiful.

He is an intelligent boy.

☞ Each sentence mentioned above talks about only one noun.

Comparative Degree

When we compare two persons or two things with each other, we can use both the Positive degree and the Comparative degree.

Example:

(i) This house is bigger than that one. (Comparative degree)

This house is not as big as that one. (Positive degree)

The term 'bigger' is comparative version of the term 'big'.

Both these sentences convey the same meaning.

(ii) This flower is more beautiful than that. (Comparative)

This flower is not as beautiful as that. (Positive)

The term "more beautiful" is comparative version of the term 'beautiful'.

Both these sentences convey the same meaning.

(iii) He is more intelligent than this boy. (Comparative)

He is not as intelligent as this boy. (Positive)

The term 'more intelligent' is comparative version of the term 'intelligent'.

Both these sentences convey the same meaning.

(iv) He is taller than Mr. Hulas. (Comparative)

He is not as tall as Mr. Hulas. (Positive)

The term 'taller' is comparative version of the term 'tall'.

Both these sentences convey the same meaning.

When we compare more than two persons or things with one another, we can use all the three Positive, Comparative and Superlative degrees.

Example:

(i) This is the biggest house in this street. (Superlative)

This house is bigger than any other house in this street. (Comparative)

No other house in this street is as big as this one. (Positive)

The term 'biggest' is the superlative version of the term 'big'.

All the three sentences convey the same meaning.

(ii) This flower is the most beautiful one in this garden. (Superlative)

This flower is more beautiful than any other flower in this garden. (Comparative)

No other flower in this garden is as beautiful as this one. (Positive)

The term 'most beautiful' is the superlative version of the term 'beautiful'.

All the three sentences convey the same meaning.

(iii) He is the most intelligent boy in this class. (Superlative)

He is more intelligent than other boys in the class. (Comparative)

No other boy is as intelligent as this boy. (Positive)

The term 'most intelligent' is superlative version of the term 'intelligent'.

All these sentences convey the same meaning.

(iv) He is the tallest student in this class. (Superlative)

He is taller than other students in this class. (Comparative)

No other student is as tall as this student. (Positive)

The term 'tallest' is superlative version of the term 'tall'.

Note:

Degrees of comparison are applicable only to Adjectives and Adverbs. Nouns and verbs do not have Degrees of Comparisons

He is the tallest student in the class. (The term 'tallest' is an adjective.)

Adjective

Among the members of the group, Mr. Clinton speaks most effectively. (The term 'effectively' is an adverb.)

All the terms used in the above examples are either adjectives or adverbs.

TRIVIA

There is a word in the English language with only one vowel, which occurs five times: "indivisibility."

Adjectives That Follow Verbs

Pay special attention to adjectives that follow verbs. Sometimes, the adjective follows a verb, but it describes a noun or pronoun that comes before the verb.

Example:

These strawberries taste sour.

The pickles are salty.

☞ Adjectives are used either attributively or predicatively.

Example:

The boy is clever.

The problem is easy.

☞ Most adjectives come before the word they modify.

Example:

That is a cute puppy.

She likes a high school senior.

☞ In a nutshell, adjectives define nouns and give them characteristics to differentiate them from other nouns.

Example:

He was wearing a blue shirt.

☞ Here 'blue' is an adjective as it is describing the noun 'shirt' by answering the question 'what colour of shirt?'

Example:

There are seven rooms in the house.

Here 'seven' is also an adjective as it's telling the quantity/the number of the noun 'rooms', answering the question 'how many rooms?'.

So basically, the main function of an adjective is to qualify a noun or a pronoun so that it will become more specific and interesting. Instead of just one word, a group of words with a subject and a verb, can also function as an adjective. When this happens, the group of words is called an adjective clause.

Models of Degrees of Comparison

Model-1: 'The best':

Example:

(i) This is the best hotel in this area.

No other hotel is as better as this in this area.

No other hotel is as good as this one in this area.

(ii) Unemployment is the most serious problem faced by our country.

Unemployment is more serious than any other problem faced by our country.

No other problem faced by our country is as serious as unemployment.

Model-2: 'One of the best':

Example:

(i) Kolkata is one of the largest cities in India.

Kolkata is larger than many other cities in India.

Very few cities in India are as large as Kolkata.

(ii) Sachin Tendulkar is one of the best batsmen in the world.

Sachin Tendulkar is better than many other batsmen in the world.

No other batman in the world is as good as Sachin Tendulkar.

Model-3: 'Not the best':

Example:

(i) This is not the best solution to the problem.

This is not better than few other solutions to this problem.

Other solutions to this problem are not as good as this one.

(ii) New York is not the largest city in America.

New York is not larger than many other cities in America.

Few other cities in America are at least as large as New York.

Few adjectives and adverbs get their comparative forms by simply adding 'more' before them and their superlative terms, by adding 'most' before them.

Example:

Positive	Comparative	Superlative
Beautiful	more beautiful	most beautiful
Effective	more effective	most effective
Effectively	more effectively	most effectively
Enjoyable	more enjoyable	most enjoyable
Useful	more useful	most useful
Different	more different	most different
Honest	more honest	most honest
Qualified	more qualified	most qualified

Few adjectives and adverbs get their comparative forms by simply adding 'er' after them and their superlative terms by adding 'est' after them.

Example:

Positive	Comparative	Superlative
Hard	harder	hardest
Big	bigger	biggest
Tall	taller	tallest
Long	longer	longest
Short	shorter	shortest
Costly	costlier	costliest
Simple	simpler	simplest

Degrees of comparison add beauty and variety to sentences.

MUST REMEMBER

- Adjectives are a large class of words which define more precisely the reference of a noun or pronoun.
- Possessive adjectives express the state of possession of nouns and are placed before nouns and show possession.
- When we compare two persons or two things with each other, we can use both the Positive degree and the Comparative degree.

PRACTICE EXERCISE

I. Underline the adjectives in the following sentences and identify their type.

1. The car sustained heavy damage in the accident.
2. He has written several stories.
3. A dog is very faithful to its master.
4. Every man has his duties.
5. He is a man of few words.
6. Neither party is quite in the right.
7. Which color do you prefer?
8. The way was long, the wind was cold.
9. He calls me every day.
10. I have not seen him in several days.

II. Fill in the blanks with the correct degree of comparison.

1. She is ………….. than her sister. (pretty)
2. Martha is a ………….. girl. (nice)
3. Supriya is the ………….. girl in the class. (intelligent)
4. Martin speaks English ………….. (good)
5. Russia is the ………….. country in the world. (big)
6. China is a ………….. country. (big)
7. China is ………….. than India. (big)
8. This is the ………….. book I have ever read. (interesting)
9. I am ………….. than you. (smart)
10. Take the ………….. of the two routes. (short)

HOTS

Fill in the blanks with suitable adjectives.

1. Tom doesn't take risks when he's driving. He's always _____.
2. Monica's English is very _____ although she makes a lot of mistakes.
3. Everything was very quiet. There was _____ silence.
4. The driver of the car had sustained _____ injuries.
5. There was a _____ change in the weather.

Articles and Prepositions

Learning Objectives : In this chapter, students will learn about:
- ✓ Articles and its Types
- ✓ Preposition and different Types

CHAPTER SUMMARY

An article is a word that is used with a noun to indicate the type of reference being made by the noun. There are three articles in English language: A, An, and The.

Example:
(i) A cat jumped over the pipe.
(ii) I need an umbrella.
(iii) The dog is still barking.

In fact, the articles *a, an* and *the* function as special adjectives.

Types of Articles
They can be classified into Indefinite and Definite Articles.

Indefinite Articles — A, An
An is used before singular count nouns beginning with a vowel (a, e, i, o, u) or vowel sound: An apple, an elephant, an issue, an orange.

A is used before singular count nouns beginning with consonants (other than a, e, i, o, u) or consonant sound: a stamp, a desk, a TV, a cup, a book, a unicorn.

Usage of 'A' and 'An'

☞ 'A' is used before singular nouns that are unspecified:
Example:
a pencil

☞ 'A' is used before number collectives and some numbers:

Example:
a dozen
a gallon

☞ 'A' is used before a singular noun followed by a restrictive modifier:
Example:
a girl who was wearing a yellow hat

☞ 'A' is used with nouns to form adverbial phrases of quantity, amount, or degree:
Example:
I felt a bit depressed.

☞ 'An' is used before:
1. Words beginning with a vouel (a, e, i, o, u)
   Example:
   An area, an ox, an umbrella, an excuse
2. Words beginning with a silent 'h' (before a vowel)
   Example:
   An hour, an honest man, an honourable man.

Definite Article — The
The word 'the' is one of the most common words in English. It is our only definite article. Nouns in English are preceded by the definite article when the speaker believes that the listener already knows what he is referring to. The speaker may believe this for many different reasons, some of which are listed below.

When to Use 'The'

☞ Use 'the' to refer to something which has already been mentioned.
Example:
(i) On Monday, an unarmed man stole $1,000 from the bank. The thief hasn't been caught yet.
(ii) I was walking past Benny's Bakery when I decided to go into the bakery to get some bread.
(iii) There's a position available in my team. The job will involve some international travel.

☞ Use 'the' when you assume there is just one of something in that place, even if it has not been mentioned before.
Example:
(i) We went on a walk in the forest yesterday.
(ii) Where is the bathroom?
(iii) Turn left and go to number 45. Our house is across the Italian restaurant.
(iv) My father enjoyed the book you gave him.

☞ Use 'the' in sentences or clauses where you define or identify a particular person or object.
Example:
(i) The man who wrote this book is famous.
(ii) I scratched the red car parked outside.
(iii) I live in the small house with a blue door.
(iv) He is the doctor I came to see.

☞ Use 'the' to refer to people or objects that are unique.
Example:
(i) The sun rose at 6:17 this morning.
(ii) You can go anywhere in the world.
(iii) Clouds drifted across the sky.
(iv) The president will be speaking on TV tonight.
(v) The CEO of Total petro company is coming to our meeting.

☞ Use 'the' before superlatives and ordinal numbers.
Example:
(i) This is the highest building in New York.
(ii) She read the last chapter of her new book first.
(iii) You are the tallest person in our class.
(iv) This is the third time I have called you today.

☞ Use 'the' with adjectives, to refer to a whole group of people.
Example:
(i) The French enjoy cheese.
(ii) The elderly require special attention.
(iii) She has given a lot of money to the poor.

☞ Use 'the' with decades.
Example:
(i) He was born in the seventies.
(ii) This is a painting from the 1820's.

☞ Use 'the' with clauses introduced by only.
Example:
(i) This is the only day we've had sunshine during the week.
(ii) You are the only person he will listen to.
(iii) The only tea I like is black tea.

☞ Use 'the' with names of geographical areas, rivers, mountain ranges, groups of islands, canals, and oceans.
Example:
(i) They are travelling in the Arctic.
(ii) Our ship crossed the Atlantic in seven days.
(iii) I will go on a cruise down the Nile.
(iv) Hiking across the Rocky Mountains would be difficult.

☞ Use 'the' with countries that have plural names.
Example:
(i) I have never been to the Netherlands.
(ii) Do you know anyone who lives in the Philippines?

☞ Use 'the' with countries that include the words 'republic', 'kingdom', or 'states' in their names.
Example:
(i) She is visiting the United States.
(ii) James is from the Republic of Ireland.

☞ Use 'the' with newspaper names.
Example:
(i) I read it in the Guardian.
(ii) She works for the New York Times.

☞ Use 'the' with the names of famous buildings, works of art, museums, or monuments.
Example:
(i) Have you been to the Vietnam Memorial?
(ii) We went to the Louvre and saw the Mona Lisa.
(iii) I would like to visit the Eiffel Tower.
(iv) I saw King Lear at the Globe.

☞ Use 'the' with the names of hotels & restaurants, unless these are named after a person.
Example:
(i) They are staying at the Hilton on 6th street.
(ii) We ate at the Golden Lion.

☞ Use 'the' with the names of families, but not with the names of individuals.
Example:
(i) We're having dinner with the Smiths tonight.
(ii) The Browns are going to the play with us.

TRIVIA

Over 80% of the information stored on computers worldwide is in English.

When Not to Use 'The'

☞ Do not use 'the' with names of countries (except for the special cases above).
Example:
(i) Germany is an important economic power.
(ii) He's just returned from Zimbabwe.

☞ Do not use 'the' with the names of languages.
Example:
(i) French is spoken in Tahiti.
(ii) English uses many words of Latin origin.
(iii) Indonesian is a relatively new language.

☞ Do not use 'the' with the names of meals.
Example:
(i) Lunch is my favorite meal.
(ii) I like to eat breakfast early.

☞ Do not use 'the' with people's names.
Example:
(i) John is coming over later.
(ii) Mary Carpenter is my boss.

☞ Do not use 'the' with titles when combined with names.
Example:
(i) Prince Charles is Queen Elizabeth's son.
(ii) President Kennedy was assassinated in Dallas.

☞ Do not use 'the' after the 's possessive case.
Example:
(i) His brother's car was stolen.
(ii) Peter's house is over there.

☞ Do not use 'the' with professions.
Example:
(i) Engineering is a well-paid career.
(ii) He'll probably study medicine.

☞ Do not use 'the' with names of shops.

Example:
(i) I'll get the card at Smith's.
(ii) Can you go to Boots for me?

☞ Do not use 'the' with years.
Example:
(i) 1948 was a wonderful year.
(ii) He was born in 1995.

☞ Do not use 'the' with uncountable nouns.
Example:
(i) Rice is an important food item in Asia.
(ii) Milk is often added to tea in England.
(iii) War is destructive.

☞ Do not use 'the' with the names of individual mountains, lakes and islands.
Example:
(i) Mount McKinley is the highest mountain in Alaska.
(ii) She lives near Lake Windermere.
(iii) Have you visited Long Island?

☞ Do not use 'the' with most names of towns, streets, stations and airports.
Example:
(i) Victoria Station is in the centre of London.
(ii) Can you direct me to Bond Street?
(iii) She lives in Florence.
(iv) They're flying to Heathrow.

Preposition

A word governing, and usually preceding, a noun or pronoun and expressing a relation to another word or element in the clause, as in 'the man on the platform', 'she arrived after dinner', 'what did you do it for?' Is known as preposition.

Types of Preposition

The different types of preposition are as follows:
(i) Preposition for Time
(ii) Preposition for Place
(iii) Preposition for Direction
(iv) Preposition for Agent
(v) Preposition for Instrument
(vi) Prepositional Phrase

Prepositions for Time (in, on, at)

Prepositions used for time of different natures are in, on at etc.

Uses of In

☞ Month or Year.
Example:
In January, in 1985.

☞ Particular time of day or month or year.
Example:
In morning, in evening, in the first week of January, in summer, in winter.

☞ Century or specific time in past, etc.
Example:
In 21st century, in stone age, in past, in future, in present.

Uses of On

☞ Day.
Example:
On Monday

☞ Date.
Example:
On 5th of March, on March 5

☞ Particular day.
Example:
On Independence Day, on my birthday

Uses of At

☞ Time of clock.
Example:
At 5 O'clock, at 7:30 PM

☞ Short and precise time.
Example:
at noon, at sunset, at lunch time, at bed time, at the moment, at the same time.

Example:
He was born in 1945.
She will go to New York on 25th of March.
The concert will begin at 7 O'clock.
He gets up early in the morning.
We enjoyed a lot in the summer.

The president will deliver speech to public on Independence Day.

She received a lot of gifts on her birthday.

Where were you at the lunchtime?

I will call you at 12 A.M.

Prepositions for Place (in, on, at)

Prepositions "in, on or at" are usually used for different places.

Uses of In

☞ To refer to a place having some boundary (physical or virtual boundary)

Example:

In hall, in school, in a building, in a box, in a car, in library, in garden, in America, in room, in cupboard

Uses of On

☞ To refer to the surface of something.

Example:

On a table, on blackboard, on a page, on the wall, on the roof, on a map

Uses of At

☞ To refer to a specific place.

Example:

At the entrance, at the bottom of glass, at front of the chair, at bus stop, at the edge of roof

Example:

She lives in New York.

Students study in library.

The wedding ceremony will be held in the hall.

There are some books on the table.

The teacher wrote a sentence on blackboard.

He was flying kite on the roof.

Her parents were waiting for her at the entrance of school.

There was a huge gathering at bus stop.

His house is at the end of street.

Prepositions for Direction (to, toward, through, into)

Prepositions like to, towards, through, and into are used to describe the direction.

Example:

She went to the library.

He jumped into the river.

He ran away when he felt that someone was coming toward him.

Prepositions for Agent (by, with)

Preposition for agent is used for a thing which is a cause of another thing in the sentence. Such prepositions are by, with, etc.

Example:

This book is written by Shakespeare.

The work was completed by him.

The room was decorated by her.

The tub is filled with water.

Prepositions for device, instrument or machine (by, with, on)

Different preposition are used by different devices, instruments or machines. e.g. by, with, on, etc.

Example:

She comes by bus daily.

He opened the lock with key.

Prepositional Verb

A prepositional phrase is a combination of a verb and a preposition. It is just a verb followed by a preposition.

Prepositional Verb = Verb + Preposition

Some verbs need particular prepositions to be used after them in sentences having a direct object. Such a verb with its required preposition is called a prepositional verb.

Example:

He knocks at the door.

In above sentence, "knock at" is a prepositional verb, which contains a verb "knock" and a preposition "at". Without the use of correct preposition after a prepositional verb in a sentence, the sentence is considered to be grammatically wrong.

Example:

If we say "he knocks the door", it is wrong because it lacks the required preposition "at".

So the correct sentence is "he knocks at the door".

Prepositional verbs are transitive and they have a direct object in sentence. Some of the frequently used prepositional verbs are laugh at, knock at, listen to, look at, look for, look after, wait for, agree to, agree with, talk about, talked to, etc.

Example:
She is listening to music.
She looked at the blackboard.
We believe in God.
They were waiting for the teacher.
Do you agree with me?
Do you agree to my proposal?
Someone is knocking at the door.
You should not rely on her.

MUST REMEMBER

- An article is a word that is used with a noun to indicate the type of reference being made by the noun.
- An is used before singular count nouns beginning with a vowel (a, e, i, o, u) or vowel sound.
- A is used before singular count nouns beginning with consonants or consonant sound.
- Nouns in English are preceded by the definite article when the speaker believes that the listener already knows what he is referring to.
- A word governing, and usually preceding, a noun or pronoun and expressing a relation to another word or element in the clause, as in 'the man on the platform', 'she arrived after dinner', 'what did you do it for?' Is known as preposition.
- Preposition for agent is used for a thing which is a cause of another thing in the sentence.
- Prepositional verbs are transitive and they have a direct object in sentence.

PRACTICE EXERCISE

I. Choose the correct article in each sentence.
1. Did you bring (a, an, the) umbrella?
2. Are you looking for (a, an, the) shampoo?
3. I checked (a, an, the) mailbox again.
4. Can I have (a, an, the) spoon please?
5. I was born into (a, an, the) poor family.
6. She will come back in (a, an, the) hour.
7. Have you been to (a, an, the) Space Needle Tower in Seattle?
8. I would love to talk to one of (a, an, the) managers.
9. What (a, an, the) amazing view!
10. The helicopter landed on (a, an, the) roof of a building.

II. Fill in the blanks with the articles (a/an/the). Write nothing if the blank needs no article.
1. _____ price of gas keeps rising.
2. John traveled to _____ Mexico.
3. Juan is _____ Spanish.
4. I read _____ amazing story yesterday.
5. My brother does not eat _____ chicken.
6. _____ love is such _____ beautiful thing.
7. I live in _____ apartment. _____ apartment is new.
8. I would like _____ piece of cake.
9. I was in _____ Japanese restaurant. _____ restaurant served good food.
10. Sara can play _____ guitar.

III. Fill in the blanks with the correct preposition.
1. The picture is ____ the wall.
   (a) in   (b) under
   (c) on   (d) at
2. The desks are ____ the blackboard in the classroom.
   (a) opposite   (b) between
   (c) above   (d) behind
3. The cat always sleeps ____ my bed.
   (a) under   (b) above
   (c) between   (d) over
4. The lamp is ____ the table.
   (a) in   (b) above
   (c) on   (d) under
5. The book is ____ the mug and the pen.
   (a) in   (b) between
   (c) on   (d) above
6. There is a bench ____ my house.
   (a) under   (b) on
   (c) in front of (d) above
7. There are apple trees ____ the house.
   (a) behind   (b) in
   (c) on   (d) at
8. The bookshop is ____ the bank.
   (a) between   (b) above
   (c) next to   (d) over
9. There is a museum ____ the school.
   (a) in   (b) opposite
   (c) under   (d) over
10. There is a bed ____ my room.
    (a) in   (b) on
    (c) under   (d) over
11. The mouse is ____ the cats.
    (a) on   (b) between
    (c) above   (d) over
12. The pillow is ____ the blanket.
    (a) in   (b) between
    (c) under   (d) between
13. The books are ____ my schoolbag.
    (a) above   (b) in
    (c) between   (d) at
14. You sit ____ me in the classroom.
    (a) between   (b) on
    (c) in front of (d) at
15. My mother's plant is ____ the TV.
    (a) above   (b) in
    (c) in front of (d) over

16. Mike often hides ____ that tree.
    (a) in   (b) above
    (c) behind   (d) at
17. The computer is ____ the telephone.
    (a) under   (b) next to
    (c) between   (d) on
18. Sam usually sits ____ this chair.
    (a) on   (b) in
    (c) above   (d) over
19. Mary sometimes sits ____ John and Jill.
    (a) between   (b) on
    (c) in front of (d) over
20. The books are ____ the shelf.
    (a) in   (b) next to
    (c) on   (d) opposite
21. She is gifted ____ common sense.
    (a) on   (b) by
    (c) with   (d) over
22. Sheela burst ____ the room when Mohini was writing a letter.
    (a) on   (b) in
    (c) of   (d) out
23. The players have gone _____ the playground.
    (a) in   (b) over
    (c) with   (d) to
24. He has not met his mother ____ long.
    (a) for   (b) with
    (c) since   (d) by
25. The land was divided ____ the two sisters.
    (a) among   (b) between
    (c) with   (d) for
26. The terrorist shot the policeman ____ his gun.
    (a) by   (b) for
    (c) with   (d) in
27. Compare Gandhi ____ Karl Marx.
    (a) to   (b) with
    (c) over   (d) in.
28. Janardhan was appointed ____ the post of section officer.
    (a) to   (b) on
    (c) with   (d) for
29. My Mother-in-law is blind ____ one eye.
    (a) from   (b) in
    (c) on   (d) of
30. He prevented me ____ going to the school.
    (a) from   (b) for
    (c) with   (d) on
31. Sabina has invited his friends ____ dinner.
    (a) for   (b) to
    (c) with   (d) over
32. The water supply at last gave ____
    (a) out   (b) off
    (c) of   (d) about
33. He has copied this letter word ____ word.
    (a) by   (b) in
    (c) for   (d) from
34. He is very grateful____ me.
    (a) for   (b) to
    (c) from   (d) with
35. There is an exception ____ every rule.
    (a) to   (b) in
    (c) for   (d) with
36. He was excluded ____ the team.
    (a) on   (b) from
    (c) by   (d) for
37. Ram was engrossed ____ his studies.
    (a) on   (b) with
    (c) in   (d) over
38. She is enraged ____ me.
    (a) with   (b) on
    (c) in   (d) over
39. He feels ____ the well being of the poor people.
    (a) in   (b) on
    (c) for   (d) by
40. The teacher frowned ____ the students.
    (a) at   (b) on
    (c) in   (d) with
41. Rich men are greedy ____ money.
    (a) for   (b) of
    (c) in   (d) with

42. She is hopeful ____ her success in the I.A.S. examination.
    (a) in   (b) by
    (c) of   (d) on
43. You should not include ____ idle talks.
    (a) on   (b) over
    (c) about   (d) in
44. I am indebted ____ you for this kind favour.
    (a) with   (b) for
    (c) to   (d) in
45. He is completely involved _____ his family affairs.
    (a) in   (b) on
    (c) with   (d) over
46. A cat differs ____ a dog.
    (a) with   (b) from
    (c) or   (d) in
47. The watch has run ____.
    (a) out   (b) about
    (c) down   (d) in
48. Do not despair ____ failures in life.
    (a) on   (b) in
    (c) over   (d) of
49. This is the book I was telling you ____.
    (a) about   (b) of
    (c) on   (d) for
50. I am very grateful ____ Mr. Nair for his timely help.
    (a) for   (b) to
    (c) by   (d) with
51) I could not guess ____ the answer to this question.
    (a) in   (b) for
    (c) at   (d) on
52. He got ____ his illness in two weeks.
    (a) on   (b) by
    (c) with   (d) over
53. There was no jest ____ his poverty.
    (a) in   (b) at
    (c) for   (d) with
54. He is not known ____ my brother.
    (a) with   (b) about
    (c) for   (d) to
55. I long ____ a quite life in a hill station.
    (a) in   (b) by
    (c) for   (d) with
56. One should live ____ honest labours.
    (a) by   (b) with
    (c) on   (d) for
57. Rama was married ____ Sita.
    (a) by   (b) to
    (c) with   (d) for
58. I am badly in need ____ money.
    (a) of   (b) for
    (c) with   (d) on
59. She was mistaken ____ her sister.
    (a) with   (b) as
    (c) for   (d) from
60. I took strong objection ____ the proposal.
    (a) on   (b) to
    (c) against   (d) with
61. Radha parted ____ her parents in tears.
    (a) from   (b) of
    (c) with   (d) by
62. You should not trifle ____ his feelings.
    (a) on   (b) after
    (c) over   (d) with
63. Good triumphs ____ evil in the long run.
    (a) on   (b) over
    (c) with   (d) against
64. Trust ____ God and do the right.
    (a) in   (b) on
    (c) with   (d) by
65. He fell a victim ____ plague.
    (a) on   (b) to
    (c) in   (d) for
66. I warned him ____ the pick pockets.
    (a) about   (b) in
    (c) from   (d) against
67. Mr. Mani is worth ____ the honour.
    (a) with   (b) of
    (c) on   (d) over
68. One should never be a traitor ____ one's country.
    (a) of   (b) in
    (c) to   (d) with

Articles and Prepositions

69. I am no longer interested ____ his affairs.
    (a) on   (b) with
    (c) for   (d) in
70. She always jumps ____ the conclusion.
    (a) in   (b) on
    (c) to   (d) with
71. He lamented ____ the loss of his property.
    (a) with   (b) in
    (c) on   (d) for
72. I did not hinder her ____ going there.
    (a) from   (b) in
    (c) for   (d) on
73. He is not eligible ____ the post of manager.
    (a) in   (b) of
    (c) on   (d) for
74. I reminded him ____ his promise.
    (a) with   (b) for
    (c) of   (d) from
75. I have referred the matter ____ the principal.
    (a) with   (b) by
    (c) to   (d) on
76. They have run short ____ fuel.
    (a) of   (b) with
    (c) for   (d) in
77. He is not satisfied ____ his lot.
    (a) for   (b) in
    (c) with   (d) over
78. This medicine has relieved him ____ his pain.
    (a) in   (b) of
    (c) with   (d) over
79. Please send ____ the doctor at once.
    (a) on   (b) by
    (c) for   (d) with
80. We are sick ____ him.
    (a) of   (b) by
    (c) with   (d) on

HOTS

I. Fill in the blanks with the suitable article (a/an/the):

1. I like _____ blue shirt over there better than _____ red one.
2. Carla's father is _____ electrician.
3. I have _____ good idea.
4. Do the Smiths have _____ yellow van?
5. _____ cat, which had entered our kitchen yesterday, had come in again today morning.

II. Use the correct preposition to fill in the blanks below.

1. What are you doing _____ Saturday?
2. I haven't been to the countryside _____ December.
3. We live _____ London.
4. Would you like to go _____ the cinema tonight?
5. Luke is very pleased _____ his exam results.

Verbs, Adverbs, Phrasal Verbs and Modals — 4

Learning Objectives : In this chapter, students will learn about:
- ✓ Finite and Non-finite Verbs
- ✓ Uses of Verbs
- ✓ Uses of Modal Verbs
- ✓ Adverbs and their types
- ✓ Phrasal Verbs

CHAPTER SUMMARY

A word (such as jump, think, happen, or exist) that is usually one of the main parts of a sentence and that expresses an action, an occurrence, or a state of being is known as verb.

A sentence has two parts– Subject and Predicate. Subject tells what the sentence is about the predicate gives a statements about the subjects. For example in the sentence below the underlined text is predicate.

1. The girl sang a song.
2. The captain was happy. The words 'sang' & 'was' are verbs.

Verbs can be divided into two categories–Finite and Non-finite.

Finite Verbs

Finite Verbs are those verbs that have a definite relation with the subject or noun. These verbs are usually the main verb of a clause or sentence and can be changed according to the noun. They are used only in present and past tense. They can be indicative of passive or active voice and also of number (singular or plural).

Example:

She walks home. – Here we see that the finite verb is walks and the pronoun is 'she'.

She walked home. – Here we can see how the verb changed/modified to change the tense of the sentence.

Non-Finite Verbs

These verbs cannot be the main verb of a clause or sentence as they do not talk about the action that is being performed by the subject or noun. They do not indicate any tense, mood or gender. They are used as nouns, adverbs and adjectives. They are also used to form non-finite clauses which are simply dependent clauses that use non-finite verbs.

Example:

He loves camping in the woods.

Here the non-finite verb is camping and it is used as a noun. These kind of non-finite verbs are called Gerunds.

I need to go to sleep.

Here the non-finite verb to sleep is acting as a noun. Non-finite verbs that use 'to' before them are called Infinitives.

The sleeping dog caused a delay. The non-finite verbs that have '-ing' or '-ed' as suffixes and cause the verb to become an adjective are called Participles.

Participles, Gerunds and Infinitives together are called verbals. Verbals are words which are formed from a verb but which function as a different part of speech.

Participle

A participle is usually formed by adding –ing or –ed to a verb. It functions as an adjective.

Example:

The singing bird was the main attraction at the event.

The injured man was waiting for the doctor.

Gerund

A gerund is formed by adding –ing to a verb. It functions as a noun.

Example:

Swimming is very good for the body.

Smoking is prohibited in the hospital.

Infinitive

An infinitive is formed by using the word 'to' before the verb in its stem word. It functions as a noun, adjective or adverb.

Example:

He was made to clean his room.

Shalini loves to talk.

Types of Verbs

Verbs are words that express action or state of being. There are three types of verbs: action verbs, linking verbs, and helping verbs.

Action Verbs

Action verbs are words that express action (give, eat, walk, etc.) or possession (have, own, etc.). Action verbs can be either transitive or intransitive.

Transitive Verbs

A transitive verb always has a noun that receives the action of the verb, called the direct object.

Example:

Laurissa raises her hand.

The verb is raises. Her hand is the object receiving the verb's action. Therefore, raises is a transitive verb.

Transitive verbs sometimes have indirect objects, which name the object to whom or for whom the action was done.

Example:

Abdus gave Becky the pencil.

The verb is gave. The direct object is the pencil. (What did he give? The pencil.)

The indirect object is Becky. (To whom did he give it? To Becky.)

Intransitive Verbs

An intransitive verb never has a direct or indirect object. Although an intransitive verb may be followed by an adverb or adverbial phrase, there is no object to receive its action.

Example:

Laurissa rises slowly from her seat.

The verb is rises. The phrase, slowly from her seat, modifies the verb, but no object receives the action.

Transitive or Intransitive

To determine whether a verb is transitive or intransitive, follow these two steps:

Step 1: Find the verb in the sentence.

Example:

Dustin will lay down his book. What is the action? will lay

His book will lie there all day. What is the action? will lie

Step 2: Ask yourself, "What is receiving the action of the verb?" If there is a noun receiving the action of the verb, then the verb is transitive. If there is no direct object to receive the action, and if the verb does not make sense with a direct object, then it is intransitive.

Example:

Dustin will lay down his book.

Dustin will lay down what? His book.

Since the verb can take a direct object, it is transitive.

His book will lie there all day.

His book will lie what? Nothing. It does not make sense to "lie something."

Since the verb has no direct object, it is intransitive.

Linking Verbs

A linking verb connects the subject of a sentence to a noun or adjective that renames or describes the subject. This noun or adjective is called the subject complement.

Example:

Jason became a business major.

The verb, became, links the subject, Jason, to its complement, a business major.

Lisa is in love with Jason.

The verb, is, links the subject, Lisa, to the subject complement, in love with Jason (describing Lisa).

The most common linking verb is the verb to be in all of its forms (am, are, is, was, were, etc.). This verb may also be used as a helping verb (see next section). To become and to seem are always linking verbs.

Other verbs may be linking verbs in some cases and action verbs in others:

to appear, to feel, to look, to remain, to stay, to taste, to continue, to grow, to prove, to sound, to smell, to turn

LINKING: Libby appeared happy. (Appeared links Libby to the subject complement, happy.)

ACTION: Deon suddenly appeared. (Here, appeared is an intransitive action verb.)

Helping Verbs

Helping verbs are used before action or linking verbs to convey additional information regarding aspects of possibility (can, could, etc.) or time (was, did, has, etc.). The main verb with its accompanying helping verb is called a verb phrase.

Example:

Teju is (helping verb) going (main verb) to Florida.

The trip might (helping verb) be (main verb) dangerous.

The following words, called modals, always function as helping verbs:

can, may, must, shall, will, could, might, ought, to, should, would

Example:

Tanya could learn to fly helicopters. (Could helps the main verb, learn.)

Janine will drive to Idaho tomorrow. (Will helps the main verb, drive.)

In addition, the following forms of the verbs to be, to do, and to have sometimes serve as helping verbs.

(Note: In other cases, they may serve as action or linking verbs.)

am, be, being, do, had, have, was, are, been, did, does, has, is, were

HELPING: Jana is moving to a new house.

LINKING: Jana is ready to go.

HELPING: Dustin did eat his vegetables!

ACTION: Dustin did his homework last night. (transitive verb)

Uses of Verbs

☞ We use the present simple:

(a) To talk about something happening regularly in the present.

Example:

The children come home from school at about four.

We often see your brother at work.

(b) To talk about something happening continually in the present.

Example:

They live next door to us.

He works for the Post Office.

(c) To talk about things which are generally true.

Example:

Water boils at 100 degrees Celsius.

The Nile is the longest river in Africa.

☞ We use the present continuous:

(a) To show that something in the present is temporary.

Example:

We are living in a rented flat at present.

My wife usually goes to the office, but she is working at home today.

(b) For something happening regularly in the present before and after a given time.

Example:

I'm usually getting ready for work at eight o'clock.

When I see George he's always reading his newspaper.

(c) For something happening before and after the moment of speaking.

Example:

I can't hear you. I'm listening to my iPod.

Be quiet. The children are sleeping.

☞ We use modal verbs:

(a) To talk about the present when we are not sure of something.

Example:

I don't know where Henry is. He might be playing tennis.

Who's knocking at the door? I don't know. It could be the police.

Uses of Modal Verbs

To indicate that something is probable or possible, or not so.

Example:

It is sunny today; it must be warm outside. = It is sunny today; it is probably warm outside.

His mobile is not reachable; he may/might/could be travelling by metro. = His mobile is not reachable; it is possible that he is travelling by metro.

This can't be our bill. = It is not possible that this is our bill.

☞ 'Can' and 'could' are used to refer to skills and abilities.

Example:

He can cover a hundred metres in under ten seconds.

My father could see perfectly before the age of fifty.

I can't ride a horse.

☞ 'Must' is used to indicate that something is necessary or of extreme importance, and 'should' is used to suggest that something is advisable.

Example:

You must do your homework.

You mustn't skip school.

You should say sorry.

You shouldn't smoke.

☞ 'Can', 'could' and 'may' are used to ask for, give and withhold permission.

Example:

Can I try my hand at it?

Could we disperse early today?

You may not enter the premises.

☞ 'Will' and 'would' are used to refer to habits and inclinations.

Example:

When I was a child, I would often climb trees.

I will never refuse you anything.

He would never do such a thing.

Subject-Verb Agreement

Basic Rule: A singular subject (she, Rohan, car) takes a singular verb (is, goes, shines), whereas a plural subject takes a plural verb.

Example:

The list of items is/are on the desk.

If you know that list is the subject, then you will choose 'is' for the verb.

Rule 1: A subject will come before a phrase beginning with 'of'. This is a key rule for understanding subjects. The word 'of' is the culprit in many, perhaps most, subject-verb mistakes.

Incorrect: A bouquet of yellow roses lend colour and fragrance to the room.

Correct: A bouquet of yellow roses lends colour and fragrance to the room. (bouquet lends, not roses lend)

Rule 2: Two singular subjects connected by or, either/or, or neither/nor require a singular verb.

Example:

My aunt or my uncle is arriving by train today.

Neither Juan nor Carmen is available.

Either Kiana or Casey is helping today with stage decorations.

Rule 3: The verb in an/or, either/or, or neither/nor sentence agrees with the noun or pronoun closest to it.

Example:
Neither the plates nor the serving bowl goes on that shelf.

Neither the serving bowl nor the plates go on that shelf.

For example, if I is one of two (or more) subjects, it could lead to this odd sentence:

Incorrect: Neither she, my friends, nor I am going to the festival.

Correct: Neither she, I, nor my friends are going to the festival.

Or

She, my friends, and I are not going to the festival.

Rule 4: As a general rule, use a plural verb with two or more subjects when they are connected by 'and'.

Example:
A car and a bike are my means of transportation.

But note these exceptions:

Exceptions:
Breaking and entering is against the law.

The bed and breakfast was charming.

In those sentences, breaking and entering and bed and breakfast are compound nouns.

Rule 5: Sometimes the subject is separated from the verb by words like "along with", as well as, besides, not, etc. These words and phrases are not part of the subject. Ignore them and use a singular verb when the subject is singular.

Example:
The politician, along with the newsmen, is expected shortly.

Excitement, as well as nervousness, is the cause of her shaking.

Rule 6: In sentences beginning with here or there, the true subject follows the verb.

Example:
There are four hurdles to jump.

There is a high hurdle to jump.

Here are the keys.

Note:
The word there's, a short form of "there is", it leads to casual language in informal sentences like 'There's a lot of people here today,' because it's easier to say 'there's' than 'there are.' Take care never to use there's with a plural subject.

Rule 7: Use a singular verb with distances, periods of time, sums of money, etc., when considered as a unit.

Example:
Three miles is too far to walk. (i.e. a distance of three miles)

Five years is the maximum sentence for that offence. (i.e. a period of five years)

Ten dollars is a high price to pay. (i.e. the amount of ten dollars)

BUT

Ten dollars were scattered on the floor. (i.e., ten dollar bills)

Rule 8: With words that indicate portions e.g., a lot, a majority, some, all — Rule 1 given earlier in this section is reversed, and we are guided by the noun after of. If the noun after of is singular, use a singular verb. If it is plural, use a plural verb.

Example:
(i)   A lot of the pie has disappeared.
(ii) A lot of the pies have disappeared.
(iii) A third of the city is unemployed.
(iv) A third of the people are unemployed.
(v)   All of the pie is gone.
(vi) All of the pies are gone.
(vii) Some of the pie is missing.
(viii) Some of the pies are missing.

Note:

In recent years, none has come to be considered singular. However, according to Merriam-Webster's Dictionary of English Usage: "Clearly none has been both singular and plural since Old English and still is. The notion that it is singular only is a myth of unknown origin that appears to have arisen in the 19th century. If in context it seems like a singular to you, use a singular verb; if it seems like a plural, use a plural verb. Both are acceptable beyond serious criticism." When none is clearly intended to mean "not one," it is followed by a singular verb.

Rule 9: With collective nouns such as group, jury, family, audience, population, the verb might be singular or plural, depending on the writer's intent.

Example:

All of my family has arrived OR have arrived.

Most of the jury is here OR are here.

A third of the population was not in favour OR were not in favour of the bill.

Note:

Anyone who uses a plural verb with a collective noun must take care to be accurate—and also consistent. It must not be done carelessly. The following is the sort of flawed sentence one sees and hears a lot these days.

The staff is deciding how they want to vote.

Careful speakers and writers would avoid assigning the singular verb is and the plural pronoun they to the noun staff in the same sentence.

Consistent: The staff are deciding how they want to vote.

Rewriting such sentences is recommended whenever possible. The preceding sentence would read even better as:

The staff members are deciding how they want to vote.

Rule 10: The word were replaces was in sentences that express a wish or are contrary to facts:

Example:

If Joe were here, you'd be sorry.

Shouldn't Joe be followed by was, not were, given that Joe is singular? But Joe isn't actually here, so we use were, not was. The sentence demonstrates the subjunctive mood, which is used to express things that are hypothetical, wishful, imaginary, or factually contradictory. The subjunctive mood pairs singular subjects with what we usually think of as plural verbs.

Example:

I wish it were Friday.

She requested that he raise his hand.

In the first example, a wishful statement, not a fact, is being expressed; therefore, were, which we usually think of as a plural verb, is used with the singular subject I.

Normally, he raise would sound terrible to us. However, in the second example, where a request is being expressed, the subjunctive mood is correct.

Note:

The subjunctive mood is losing ground in spoken English but should still be used in formal speech and writing.

TRIVIA

The word 'Goodbye' originally comes from an Old English phrase meaning 'God be with you'.

Adverb

An adverb is a word or set of words that modifies verbs, adjectives, or other adverbs. Adverbs answer how, when, where, why, or to what extent—how often or how much (e.g., daily, completely).

Example:

He speaks slowly. (tells how)

He speaks very slowly. (the adverb very tells how slowly)

She arrived today. (tells when)

She will arrive in an hour. (this adverb phrase tells when)

Let's go outside. (tells where)

We looked in the basement. (this adverb phrase tells where)

Bernie left to avoid trouble. (this adverb phrase tells why)

George works out strenuously. (tells to what extent)

George works out whenever possible. (this adverb phrase tells to what extent)

Kinds of Adverbs

There are different kinds of adverbs expressing different meaning. The following are some of the common ones.

I. Adverb of Time

An adverb of time tells us when something is done or happens. We use it at the beginning or at the end of a sentence. We use it as a form of emphasis when we place it at the beginning. Adverbs of time include afterwards, already, always, immediately, last month, now, soon, then, and yesterday.

Example:

He collapsed and died yesterday.

His factory was burned down a few months ago.

Last week, we were stuck in the lift for an hour.

II. Adverb of Place

An adverb of place tells us where something is done or happens. We use it after the verb, object or at the end of a sentence. Adverbs of place include words, such as, above, below, here, outside, over there, there, under, and upstairs.

Example:

We can stop here for lunch.

The school boy was knocked over by a school bus.

They rushed for their lives when fire broke out in the floor below.

III. Adverb of Manner

An adverb of manner tells us how something is done or happens. Most adverbs of manner end in –ly, such as, badly, happily, sadly, slowly, quickly, and others that include well, hard, fast, etc.

Example:

The brothers were badly injured in the fight.

They had to act fast to save the others floating in the water.

At the advanced age of 88, she still sang very well.

IV. Adverb of Degree

An adverb of degree tells us the level or extent at which something is done or happens. Words of adverb of degree are almost, much, nearly, quite, really, so, too, very, etc. They express quality.

Example:

It was too dark for us to find our way out of the cave. (Before adjective)

The referee had to stop the match when it began to rain very heavily. (Before adverb)

Her daughter is quite fat for her age.

The accident victim nearly died from his injuries.

After all these years, she is still feeling very sad about her father's death.

V. Adverb of Frequency

An adverb of frequency tells us how often something is done or happens. Words used as adverbs of frequency include again, almost, always, ever, frequently, generally, hardly ever, nearly, nearly always, never, occasionally, often, rarely, seldom, sometimes, twice, usually, and weekly.

Example:

They were almost fifty when they got married.

He hardly ever says something nice to his wife.

While overseas, he frequently phoned home.

She is not nearly always right although she thinks she is always right.

Verbs, Adverbs, Phrasal Verbs and Modals

He complained that she never smiled back.

We only write to each other very occasionally.

Peter seldom reads the Bible.

Sometimes he stays late in the office to complete his work.

Our cat was bitten twice by the same dog.

The man usually proposes marriage.

VI. Interrogative Adverbs

The adverbs used to ask questions are called Interrogative Adverbs.

Example:

(1) Why is she standing?

(ii) Where do you live?

(iii) When the train will arrive?

The question words "why", "when" & "where" are called Interrogative Adverbs.

Rules of Adverbs

Rule 1: Many adverbs end in -ly, but many do not. Generally, if a word can have -ly added to its adjective form, place it there to form an adverb.

Example:

She thinks quick/quickly.

How does she think? Quickly.

She is a quick/quickly thinker.

Quick is an adjective describing thinker, so no -ly is attached.

She thinks fast/fastly.

Fast answers the question how, so it is an adverb. But fast never has -ly attached to it.

We performed bad/badly.

Badly describes how we performed, so -ly is added.

Rule 2: Adverbs that answer the question how sometimes cause grammatical problems. It can be a challenge to determine if -ly should be attached. Avoid the trap of -ly with linking verbs such as taste, smell, look, and feel, which pertain to the senses. Adverbs are often misplaced in such sentences, which require adjectives instead.

Example:

Roses smell sweet/sweetly.

Do the roses actively smell with noses? No; in this case, smell is a linking verb — which requires an adjective to modify roses — so no -ly.

The woman looked angry/angrily to us.

Did the woman look with her eyes, or are we describing her appearance? We are describing her appearance (she appeared angry), so no -ly.

The woman looked angry/angrily at the paint splotches.

Here the woman actively looked (used her eyes), so the -ly is added.

She feels bad/badly about the news.

She is not feeling with fingers, so no -ly.

Rule 3: The word good is an adjective, whose adverb equivalent is well.

Example:

You did a good job.

Good describes the job.

You did the job well.

Well answers how.

You smell good today.

Good describes your fragrance, not how you smell with your nose, so using the adjective is correct.

You smell well for someone with a cold.

You are actively smelling with your nose here, so use the adverb.

Rule 4: The word well can be an adjective, too. When referring to health, we often use well rather than good.

Example:

You do not look well today.

I don't feel well, either.

Rule 5: There are three degrees of adverbs. In formal usage, do not drop the -ly from an adverb when using the comparative form.

Incorrect: She spoke quicker than he did.

Correct: She spoke more quickly than he did.

Incorrect: Talk quieter.

Correct: Talk more quietly.

Phrasal Verbs

Phrasal verbs are usually two-word phrases consisting of verb + adverb or verb + preposition. Think of them as you would any other English vocabulary. Study them as you come across them, rather than trying to memorize many at once. Use the list below as a reference guide when you find an expression that you don't recognize. The example sentences will help you understand the meanings. If you think of each phrasal verb as a separate verb with a specific meaning, you will be able to remember it more easily. Like many other verbs, phrasal verbs often have more than one meaning.

The following list shows about 200 common phrasal verbs, with meanings and examples. Only the most usual meanings are given. Some phrasal verbs may have additional meanings.

Phrasal verb	Meaning	Example
ask somebody out	invite on a date	Brian asked Judy out to dinner and a movie.
ask around	ask many people the same question	I asked around but nobody has seen my wallet.
add up to something	equal	Your purchases add up to $205.32.
back something up	reverse	You'll have to back up your car so that I can get out.
back somebody up	support	My wife backed me up over my decision to quit my job.
blow up	explode	The racing car blew up after it crashed into the fence.
blow something up	add air	We have to blow 50 balloons up for the party.
break down	stop functioning (machine)	Our car broke down on the highway due to snowstorm.
break down	get upset	The woman broke down when the police told her that her son had died.
break something down	divide into smaller parts	Our teacher broke the final project down into three separate parts.
break in	force entry to a building	Somebody broke in last night and stole our stereo.
break into something	enter forcibly	The firemen had to break into the room to rescue the children.
break in	interrupt	The TV station broke in to report the news of the president's death.
break up	end a relationship	My boyfriend and I broke up before I moved to America.

Verbs, Adverbs, Phrasal Verbs and Modals

break up	start laughing	The kids just broke up as soon as the clown started talking.
break out	escape	The prisoners broke out of jail when the guards weren't looking.
break out in something	develop a skin condition	I broke out in a rash after our camping trip.
bring somebody down	make unhappy	This sad music is bringing me down.
bring somebody up	raise a child	My grandparents brought me up after my parents died.
bring something up	start talking about a subject	My mother walks out of the room when my father brings up sports.
bring something up	vomit	He drank so much that he brought his dinner up in the toilet.
call around	make phone calls	We called around but we weren't able to find the car part we needed.
call somebody back	return a phone call	I called the company back but the offices were closed for the weekend.
call something off	cancel	Jason called the wedding off because he wasn't in love with his fiancé.
call on somebody	ask for an answer	The professor called on me for question 1.
call on somebody	visit somebody	We called on you last night but you weren't home.
call somebody up	phone	Give me your phone number and I will call you up when we are in town.
calm down	relax after being angry	You are still mad. You need to calm down before you drive the car.
catch up	get to the same point as somebody else	You'll have to run faster than that if you want to catch up with Marty.
check in	arrive and register at a hotel or airport	We will get the hotel keys when we check in.

check out	leave a hotel	You have to check out of the hotel before 11:00 AM.
check somebody/something out	look at carefully, investigate	The company checks out all new employees.
check out somebody/something	look at	Check out the crazy hair on that guy!
cheer up	become happier	She cheered up when she heard the good news.
cheer somebody up	make happier	I brought you some flowers to cheer you up.
chip in	help	If everyone chips in we can get the kitchen painted by noon.
clean something up	tidy, clean	Please clean up your bedroom before you go outside.
come across something	find unexpectedly	I came across these old photos when I was tidying the closet.
come apart	separate	The top and bottom come apart if you pull hard enough.
come down with something	become sick	My nephew came down with chicken pox this weekend.
come forward	volunteer for a task or evidence	The woman came forward with her husband's finger prints.
come from somewhere	originate in	The art of origami comes from Asia.
count on somebody/something	rely on	I am counting on you to make dinner while I am out.
cross something out	draw a line through	Please cross out your old address and write your new one.
cut back on something	consume less	My doctor wants me to cut back on sweets and fatty foods.
cut something down	make something fall to the ground	We had to cut the old tree in our yard down after the storm.
cut in	interrupt	Your father cut in while I was dancing with your uncle.
cut in	pull in closely in front of another vehicle	The bus driver got angry when that car cut in.

Verbs, Adverbs, Phrasal Verbs and Modals

cut in	start operating (of an engine or electrical device)	The air conditioner cuts in when the temperature gets to 22°C.
cut something off	remove with something sharp	The doctors cut off his leg because it was severely injured.
cut something off	stop providing	The phone company cut off our phone because we didn't pay the bill.
cut somebody off	take out of a will	My grandparents cut my father off when he remarried.
cut something out	remove part of something (usually with scissors and paper)	I cut this ad out of the newspaper.
do somebody/something over	beat up, ransack	He's lucky to be alive. His shop was done over by a street gang.
do something over	do again	My teacher wants me to do my essay over because she doesn't like my topic.
do away with something	discard	It's time to do away with all of these old tax records.
do something up	fasten, close	Do your coat up before you go outside. It's snowing!
dress up	wear nice clothing	It's a fancy restaurant so we have to dress up.
drop back	move back in a position/group	Andrea dropped back to third place when she fell off her bike.
drop in/by/over	come without an appointment	I might drop in/by/over for tea sometime this week.
drop out	quit a class, school etc	I dropped out of Science because it was too difficult.
eat out	eat at a restaurant	I don't feel like cooking tonight. Let's eat out.
end up	eventually reach/do/decide	We ended up renting a movie instead of going to the theatre.
fall apart	break into pieces	My new dress fell apart in the washing machine.
fall down	fall to the ground	The picture that you hung up last night fell down this morning.
fall out	separate from an interior	The money must have fallen out of my pocket.

fall out	(of hair, teeth) become loose and unattached	His hair started to fall out when he was only 35.
figure something out	understand, find the answer	I need to figure out how to fit the piano and the bookshelf in this room.
fill something in	to write information in blanks, as on a form	Please fill in the form with your name, address, and phone number.
fill something out	to write information in blanks, as on a form	The form must be filled out in capital letters.
fill something up	fill to the top	I always fill the water jug up when it is empty.
find out	discover	We don't know where he lives. How can we find out?
find something out	discover	We tried to keep the time of the party a secret, but Samantha found it out.
get something across/over	communicate, make understandable	I tried to get my point across/over to the judge but she wouldn't listen.
get along/on	like each other	I was surprised how well my new girlfriend and my sister got along/on.
get around	have mobility	My grandfather can get around fine in his new wheelchair.
get away	go on a vacation	We worked so hard this year that we had to get away for a week.
get away with something	do without being noticed or punished	Jason always gets away with cheating in his maths tests.
get back	return	We got back from our vacation last week.
get something back	receive something you had before	Liz finally got her Science notes back from my room-mate.
get back at somebody	retaliate, take revenge	My sister got back at me for stealing her shoes. She stole my favourite hat.
get back into something	become interested in something again	I finally got back into my novel and finished it.

get on something	step onto a vehicle	We're going to freeze out here if you don't let us get on the bus.
get over something	recover from an illness, loss, difficulty	I just got over the flu and now my sister has it.
get over something	overcome a problem	The company will have to close if it can't get over the new regulations.
get round to something	finally find time to do	I don't know when I am going to get round to writing the thank you cards.
get together	meet (usually for social reasons)	Let's get together for a party this weekend.
get up	get out of bed	I got up early today to study for my exam.
get up	stand	You should get up and give the elderly man your seat.
give somebody away	reveal hidden information about somebody	His wife gave him away to the police.
give somebody away	take the bride to the altar	My father gave me away at my wedding.
give something away	ruin a secret	My little sister gave the surprise party away by accident.
give something away	give something to somebody for free	The library was giving away old books on Friday.
give something back	return a borrowed item	I have to give these skates back to Franz before his hockey game.
give in	reluctantly stop fighting or arguing	My friend didn't want to go to the ballet, but he finally gave in.
give something out	give to many people (usually at no cost)	They were giving out free perfume samples at the department store.
give something up	quit a habit	I am giving up smoking as of January 1st.
give up	stop trying	My maths homework was too difficult so I gave up.
go after somebody	follow somebody	My brother tried to go after the thief in his car.

go after something	try to achieve something	I went after my dream and now I am a published writer.
go against somebody	compete, oppose	We are going against the best soccer team in the city tonight.
go ahead	start, proceed	Please go ahead and eat before the food gets cold.
go back	return to a place	I have to go back home and get my lunch.
go out	leave home to go on a social event	We're going out for dinner tonight.
go out with somebody	date	Jesse has been going out with Luke since they met last winter.
go over something	review	Please go over your answers before you submit your test.
go over	visit somebody nearby	I haven't seen Tina for a long time. I think I'll go over for an hour or two.
go without something	suffer, lack or deprivation	When I was young, we went without winter boots.
grow apart	stop being friends over time	My best friend and I grew apart after she changed schools.
grow back	regrow	My roses grew back this summer.
grow up	become an adult	When Jack grows up he wants to be a fireman.
grow out of something	get too big for	Elizabeth needs a new pair of shoes because she has grown out of her old ones.
grow into something	grow big enough to fit	This bike is too big for him now, but he should grow into it by next year.
hand something down	give something used	I handed my old comic books down to my little cousin.
hand something in	submit	I have to hand in my essay by Friday.
hand something out	to distribute to a group of people	We will hand out the invitations at the door.
hand something over	give (usually unwillingly)	The police asked the man to hand over his wallet and his weapons.

Verbs, Adverbs, Phrasal Verbs and Modals

hang in	stay positive	Hang in there. I'm sure you'll find a job very soon.
hang on	wait a short time	Hang on while I grab my coat and shoes!
hang out	spend time relaxing	Instead of going to the party we are just going to hang out at my place.
hang up	end a phone call	He didn't say goodbye before he hung up.
hold somebody/ something back	prevent from doing/going	I had to hold my dog back because there was a cat in the park.
hold something back	hide an emotion	Jamie held back his tears at his grandfather's funeral.
hold on	wait a short time	Please hold on while I transfer you to the Sales Department.
hold onto somebody/ something	hold firmly using your hands or arms	Hold onto your hat because it's very windy outside.
keep on doing something	continue doing	Keep on stirring until the liquid comes to a boil.
keep something from somebody	not tell	We kept our relationship from our parents for two years.
keep somebody/ something out	stop from entering	Try to keep the wet dog out of the living room.
keep something up	continue at the same rate	If you keep those results up you will get into a great college.
let somebody down	fail to support or help, disappoint	I need you to be on time. Don't let me down this time.
let somebody in	allow to enter	Can you let the cat in before you go to school?
log in	sign in (to a website, database etc)	I can't log in to Facebook because I've forgotten my password.
log out (or off)	sign out (of a website, database etc)	If you don't log off somebody could get into your account.
look after somebody	take care of	I have to look after my sick grandmother.
look down on somebody	think less of	Ever since we stole that chocolate bar your dad has looked down on me.

look for somebody/something	try to find	I'm looking for a red dress for the wedding.
look forward to something	be excited about the future	I'm looking forward to the Christmas break.
look into something	investigate	We are going to look into the price of snowboards today.
look out	be careful	Look out! That car's going to hit you!
look out for	be vigilant for	Don't forget to look out for snakes on the hiking trail.
look something over	check, examine	Can you look over my essay for spelling mistakes?
look something up	search and find information	We can look her phone number up on the Internet.
look up to somebody	have a lot of respect for	My little sister has always looked up to me.
make something up	invent, lie about something	Josie made up a story about why we were late.
make up	apply cosmetics to	My sisters put makeup on me for my graduation party.
make somebody up	forgive each other	We were angry last night, but we made up at breakfast.
mix something up	confuse two or more things	I mixed up the twins' names again!
not care for somebody/something	not like	I don't care for his behaviour.
pass away	die	His uncle passed away last night after a long illness.
pass out	faint	It was so hot in the church that an elderly lady passed out.
pass something out	give the same thing to many people	The professor passed the textbooks out before class.
pass something up	decline	I passed up the job because I am afraid of change.
pay somebody back	return owed money	Thanks for buying my ticket. I'll pay you back on Friday.

Verbs, Adverbs, Phrasal Verbs and Modals

pay for something	be punished for doing something bad	That bully will pay for being mean to my little brother.
pick something out	choose	I picked out three sweaters for you to try on.
point somebody/ something out	indicate with your finger	I'll point my boyfriend out when he runs by.
put something down	put what you are holding on a surface or floor	You can put the groceries down on the kitchen counter.
put somebody down	insult	The students put the substitute teacher down because his pants were too short.
put something off	postpone	We are putting off our trip until January because of the hurricane.
put something out	extinguish	The neighbours put the fire out before the firemen arrived.
put something together	assemble	I have to put the crib together before the baby arrives.
put up with somebody/ something	tolerate	I don't think I can put up with three small children in the car.
put something on	put clothing/ accessories on your body	Don't forget to put on your new earrings for the party.
run into somebody/ something	meet unexpectedly	I ran into an old school-friend at the mall.
run over somebody/ something	drive a vehicle over a person or thing	I accidentally ran over your bicycle in the driveway.
run over/through something	rehearse, review	Let's run over/through these lines one more time before the show.
run away	leave unexpectedly, escape	The child ran away from home and has been missing for three days.
run out	have none left	We ran out of shampoo so I had to wash my hair with soap.
send something back	return (usually by mail)	My letter got sent back to me because I used the wrong stamp.
set something up	arrange, organize	Our boss set a meeting up with the president of the company.

set somebody up	trick, trap	The police set up the car thief by using a hidden camera.
shop around	compare prices	I want to shop around a little before I decide on these boots.
show off	act extra special	He always shows off on his skateboard.
sleep over	stay somewhere for the night	You should sleep over tonight if the weather is too bad to drive home.
sort something out	organize, resolve a problem	We need to sort the bills out before the first of the month.
stick to something	continue doing something	You will lose weight if you stick to the diet.
switch something off	stop the energy flow, turn off	The light's too bright. Could you switch it off.
switch something on	start the energy flow, turn on	We heard the news as soon as we switched on the car radio.
take after somebody	resemble a family member	I take after my mother. We are both impatient.
take something back	return an item	I have to take our new TV back because it doesn't work.
take off	start to fly	My plane takes off in five minutes.
take something off	remove something (usually clothing)	Take off your socks and shoes and come in the lake!
take something out	remove from a place or thing	Can you take the garbage out to the street for me?
take somebody out	pay for somebody to go somewhere with you	My grandparents took us out for dinner and a movie.
tear something up	rip into pieces	I tore up my ex-boyfriend's letters and gave them back to him.
think back	remember (often + to, sometimes + on)	When I think back on my youth, I wish I had studied harder.
think something over	consider	I'll have to think this job offer over before I make my final decision.
throw something away	dispose of	We threw our old furniture away when we won the lottery.

Verbs, Adverbs, Phrasal Verbs and Modals

turn something down	decrease the volume	Please turn the TV down while the guests are here.
turn something down	refuse	I turned the job down because I don't want to move.
turn something off	stop the energy flow, switch off	Your mother wants you to turn the TV off and come for dinner.
turn something on	start the energy, switch on	It's too dark in here. Let's turn some lights on.
turn something up	increase the volume or strength	Can you turn the music up? This is my favourite song.
turn up	appear	Our cat turned up after we put posters up all over the neighbourhood.
try something on	sample clothing	I'm going to try these jeans on, but I don't think they will fit.
try something out	test	I am going to try this new brand of detergent out.
use something up	finish the supply	The kids used all of the toothpaste up so we need to buy some more.
wake up	stop sleeping	We have to wake up early for work on Monday.
warm up	prepare body for exercise	I always warm up by doing sit-ups before I go for a run.
wear off	fade away	Most of my make-up wore off before I got to the party.
work out	exercise	I work out at the gym three times a week.
work out	be successful	Our plan worked out fine.
work something out	make a calculation	We have to work out the total cost before we buy the house.

Modal Verb

A modal verb is a type of verb that is used to indicate modality – that is, likelihood, ability, permission, and obligation. Examples include the English verbs can/could, may/might, must, will/would, and shall/should. In English, modal verbs are often distinguished as a class based on certain grammatical properties.

Function

A modal auxiliary verb gives information about the function of the main verb that it governs. Modals have a wide variety of communicative functions, but these functions can generally be related to a scale ranging from possibility ("may") to necessity ("must"), in terms of one of the following types of modality:

- 'Epistemic modality,' concerned with the theoretical possibility of propositions being true or not true (including likelihood and certainty)
- 'Deontic modality,' concerned with possibility and necessity in terms of freedom to act (including permission and duty)
- 'Dynamic modality,' which may be distinguished from deontic modality, in that with dynamic modality, the conditioning factors are internal – the subject's own ability or willingness to act

Can, Could, Be Able To

"Can" is one of the most commonly used modal verbs. It can be used to express ability or opportunity, to request or offer permission, and to show possibility or impossibility.

"Can", "could" and "be able to" are used to express a variety of ideas:

☞ **Ability/Lack of Ability**

Present and Future:
can/can't + base form of the verb

Example:
(i) Tom can write poetry very well.
(ii) I can help you with that next week.
(iii) Lisa can't speak French.

am / is / are / will be + able to + base form of the verb
am not/ isn't / aren't/ won't be + able to + base form of the verb

Example:
(i) Mike is able to solve complicated math equations.
(ii) The support team will be able to help you in about ten minutes.
(iii) I won't be able to visit you next summer.

Past:
Could / couldn't + base form of the verb

Example:
When I was a child, I could climb trees.
was / were + able to + base form of the verb
wasn't / weren't + able to + base form of the verb
hasn't / haven't + been able to + base form of the verb

Example:
I wasn't able to visit her in the hospital.
He hasn't been able to get in touch with the client yet.

> **Note:**
> Can and could do not take an infinitive (to verb) and do not take the future auxiliary will.

I can to help you this afternoon. (Incorrect)
I can help you this afternoon. (Correct)
I will (I'll) be able to help you this afternoon. (Correct)

☞ **Possibility / Impossibility**
can / can't + base form of the verb

Example:
You can catch that train at 10:43.
He can't see you right now. He's in surgery.

could + base form of the verb

Example:
I could fly via Amsterdam if I leave the day before.

☞ **Ask Permission / Give Permission**
Can + Subject + base form of the verb (informal)

Example:
Can you lend me ten dollars?
Can + base form of the verb (informal)

Example:
You can borrow my car.
Could + subject + base form of the verb (polite)

Example:
Could I have your number?
Could I talk to your supervisor please?

☞ **Make a suggestion** – To make a suggestion use:
Could + base form of the verb (informal)

Example:
You could take the tour of the castle tomorrow.

☞ **Formal Permission / Formal Prohibition**

may / may not + base form of the verb

Example:

You may start your exam now.

You may not wear sandals to work.

☞ **Polite Request**

May + subject + base form of the verb

Example:

May I help you?

☞ **Possibility / Negative Possibility**

may / might + base form of the verb

Example:

(i) We may go out for dinner tonight. Do you want to join us?

(ii) Our company might get the order if the client agrees to the price.

may not / might not + base form of the verb

Example:

(i) Adam and Sue may not buy that house. It's very expensive.

(ii) They might not buy a house at all.

☞ **To Make a Suggestion (when there is no better alternative)**

may as well / might as well + base form of the verb

Example:

(i) You may as well come inside. John will be home soon.

(ii) We might as well take Friday off. There's no work to be done anyway.

☞ **Polite Suggestion**

might + base form of the verb

Example:

You might like to try the salmon fillet. It's our special today.

Shall, Should, Ought to

☞ **To Offer Assistance or Polite Suggestion (When you are quite sure of a positive answer)**

Shall + subject + base form of the verb

Example:

Shall we go for a walk?

Note:
Shall is only used with I or we. It is used instead of will only in formal English.

☞ **To Offer of Assistance or Polite Suggestion (When you are not sure of a positive answer)**

Should + subject + base form of the verb

Example:

Should I call a doctor?

☞ **A Prediction or Expectation that Something Will Happen**

Should / shouldn't + base form of the verb.

Example:

(i) The proposal should be finished on time.

(ii) I shouldn't be late. The train usually arrives on time.

☞ **To Give Advice**

Should / ought to + base form of the verb.

Example:

(i) You should check that document before you send it out.

(ii) You ought to have your car serviced before the winter.

☞ **To Give Advice (about something you think wrong or unacceptable)**

Shouldn't + base form of the verb

Example:

James shouldn't teach him words like those.

Must, Have to, Need to, Don't have to, Needn't

☞ **Necessity or Requirement**

Present and Future:

must / have to / need to + base form of the verb

Example:

(i) You must have a passport to cross the border.

(ii) Elisabeth has to apply for her visa by March 10th.

(iii) I need to drop by his room to pick up a book.

Past:

had to / needed to + base form of the verb

Example:
(i) I had to work till late last night.
(ii) I needed to drink a few cups of coffee in order to stay awake.

Note:
have to and need to are often used in the same context, but many times, need to is used to express something that is less urgent, something in which you have a choice.

☞ **Almost 100% Certain**
must + base form of the verb
Example:
Thomas has lived in Paris for years. His French must be very good.

☞ **To Persuade**
must / have to + base form of the verb
Example:
(i) You must try this wine. It's excellent.
(ii) You have to visit us while you're in town.

☞ **Prohibited or Forbidden**
must not / mustn't + base form of the verb
Example:
(i) You must not drive over the speed limit.
(ii) You mustn't leave medicines where children can get to them.

☞ **Lack of Necessity**
don't /doesn't /didn't + have to + base form of the verb
Example:
(i) You don't have to park the car. The hotel valet will do it for you.
(ii) Tim doesn't have to go to school today. It's a holiday.
(iii) You didn't have to shout. Everyone could hear you.

needn't + base form of the verb
Example:
You needn't worry about me. I'll be fine.

Difference between Must and Have To?
Must and have to are modal verbs in English.

☞ **Must**
1. We use 'must' to make a logical deduction based on evidence. It indicates that the speaker is certain about something.
   Example:
   It has rained all day, it must be very wet outside.
   The weather is fantastic in California. It must be a lot fun to live there.
2. Must is also used to express a strong obligation.
   Example:
   Students must arrive in class on time.
   You must stop when the traffic lights are red.
   I must go to bed.

☞ **Have to:** Like must, have to is used to express strong obligation, but when we use have to, there is usually a sense of external obligation. Some external circumstance makes the obligation necessary.
Example:
(i) I have to send an urgent email.
(ii) I have to take this book back to the library.

Will / Would
will / won't + base form of the verb
Example:
(i) John will pick you up at 7:00 am.
(ii) Beth won't be happy with the results of the exam.

☞ **Polite Request or Statement**
Will / Would + base form of the verb
Example:
(i) Will you please take the trash out?
(ii) Would you mind if I sit here?
(iii) I'd (I would) like to sign up for your workshop.

☞ **Habitual Past Action**
Would/Wouldn't + base form of the verb
Example:
When I was a child, I would spend hours playing with my train set.

Verbs, Adverbs, Phrasal Verbs and Modals

Peter wouldn't eat broccoli when he was a kid. He loves it now.

Difference between shall and will

Shall is not used often in modern English. In fact, shall and will have the same meaning and are used to refer to the simple future. They are used as follows:

will is used with all persons: I, you, he, she, it, we, they will go there

shall is used with the first person singular and plural : I, we shall go

The short form of will and shall is 'll

Example:

(i) I, you, he, she, it, we, they will or 'll call you

(ii) I, we shall or 'll call you

In the negative, the short forms of will not and shall not are won't and shan't respectively

Example:

(i) I, you, he, she, it, we, they won't give up

(ii) I, we shan't give up

Uses of shall

☞ It should be noted that shall is often used to make suggestions, offers or ask for advice. It is used in questions as follows:

Example:

(i) Shall we stay or go out?

(ii) Shall we dance?

(iii) Shall I get his phone number if I meet him?

(iv) What shall I do to get rid of my acne?

☞ As said above, shall is used with first person singular and plural (I and we) But there is a very special use of shall with other persons to make a promise, command or threat as noted below:

Example:

(i) You shall not get in! (Command)

(ii) You shall pay for it. (Threat)

(iii) You shall get your money back soon. (Promise)

In American English, shall is mainly used in formal or legal documents:

Example:

(i) You shall abide by the law.

(ii) There shall be no trespassing on this property.

(iii) Students shall not enter this room.

- A word that is usually one of the main parts of a sentence and that expresses an action, an occurrence, or a state of being is known as verb.
- Finite Verbs are those verbs that have a definite relation with the subject or noun.
- The non-finite verbs that have '-ing' or '-ed' as suffixes and cause the verb to become an adjective are called Participles.
- A gerund is formed by adding –ing to a verb. It functions as a noun.
- An infinitive is formed by using the word 'to' before the verb in its stem word. It functions as a noun, adjective or adverb.
- Action verbs can be either transitive or intransitive.
- A transitive verb always has a noun that receives the action of the verb, called the direct object.
- An intransitive verb never has a direct or indirect object.
- A linking verb connects the subject of a sentence to a noun or adjective that renames or describes the subject.
- Helping verbs are used before action or linking verbs to convey additional information regarding aspects of possibility or time.
- 'Must' is used to indicate that something is necessary or of extreme importance, and 'should' is used to suggest that something is advisable.
- An adverb of time tells us when something is done or happens. We use it at the beginning or at the end of a sentence.
- An adverb of place tells us where something is done or happens. We use it after the verb, object or at the end of a sentence.
- An adverb of manner tells us how something is done or happens.
- An adverb of degree tells us the level or extent at which something is done or happens.
- An adverb of frequency tells us how often something is done or happens.
- The adverbs used to ask questions are called Interrogative Adverbs.
- Phrasal verbs are usually two-word phrases consisting of verb + adverb or verb + preposition.
- If you think of each phrasal verb as a separate verb with a specific meaning, you will be able to remember it more easily.
- A modal verb is a type of verb that is used to indicate modality – that is, likelihood, ability, permission, and obligation.
- A modal auxiliary verb gives information about the function of the main verb that it governs.

Verbs, Adverbs, Phrasal Verbs and Modals

PRACTICE EXERCISE

I. Identify if the underlined words are finite or non-finite verbs.

1. Nancy <u>does</u> her homework every day
2. Nancy is <u>doing</u> her homework at the moment
3. They <u>are</u> writing a letter.
4. She <u>speaks</u> Chinese very well.
5. He <u>has</u> a big car.
6. The proposal has <u>been</u> examined today.
7. She <u>tried</u> to help him.
8. It is healthy to <u>laugh</u> problems.
9. <u>Finding</u> the gates widely open, the thief went inside
10. He had his car <u>cleaned</u>.

II. Fill in the blanks with appropriate verb form and identify if you've used the verb in the gerund, infinitive or participle form.

1. I don't fancy _____ (go) out tonight.
2. He decided _____ (study) Biology.
3. She avoided _____ (tell) him about her plans.
4. I am learning _____ (speak) English.
5. I promise _____ (help) you tomorrow.
6. I would like _____ (come) to the party with you.
7. _____ (Hear) a loud noise, we ran to the window.
8. He ruined his sight by _____ (watch) TV all day.
9. We saw a clown _____ (stand) on his head.
10. _____ (Ask) questions is a whole lot easier than _____ (answer) them.

III. Fill in the blanks with the correct option given in brackets.

1. I found his home very _____.
(easily, difficultly, frequently)
2. Rohan behaves very _____ with his elders.
(goodly, badly, easily)
3. My father will be _____ of town this weekend.
(inside, outside, out)
4. Rohan plays football _____.
(aggressively, sympathetically, hardly)
5. They called the police _____ after the accident.
(immediately, slowly, peacefully)
6. Kiran is a _____ paid employee of this company.
(lowly, highly, hardly)
7. I was stuck in the jam for _____ two hours.
(nearly, simply, correctly)
8. How _____ do you go there?
(never, seldom, often)
9. Thomas was _____ happy when he got his first job.
(extremely, fully, halfly)
10. My elder brother is 25, he still feels _____ when he sees cockroach.
(frightender, frightened, frightendest)
11. Mr. Sharma felt very _____ when his son failed the final examination.
(more disappointed, most disappointed, disappointed)
12. I feel _____on Sundays.
(relaxed, relaxing, relaxful)
13. Rohan felt _____ when his manager shouted at him in front of his juniors.
(proud, honoured, ashamed)
14. He doesn't seem _____ in your offer.
(interested, interesting, exciting)
15. I _____ dancing.
(often go, go often)
16. She _____ in the morning.
(smokes never, never smokes)
17. _____ drink wine at lunchtime.
(I rarely, rarely I)

18. I _____ some gardening at the weekend if the weather's nice.
    (do usually, usually do)
19. He _____ into work on time.
    (gets hardly ever, hardly ever gets)
20. She _____ reading the novel she started yesterday.
    (already has finished, has already finished)
21. _____ not accept this deal.
    (I will definitely, Definitely I will)
22. I _____ like fish very much; I can eat it, but I wouldn't choose to eat it.
    (really don't, don't really)
23. When we were young, we _____ on camping holidays to France.
    (went always, always went)
24. _____ seen such a mess as his bedroom.
    (Seldom have I, I seldom have)
25. I _____ be able to make it tomorrow.
    (won't probably, probably won't)
26. _____ so insulted.
    (I never have been, I have never been)
27. Hardly ever _____ it.
    (I do, do I, do I do)

IV. Fill in the blanks with the correct option given in brackets.

1. _____ I met my childhood friend Meeta.
   (Yesterday/Tomorrow/This Sunday)
2. You need to run _____ to win this race.
   (slow/steadily/fast)
3. I won't say it _____.
   (progressively/repeatedly/necessarily)
4. Speak _____, I cannot hear you.
   (loudly/slowly/hardly)
5. You should _____ smoke as it is dangerous for your health.
   (always/usually/never)
6. We searched _____ but were unable to find her lost jewellery.
   (nowhere/anywhere/everywhere)
7. I hope to see you _____!
   (soon/never/random)
8. Deepak never dresses _____ for work.
   (formally/coolly/dirtily)

V. Fill in the blanks with the correct option.

1. Carlos is an excellent student. He _____ goes to class.
   (a) always   (b) usually
   (c) sometimes   (d) seldom
   (e) never
2. I hate vegetables. I _____ eat carrots.
   (a) always   (b) usually
   (c) sometimes   (d) seldom
   (e) never
3. Robert goes to the gym only two or three times a year. He _____ goes to the gym.
   (a) always   (b) never
   (c) usually   (d) seldom
4. Harold never leaves the college on Friday. He _____ eats at the cafeteria on Fridays.
   (a) always   (b) never
   (c) seldom
5. Ms. Biethan is always in a good mood. She is _____ sad.
   (a) always   (b) usually
   (c) never
6. Teresa is not a pleasant person. She is _____ in a bad mood.
   (a) never   (b) seldom
   (c) always
7. My sister usually drives to work with a friend. She _____ drives alone.
   (a) never   (b) always
   (c) usually   (d) seldom
8. I never lend money to Curtis. He _____ pays me back.
   (a) sometimes   (b) always
   (c) never   (d) usually
9. Susan goes to the beach whenever she can. She _____ misses a chance to go to the ocean.
   (a) never   (b) always
   (c) usually

Verbs, Adverbs, Phrasal Verbs and Modals

10. It almost always rains in Seattle. The sun _____ shines there.
    (a) always (b) usually
    (c) seldom

VI. Select the right option to fill in the blanks.

1. Could you turn _____ the TV? The soap opera is about to start.
   (a) back (b) on
   (c) off (d) out

2. There was nothing good on TV so I turned it _____ and went to bed.
   (a) off (b) up
   (c) in (d) down

3. The TV is too loud. Can you turn it _____ a bit?
   (a) up (b) out
   (c) off (d) down

4. The TV is too quiet. Can you turn it _____ a bit?
   (a) back (b) off
   (c) up (d) over

5. I've been looking _____ my car keys for half an hour. Have you seen them anywhere?
   (a) up (b) for
   (c) after (d) at

6. My mother has offered to look _____ the children, so we can go to the party.
   (a) for (b) into
   (c) at (d) after

7. If you don't know what the word means, you'll have to look it _____ in the dictionary.
   (a) for (b) up
   (c) out (d) off

8. The meeting has been put _____ to Friday as many people have got the flu.
   (a) up (b) in
   (c) back (d) out

9. The meeting has been brought _____ to Monday due to the seriousness of the situation.
   (a) on (b) out
   (c) down (d) forward

10. The company is taking _____ new workers to meet this projected demand.
    (a) at (b) on
    (c) up (d) over

VII. Select correct Phrasal verb to fill in the blanks.

1. Has the advertising agency _____ the new promotional material yet? I need it by this afternoon.
   (a) dropped off (b) dropped in
   (c) dropped out (d) dropped by

2. We need to _____ the price of the product, which is relatively high, and focus on its quality as a selling point.
   (a) back down
   (b) break down
   (c) play down
   (d) settle down

3. Have you _____ any other interesting product features that we could emphasize in the ads?
   (a) come across (b) drawn out
   (c) gotten across (d) made out

4. We've decided to _____ billboards and use more double-page spreads instead.
   (a) back off on
   (b) come down with
   (c) cut back on
   (d) drop off

5. This poster is horrible and can't be used. The colours and images are all wrong. We will have to _____ .
   (a) do it over (b) even it out
   (c) do it in (d) put it down

6. We had to reorder the printed advertisements because the printer completely forgot and _____ the free sample coupons.
   (a) kept off (b) left out
   (c) passed out (d) shaved off

7. We're going to have to _____ the advertising campaign if we can't get any TV or radio time.
   (a) call on (b) call off
   (c) drop off (d) drop out

8. This commercial doesn't seem to promote the product. Can you explain to me how dancing chickens _____ sport shoes?
   (a) pan out as   (b) hold up to
   (c) add up to   (d) have to do with
9. I like that magazine, but I think we should _____ advertising in it until its circulation has increased.
   (a) put out   (b) put back
   (c) put away   (d) put off
10. My new assistant needs to be _____ before I trust her to run an ad campaign like this one.
    (a) broken down   (b) broken in
    (c) broken up   (d) broken into

VIII. Fill in the blanks with appropriate phrasal verb.
1. What time does this afternoon's match _____?
   (a) make off   (b) take off
   (c) set off   (d) kick off
2. I'm thinking of _____ a new hobby. Maybe I'll give painting a try.
   (a) doing up   (b) setting up
   (c) taking up   (d) making up
3. I can't afford to _____ on another foreign holiday this year.
   (a) set out   (b) splash out
   (c) take out   (d) give out
4. If you need somewhere to stay, I can _____ for a few days.
   (a) set you up   (b) get you up
   (c) take you up   (d) put you up
5. If you're going to the shops, can you get us some milk. I'm afraid we've _____ again.
   (a) grown out   (b) taken out
   (c) gone out   (d) run out
6. How are you _____ with your new neighbours? Are they okay?
   (a) hitting off   (b) getting along
   (c) taking off   (d) getting through
7. Someone _____ my flat while I was away and stole my video and sound system.

(a) dropped into   (b) crashed into
(c) moved into   (d) broke into
8. Of course I was upset that I didn't get the job, but I'll soon _____ it.
   (a) do over   (b) get over
   (c) make over   (d) put over
9. If you're thinking of selling your house, you should _____ first. You'll get a better price.
   (a) do it up   (b) dream it up
   (c) make it up   (d) make it out
10. Being in hospital in the UK was a terrible experience. I don't want to have to _____ that again if I can help it.
    (a) think through   (b) get off
    (c) go through   (d) make through

IX. Fill in the correct form of can, could or be able to in the following sentences.
1. _____ Tony run long distances when he was a boy?
2. _____ you please call a tow truck for me? My car broke down. (polite)
3. The students _____ to buy their textbooks today. The bookstore is all out of them.
4. _____ you teach me how to fix my computer? You're so good at it.
5. _____ you _____ reach the customer if you call him at 4:00 his time?

X. Fill in the blanks with correct form of May or Might.
1. They _____ finish the project on time. The main engineer is ill.
2. You _____ want to stop by the museum gift shop on your way out.
3. _____ I have your autograph?
4. He _____ visit the Louvre. He's in Paris anyway.
5. You _____ park your car here. It's reserved for guests of the hotel only.

XI. Fill in should, shouldn't or ought in the following sentences.
1. He _____ encourage such bad behaviour.

Verbs, Adverbs, Phrasal Verbs and Modals

2. You _____ get your teeth cleaned at least once a year.
3. The house _____ be ready to move into by next month. It's almost finished.
4. Ron _____ to improve his attitude. If he doesn't, he might get fired.
5. _____ I get your jacket? It's cold in here.
6. You _____ put your feet on the table. It's not polite.

XII. Fill in the blanks with any one of the following modals.

must, must not, have to, has to, don't have to, doesn't have to, needn't as in the examples.
There may be more than one correct answer.

1. Shira doesn't _____ drive to the airport. She's going by taxi.
2. You _____ speak politely to the customers.
3. You _____ tell Anna about the party tomorrow night. It's a surprise! (must not, need to, doesn't have to)
4. Tina _____ register for her classes on Monday, otherwise she won't get a place in them. (doesn't have to, mustn't, has to)
5. You _____ send that fax. I've already sent it. (must, will have to, don't have to)
6. A dog _____ get special training in order to be a guide dog. (must, need to, don't have to)
7. Jeremy _____ get up early tomorrow. His class was cancelled. (mustn't, doesn't have to, don't need to)

XIII. Fill in the blanks with will, won't, would, or wouldn't.

1. _____ you please help me lift this box?
2. I _____ like to order the onion soup please.
3. The manager _____ be pleased to hear that a customer slipped on the wet floor.
4. _____ it be okay if I slept here tonight?
5. When Igor lived in Russia, he _____ call his mother as often as he does now.
6. I can assure you sir, the order _____ be shipped out tonight.

XIV. Choose the correct modal verb and fill in the blanks.

1. _____ you go already? You only arrived an hour ago!
   (a) must   (b) should
   (c) can   (d) none of these
2. When he was young, he _____ swim very well. He won medals and championships!
   (a) had to
   (b) can
   (c) could
   (d) none of these
3. The company _____ go bankrupt if they don't find a lot of money quickly!
   (a) should   (b) shouldn't
   (c) might   (d) none of these
4. You look very confused by the homework, Clive. _____ I help you?
   (a) will   (b) can
   (c) must   (d) none of these
5. I left my purse at home. Lily, _____ you lend me ten dollars?
   (a) may   (b) could
   (c) shouldn't   (d) none of these
6. It's wet and windy outside today. You _____ go out without an umbrella.
   (a) shouldn't   (b) won't
   (c) don't have to   (d) none of these
7. I think that sign means we _____ enter the building. Look, there's a security guard too.
   (a) won't   (b) have to
   (c) mustn't   (d) none of these
8. Lindsay watched the movie in French and _____ understand very much of it.
   (a) didn't have to (b) can't
   (c) couldn't   (d) none of these

XV. Fill in the blanks with the correct modal verb.

1. _____ I have more cheese on my sandwich?
   (a) Must   (b) Could
   (c) Would   (d) Have to

2. You _____ eat more vegetables.
   (a) should (b) might
   (c) may (d) could
3. I _____ like to buy the same television for my house.
   (a) could (b) must
   (c) would (d) have to
4. _____ I have a coffee, please?
   (a) Must (b) Have to
   (c) May (d) Would
5. You _____ smoke near children.
   (a) have to (b) may
   (c) shouldn't (d) couldn't
6. The passengers _____ wear their seat belts at all times.
   (a) could (b) must
   (c) can (d) may
7. We _____ go to the concert if the rain stops. We don't know for sure.
   (a) mustn't (b) might
   (c) have to (d) wouldn't
8. I _____ ice skate very well.
   (a) can (b) may
   (c) must (d) should
9. The boys _____ wake up earlier than 7:30 am. They have class at 8:00 am.
   (a) would (b) can't
   (c) could (d) have to
10. The rock band _____ play very well last year. Now they are much better.
    (a) must (b) couldn't
    (c) can (d) should
11. It _____ be ready by Friday, as long as we don't have any unexpected problems.
    (a) may (b) might
    (c) should (d) must
12. She _____ to lunch. She usually goes at this time.
    (a) must go (b) should go
    (c) should have gone (d) must have gone
13. If we'd had more time we _____ have finished it.
    (a) could (b) could have
    (c) must have (d) would have
14. It was her birthday yesterday. We _____ got her a card. I feel awful.
    (a) had to (b) must have
    (c) should (d) should have
15. She _____ be here in a minute she only went out to get a newspaper.
    (a) must (b) should
    (c) could (d) might
16. Sorry I'm late, I _____ drop the kids off at school.
    (a) must (b) must have
    (c) had to (d) should have
17. I _____ replied earlier but I was out all day yesterday.
    (a) had to (b) would have
    (c) could have (d) must have
18. It _____ been a great party if a few more people had come.
    (a) would have (b) should have
    (c) must have (d) might have
19. Although we didn't have the right tools, we _____ get the work finished on time.
    (a) could have (b) could
    (c) were able to (d) managed to
20. He _____ passed easily if only he'd spent a bit more time revising.
    (a) could have (b) would have
    (c) must have (d) might have

Verbs, Adverbs, Phrasal Verbs and Modals

HOTS

I. Fill in the blanks with suitable adverb.

1. Our holiday was too short. The time passed very _____
2. Rose is _____ upset about losing her job.
3. Sally works _____. She never seems to stop.
4. Alice and Stan are very _____ married.
5. I cooked this meal _____ for you, so I hope you like it.

II. Choose the best phrasal verb to fill in the blanks.

1. It's not such a terrible thing! Don't worry! _____! (be happy, not be sad).
   (a) cheer up (b) laugh away
   (c) cheer out (d) laugh out

2. After being together for twenty years, Paul and Julia _____ (end a relationship).
   (a) broke down (b) split off
   (c) broke away (d) split up

3. I've missed many lessons, so now I'll have to _____ (reach the same level, learn the same as the others) the other students.
   (a) catch up (b) catch up with
   (c) hurry up (d) learn on

4. It's your problem, so try to _____ it _____ (solve).
   (a) work, in (b) sort, off
   (c) sort, out (d) solve, in

5. It's too cold in here. Shall I _____ (increase the temperature) the heating?
   (a) turn on (b) get up
   (c) turn up (d) put on

Conjunction 5

Learning Objectives : In this chapter, students will learn about:
- ✓ Conjunction and its types

CHAPTER SUMMARY

Conjunction is a word that connects words, phrases, clauses or sentences. For example; and, but, or, nor, for, yet, so, although, because, since, unless, when, while, and where are some conjunctions.

Example:
(a) She tried but did not succeed.
(b) He does not go to school because he is ill.
(c) John and Marry went to the cinema.
(d) He thought for a moment and kicked the ball.
(e) I waited for him but he didn't come.
(f) You will be ill unless you quit smoking.
(g) We didn't go to the market because it was raining outside.

Types of Conjunction

There are three types of conjunctions:
- Coordinating Conjunction
- Subordinating Conjunction
- Correlative Conjunction

Coordinating Conjunction

Coordinating conjunctions (called coordinators) join words, phrases (which are similar in importance and grammatical structure) or independent clauses. Coordinating conjunctions are short words i.e., and, but, or, nor, for, so, yet. Coordination conjunction joins two equal parts of a sentence:
- Word + word
- Phrase + phrase
- Clause + clause
- Independent clause + independent clause.

Example:
(a) She likes tea and coffee.
(b) He may be in the room or on the roof.
(c) What you eat and what you drink affect your health.
(d) The cat jumped over the mouse and the mouse ran away.
(e) She likes pizza and cake. (pizza and cake)
(f) I bought a table and a chair. (table and chair)
(g) He may come by bus or car. (bus or car)

Note:
Independent clause is a clause which can stand alone as a sentence and have complete thought on its own.

Example:
(a) I called him, but he didn't pick up the phone.
(b) I advised him to quit smoking, but he didn't act upon my advice.
(c) He became ill, so he thought he should go to a doctor.
(d) He shouted for help, but nobody helped him.

(e) He wants to become a doctor, so he is studying Biology.

Coordinating conjunctions always come between the words or clauses that they join. A comma is used with conjunction if the clauses are long or not well-balanced. If both clauses have same subjects, the subject of 2nd clause may not be written again.

Example:
(a) She worked hard and succeeded.
(b) The player stopped and kicked the ball.
(c) He became ill but didn't go to doctor.
(d) Marry opened the book and started to study.

TRIVIA
A 672-sided shape is called a "hexahectaheptacontakaidigon"

Kinds of Coordinating Conjunctions
Coordinating conjunctions are of four kinds:

Cumulative or Copulative Conjunctions
Cumulative conjunctions merely add one statement to another. Some cumulative conjunctions are: and, both…and, as well as, not only…but also.
(a) Alice wrote the letters and Peter posted them.
(b) The cow got up and walked away slowly.

Adversative Conjunctions
Adversative conjunctions express contrast between two statements. Some adversative conjunctions are: but, still, yet, whereas, while, nevertheless, etc.

Example:
(a) The rope was thin but it was strong.
(b) She is poor but she is happy.
(c) He is hardworking whereas his brother is quite the reverse.

Disjunctive or Alternative Conjunctions
Conjunctions which present two alternatives are called disjunctive or alternative conjunctions.
Some alternative conjunctions are: or, either…or, neither…nor, neither, nor, otherwise, else, etc.

Example:
a) She must weep, or she will die.
b) Either he is mad, or he feigns madness.
c) They toil not, neither do they spin.
d) Neither a borrower, nor a lender be.

Illative Conjunctions
Some coordinating conjunctions express something inferred from another statement or fact. These are called illative conjunctions. Some illative conjunctions are: for and so.

Example:
a) Somebody came, for I heard a knock at the door.
b) He must be asleep, for there is no light in his room.
c) He has been working hard, so he will pass.

Subordinating Conjunctions
Subordinating conjunctions (called subordinators) join a subordinate clause (dependent clause) to a main clause. Most subordinating conjunctions are single words (such as because, before, when). However, some subordinating conjunctions consist of more than one word (such as even though, as long as, except that). Other examples of Subordinating conjunctions are: although, because, if, before, how, once, since, till, until, when, where, whether, while, after, no matter how, provided that, as soon as, even if, etc.

The structure of the sentence could be either of the following:

Main clause + subordinate clause

Subordinate clause + main clause

Note:
Subordinate clause is a combination of words (subject and verb) which cannot stand alone as a complete sentence. Subordinate clause is also called dependent clause because it is dependent on main clause. Subordinate clause usually starts with a relative pronoun, such as, which, who, that, whom, etc. Subordinate clause gives more information in relation to the main clause to complete the thought.

Subordinating conjunction always comes before the subordinate clause, no matter whether the subordinate clause is before the main clause or after.

Example:
(a) He does not go to school because he is ill.
(b) I will call you after I reach my home.
(c) I bought some cookies while I was coming from my office.
(d) They played football although it was raining.
(e) Although it was raining, they played football.
(f) As far as I know, this exam is very difficult.
(g) I have gone to every concert since I have lived in New York.
(h) You can get high grades in exam provided that you work hard for it.

Types of Subordinate Clause

A subordinate (dependent) clause may function as a noun, an adjective or an adverb in a sentence. On the basis of their function in a sentence, subordinate clauses can be divided into the following types:

Noun Clause

A dependent clause that functions as a noun in a sentence is called noun clause. A noun clause performs same function like a noun in a sentence.

Example:
What he did made a problem for his family.

In the above sentence, the clause "what he did" functions as a noun, hence it is a noun clause.

A noun clause works as a noun that acts as a subject, object, or predicate in a sentence. A noun clause starts with words like "that, what, whatever, who, whom, whoever, whomever".

Example:
(a) Whatever you learn will help you in future. (noun clause as a subject)
(b) What you said made me laugh. (noun clause as a subject)
(c) He knows that he will pass the test. (noun clause as an object)
(d) Now I realize what he would have thought. (noun clause as an object)

Adjective Clause

A dependent clause that functions as an adjective in a sentence is called adjective clause.

An adjective clause works like an adjective in a sentence. The function of an adjective is to modify (describe) a noun or a pronoun. Similarly a noun clause modifies a noun or a pronoun.

Example:
He wears a shirt which looks nice.

The clause "which looks nice" in above sentence is an adjective clause because it modifies noun "shirt" in the sentence.

An adjective clause always precedes the noun it modifies.

Example:
(a) I met the boy who had helped me.
(b) An apple that smells bad is rotten.
(c) The book which I like is helpful in preparation for test.
(d) The house where I live consists of four rooms.
(e) The person who was shouting needed help.

Adjective clause begins with relative pronoun (that, who, whom, whose, which, or whose) and is also relative clause.

Adjective (relative) clauses can be restrictive clause or non-restrictive clause.

Restrictive and Non-restrictive Clause

Adjective (relative) clauses can be restrictive or non-restrictive. A restrictive clause limits the meaning of preceding noun or pronoun. A non-restrictive clause tells us something about preceding noun or pronoun but does not limit the meaning of preceding noun or pronoun.

Example:
(a) The student in the class who studied a lot passed the test. (restrictive clause)
(b) The student in the class, who had attended all the lectures, passed the test. (non-restrictive clause)

In the first sentence, the clause "who studied a lot" restrict information to preceding noun (student); it means that there is only one student in the class who studied a lot, hence it is a restrictive clause.

In the second sentence, the clause "who had attended all the lectures" gives us information about preceding noun but does not limit this information to the preceding noun. It means there can be several other students in the class who had attended all the lectures.

A comma is always used before a restrictive clause in a sentence and also after non-restrictive clause if it is within a main clause. "That" is usually used to introduce a restrictive clause while "which" is used to introduce a non-restrictive clause.

Example:
(a) The table that costs $ 100 is made of steel. (restrictive clause)
(b) The table, which costs $ 100, is made of steel. (non-restrictive clause)

Adverb Clause
A dependent clause that functions as an adverb in a sentence is called adverb clause.

An adverb clause like an adverb modifies a verb, adjective clause or other adverb clause in a sentence. It modifies (describes) the situation in a main clause in terms of "time, frequency (how often), cause and effect, contrast, condition, intensity (to what extent)."

The subordinating conjunctions used for adverb clauses are as follows.

Time: when, whenever, since, until, before, after, while, as, by the time, as soon as

Cause and effect: because, since, now that, as long as, so, so that

Contrast: although, even, whereas, while, though

Condition: if, unless, only if, whether or not, even if, providing or provided that, in case

Example:
(a) Don't go before he comes.
(b) He takes medicine because he is ill.
(c) Although he tried a lot, he couldn't climb up the tree.
(d) Unless you study for the test, you can't pass it.
(e) I will go to the school unless it rains.
(f) You are safe as long as you drive carefully.
(g) You can achieve anything provided that you struggle for it.

Correlative Conjunction
These are paired conjunctions which join words, phrases or clauses which have reciprocal or complementary relationship.

The most commonly used correlative conjunctions are as follows:
(i) Either ... or
(ii) Neither ... nor
(iii) Whether ... or
(iv) Both ... and
(v) Not only ... but also

Example:
(a) Neither John nor Marry passed the exam.
(b) Give me either a cup or a glass.
(c) Both red and yellow are attractive colours.
(d) I like neither tea nor coffee.
(e) He will be either in the room or in the hall.
(f) John can speak not only English but also French.

MUST REMEMBER

- Conjunction is a word that connects words, phrases, clauses or sentences.
- Coordinating conjunctions join words, phrases or independent clauses.
- Independent clause is a clause which can stand alone as a sentence and have complete thought on its own.
- If both clauses have same subjects, the subject of 2nd clause may not be written again.
- Adversative conjunctions express contrast between two statements.
- Conjunctions which present two alternatives are called disjunctive or alternative conjunctions.
- Subordinating conjunctions (called subordinators) join a subordinate clause (dependent clause) to a main clause.
- A subordinate (dependent) clause may function as a noun, an adjective or an adverb in a sentence.
- A dependent clause that functions as a noun in a sentence is called noun clause.
- A dependent clause that functions as an adjective in a sentence is called adjective clause.
- A restrictive clause limits the meaning of preceding noun or pronoun. A non-restrictive clause tells us something about preceding noun or pronoun but does not limit the meaning of preceding noun or pronoun.
- An adverb clause like an adverb modifies a verb, adjective clause or other adverb clause in a sentence

Conjunction

PRACTICE EXERCISE

I. Complete the following sentences using an appropriate conjunction.

1. I waited for him _____ 7 o'clock and then I went home.
   (a) until
   (b) till
   (c) both (a) or (b)
2. I will make a cake _____ I have time.
   (a) if
   (b) when
   (c) unless
3. They had left _____ the time I reached their place.
   (a) by
   (b) before
   (c) as soon as
4. _____ the teacher left the classroom, the students started chatting.
   (a) No sooner
   (b) As soon as
   (c) Hardly
5. I will call you _____ I leave.
   (a) till
   (b) before
   (c) Either could be used here
6. Take this bag with you _____ you leave.
   (a) when
   (b) after
   (c) Either could be used here
7. She was depressed _____ she didn't know what to do.
   (a) because
   (b) because of
   (c) both (a) or (b)
8. We must reach there _____ he leaves.
   (a) before
   (b) until
   (c) Either could be used here
9. I cut myself _____ I was shaving.
   (a) while
   (b) whenever
   (c) Either could be used here
10. We cancelled the trip _____ it was raining.
    (a) because
    (b) in case
    (c) if

II. Point out the conjunctions in the following sentences and state whether they are coordinating or subordinating.

1. You will succeed if you work harder.
2. We arrived after they left.
3. I waited till he returned from office.
4. Bread and milk is wholesome food.
5. You will not get the prize unless you deserve it.
6. Do not go before I return from the market.
7. I can't lend you any money, for I have none.
8. Since you have apologized we will not take any further actions against you.
9. The thief fled lest he should be caught.
10. I will be upset if you don't accept my invitation.
11. She didn't come because you didn't invite her.
12. He is smarter than his boss.
13. My grandfather died when I was a child.
14. Please stay here till I return.
15. He asked whether he could go.

HOTS

Use the correct conjunction from the options provided to fill in the blanks below.

1. _____ (As, Although) he was the best qualified candidate, he didn't win the elections.
2. _____ (As, When) you come back from your trip, we'll meet to discuss the problem.
3. They said that the movie was fantastic, _____ (so, when) I watched it.
4. She went to the shops _____ (and, but) couldn't find anything that could fit her needs.
5. I don't know _____ (where, if) I can buy a pair of jeans.

Conjunction

Punctuations

Learning Objectives : In this chapter, students will learn about:
- Use of different Punctuation marks

CHAPTER SUMMARY

Punctuation is used to create sense, clarity and stress in sentences. You use punctuation marks to structure and organise your writing.

Uses of Punctuation Marks

Periods

Rule 1: Use a period at the end of a complete sentence that is a statement.

Example:
I know him well.

Rule 2: If the last item in the sentence is an abbreviation that ends in a period, do not follow it with another period.

(a) This is Alice Smith, M.D.. (Incorrect)
(b) This is Alice Smith, M.D. (Correct)
(c) Please shop, cook, etc. We will do the laundry. (Correct)

Rule 3: Question marks and exclamation points replace and eliminate periods at the end of a sentence.

Example:
(a) How are you doing these days?
(b) What a beautiful flower!

Commas

Commas and periods are the most frequently used punctuation marks. Commas customarily indicate a brief pause; they're not as final as periods.

Rule 1: Use commas to separate words and word groups in a simple series of three or more items.

Example:
My estate goes to my husband, son, daughter-in-law, and nephew.

> **Note:**
> When the last comma in a series comes before 'and' or 'or' (after daughter-in-law in the above example), it is known as the Oxford comma. Most newspapers and magazines drop the Oxford comma in a simple series, apparently feeling it's unnecessary. However, omission of the Oxford comma can sometimes lead to misunderstandings.

Example:
We had coffee, cheese and crackers and grapes.

Adding a comma after crackers makes it clear that cheese and crackers represents one dish. In cases like this, clarity demands the Oxford comma.

We had coffee, cheese and crackers, and grapes.

Fiction and non-fiction books generally prefer the Oxford comma. Writers must decide Oxford or no Oxford and not switch back and forth, except when omitting the Oxford comma could cause confusion as in the cheese and crackers example.

Rule 2: Use a comma to separate two adjectives when the order of the adjectives is interchangeable.

Example:
(a) He is a strong, healthy man.
(b) We could also say healthy, strong man.
(c) We stayed at an expensive summer resort.
(d) We would not say summer expensive resort, so no comma.

Another way to determine if a comma is needed is to mentally put and between the two adjectives. If the result still makes sense, add the comma. In the examples above, a strong and healthy man makes sense, but an expensive and summer resort does not.

Rule 3a: Many inexperienced writers run two independent clauses together by using a comma instead of a period. This results in the dreaded run-on sentence or, more technically, a comma splice.

(a) He walked all the way home, he shut the door. (Incorrect)
   There are several simple remedies:
(b) He walked all the way home. He shut the door. (Correct)
(c) After he walked all the way home, he shut the door. (Correct)
(d) He walked all the way home, and he shut the door. (Correct)

Rule 3b: In sentences, where two independent clauses are joined by connectors, such as, and, or, but, etc., put a comma at the end of the first clause.

(a) He walked all the way home and he shut the door. (Incorrect)
(b) He walked all the way home, and he shut the door. (Correct)
   Some writers omit the comma if the clauses are both quite short:

Example:
I paint and he writes.

Rule 3c. If the subject does not appear in front of the second verb, a comma is generally unnecessary.

Example:
He thought quickly but still did not answer correctly.

But sometimes a comma in this situation is necessary to avoid confusion.

Confusing: I saw that she was busy and prepared to leave.

Clearer with comma: I saw that she was busy, and prepared to leave.

Without a comma, the reader is liable to think that "she" was the one who was prepared to leave.

Rule 4.
When starting a sentence with a dependent clause, use a comma after it.

Example:
If you are not sure about this, let me know now.

But often a comma is unnecessary when the sentence starts with an independent clause followed by a dependent clause.

Example:
Let me know now if you are not sure about this.

Rule 5. Use commas to set off non-essential words, clauses, and phrases (see Who, That, Which).

(a) Jill who is my sister shut the door. (Incorrect)
(b) Jill, who is my sister, shut the door. (Correct)
(c) The man knowing it was late hurried home. (Incorrect)
(d) The man, knowing it was late, hurried home. (Correct)

In the preceding examples, note the comma after sister and late. Non-essential words, clauses, and phrases that occur mid-sentence must be enclosed by commas. The closing comma is called an appositive comma. Many writers forget to add this important comma. Following are two instances of the need for an appositive comma with one or more nouns.

(a) My best friend, Joe arrived. (Incorrect)
(b) My best friend, Joe, arrived. (Correct)
   The three items, a book, a pen, and paper were on the table. (Incorrect)
   The three items, a book, a pen, and paper, were on the table. (Correct)

Rule 6: If something or someone is sufficiently identified, the description that follows is considered non-essential and should be surrounded by commas.

Example:

Freddy, who has a limp, was in an auto accident.

If we already know which Freddy is meant, the description is not essential.

The boy who has a limp was in an auto accident.

We do not know which boy is meant without further description; therefore, no commas are used.

This leads to a persistent problem. Look at the following sentence:

Example:

My brother Bill is here.

Now, see how adding two commas changes that sentence's meaning:

My brother, Bill, is here.

Careful writers and readers understand that the first sentence means I have more than one brother. The commas in the second sentence mean that Bill is my only brother.

Why? In the first sentence, Bill is essential information: it identifies which of my two (or more) brothers I'm speaking of. This is why no commas enclose Bill.

In the second sentence, Bill is non-essential information—whom else but Bill could I mean?—hence the commas.

Comma misuse is nothing to take lightly. It can lead to a train wreck like this.

Example:

Mark Twain's book, Tom Sawyer, is a delight.

Because of the commas, that sentence states that Twain wrote only one book. In fact, he wrote more than two dozen of them.

Rule 7a: Use a comma after certain words that introduce a sentence, such as, well, yes, why, hello, hey, etc.

Example:

(a) Why, I can't believe this!

(b) No, you can't have a dollar.

Rule 7b: Use commas to set off expressions that interrupt the sentence flow (nevertheless, after all, by the way, on the other hand, however, etc.).

Example:

I am, by the way, very nervous about this.

Rule 8: Use commas to set off the name, nickname, term of endearment, or title of a person directly addressed.

Example:

(a) Will you, Aisha, do that assignment for me?

(b) Yes, old friend, I will.

(c) Good day, Captain.

Rule 9: Use a comma to separate the day of the month from the year, and — what most people forget! — always put one after the year, also.

Example:

It was in the Sun's June 5, 2003, edition.

No comma is necessary for just the month and year.

Example:

It was in a June 2003 article.

Rule 10: Use a comma to separate a city from its state, and remember to put one after the state, also.

Example:

I'm from the Akron, Ohio, area.

Rule 11: Traditionally, if a person's name is followed by Sr. or Jr., a comma follows the last name: Martin Luther King, Jr. This comma is no longer considered mandatory. However, if a comma does precede Sr. or Jr., another comma must follow the entire name when it appears midsentence.

Al Mooney Sr. is here. (Correct)

Al Mooney, Sr., is here. (Correct)

Al Mooney, Sr. is here. (Incorrect)

Rule 12: Similarly, use commas to enclose degrees or titles used with names.

Example:

Al Mooney, M.D., is here.

Rule 13a: Use commas to introduce or interrupt direct quotations.

Example:

He said, "I don't care."

"Why," I asked, "don't you care?"

This rule is optional with one-word quotations.
Example:
He said "Stop."

Rule 13b: If the quotation comes before he said, she wrote, they reported, Dana insisted, or a similar attribution, end the quoted material with a comma, even if it is only one word.
Example:
"I don't care," he said.
"Stop," he said.

Rule 13c: If a quotation functions as a subject or object in a sentence, it might not need a comma.
Example:
Is "I don't care" all you can say to me?
Saying "Stop the car" was a mistake.

Rule 14: Use a comma to separate a statement from a question.
Example:
I can go, can't I?

Rule 15: Use a comma to separate contrasting parts of a sentence.
Example:
That is my money, not yours.

Rule 16a: Use a comma before and after certain introductory words or terms, such as, namely, that is, i.e., e.g., and for instance, when they are followed by a series of items.
Example:
You may be required to bring many items, e.g., sleeping bags, pans, and warm clothing.

Rule 16b: A comma should precede the term etc. Many authorities also recommend a comma after etc. when it is placed midsentence.
Example:
Sleeping bags, pans, warm clothing, etc., are in the tent.

Semicolons

It's no accident that a semicolon is a period atop a comma. Like commas, semicolons indicate an audible pause—slightly longer than a comma's, but short of a period's full stop.

Semicolons have other functions, too. But first, a caveat: avoid the common mistake of using a semicolon to replace a colon.

I have one goal; to find her. (Incorrect)
I have one goal: to find her. (Correct)

Rule 1a: A semicolon can replace a period if the writer wishes to narrow the gap between two closely linked sentences.
Example:
Call me tomorrow; you can give me an answer then.
We have paid our dues; we expect all the privileges listed in the contract.

Rule 1b: Avoid a semicolon when a dependent clause comes before an independent clause.
Although they tried; they failed. (Incorrect)
Although they tried, they failed. (Correct)

Rule 2: Use a semicolon before such words and terms as namely, however, therefore, that is, i.e., for example, e.g., for instance, etc., when they introduce a complete sentence. It is also preferable to use a comma after these words and terms.
Example:
Bring any two items; however, sleeping bags and tents are in short supply.

Rule 4: Use a semicolon to separate units of a series when one or more of the units contain commas.
The conference has people who have come from Moscow, Idaho, Springfield, California, Alamo, Tennessee, and other places as well. (Incorrect)
Note that with only commas, that sentence is hopeless.
The conference has people who have come from Moscow, Idaho; Springfield, California; Alamo, Tennessee; and other places as well. (Correct)
(Note the final semicolon, rather than a comma, after Tennessee.)

Rule 4: A semicolon may be used between independent clauses joined by a connector, such as, and, but, or, nor, etc., when one or more commas appear in the first clause.
Example:
When I finish here, and I will soon, I'll be glad to help you; and that is a promise I will keep.

Rule 5: Do not capitalize ordinary words after a semicolon.

Incorrect: I am here; You are over there. (Incorrect)

Correct: I am here; you are over there. (Correct)

Rule 1a: Use the apostrophe to show possession. To show possession with a singular noun, add an apostrophe plus the letters.

Example:

(a) a woman's hat
(b) the boss's wife
(c) Mrs. Chang's house

Rule 1b: Many common nouns end in the letter s (lens, cactus, bus, etc.). So do a lot of proper nouns (Mr. Jones, Texas, Christmas). There are conflicting policies and theories about how to show possession when writing such nouns. There is no right answer; the best advice is to choose a formula and stay consistent.

Rule 1c: Some writers and editors add only an apostrophe to all nouns ending in s. And some add an apostrophe + s to every proper noun, be it Hastings's or Jones's.

One method, common in newspapers and magazines, is to add an apostrophe + s ('s) to common nouns ending in s, but only a stand-alone apostrophe to proper nouns ending in s.

Example:

(a) the class's hours
(b) Mr. Jones' golf clubs
(c) the canvas's size
(d) Texas' weather

Care must be taken to place the apostrophe outside the word in question. For instance, if talking about a pen belonging to Mr. Hastings, many people would wrongly write Mr. Hasting's pen (his name is not Mr. Hasting).

Mr. Hastings' pen (Correct)

Another widely used technique is to write the word as we would speak it. For example, since most people saying "Mr. Hastings' pen" would not pronounce an added s, we would write Mr. Hastings' pen with no added s. But most people would pronounce an added s in "Jones's," so we'd write it as we say it: Mr. Jones's golf clubs. This method explains the punctuation of for goodness' sake.

Rule 2a: Regular nouns are nouns that form their plurals by adding either the letter s or -es (guy, guys; letter, letters; actress, actresses; etc.). To show plural possession, simply put an apostrophe after the s.

guys' night out (guy + s + apostrophe) (Correct)

guy's night out (implies only one guy) (Incorrect)

two actresses' roles (actress + es + apostrophe) (Correct)

two actress's roles (Incorrect)

Rule 2b: Do not use an apostrophe + s to make a regular noun plural.

Apostrophe's are confusing. (Incorrect)

Apostrophes are confusing. (Correct)

We've had many happy Christmas's. (Incorrect)

We've had many happy Christmases. (Correct)

In special cases, such as when forming a plural of a word that is not normally a noun, some writers add an apostrophe for clarity.

Example:

Here are some do's and don'ts.

In that sentence, the verb do is used as a plural noun, and the apostrophe was added because the writer felt that dos was confusing. Not all writers agree; some see no problem with dos and don'ts.

However, with single lowercase letters, it is advisable to use apostrophes.

Example:

My a's look like u's.

Imagine the confusion if you wrote that sentence without apostrophes. Readers would see as and us, and feel lost.

Rule 2c: English also has many irregular nouns (child, nucleus, tooth, etc.). These nouns become plural by changing their spelling, sometimes becoming quite different words. You may find it helpful to write out the entire irregular plural noun before adding an apostrophe or an apostrophe + s.

Two childrens' hats (Incorrect)

The plural is children, not childrens.

Two children's hats (children + apostrophe + s) (Correct)

The teeths' roots (Incorrect)

The teeth's roots (Correct)

Rule 2d: Things can get really confusing with the possessive plurals of proper names ending in s, such as Hastings and Jones.

If you're the guest of the Ford family—the Fords—you're the Fords' guest (Ford + s + apostrophe). But what if it's the Hastings family?

Most would call them the "Hastings." But that would refer to a family named "Hasting." If someone's name ends in s, we must add -es for the plural. The plural of Hastings is Hastingses. The members of the Jones family are the Joneses.

To show possession, add an apostrophe.

The Hastings' dog (Incorrect)

The Hastingses' dog (Hastings + es + apostrophe) (Correct)

The Jones' car (Incorrect)

The Joneses' car (Correct)

In serious writing, this rule must be followed no matter how strange or awkward the results are.

Rule 2e: Never use an apostrophe to make a name plural.

Incorrect: The Wilson's are here. (Incorrect)

Correct: The Wilsons are here. (Correct)

Incorrect: We visited the Sanchez's. (Incorrect)

Correct: We visited the Sanchezes. (Correct)

Rule 3: With a singular compound noun (for example, mother-in-law), show possession with an apostrophe + s at the end of the word.

Example:

my mother-in-law's hat

If the compound noun (e.g., brother-in-law) is to be made plural, form the plural first (brothers-in-law), and then use the apostrophe + s.

Example:

my two brothers-in-law's hats

Rule 4: If two people possess the same item, put the apostrophe + s after the second name only.

Example:

Cesar and Maribel's home is constructed of redwood.

However, if one of the joint owners is written as a pronoun, use the possessive form for both.

(a) Maribel and my home (Incorrect)
(b) Maribel's and my home (Correct)
(c) He and Maribel's home (Incorrect)
(d) Him and Maribel's home (Incorrect)
(e) His and Maribel's home (Correct)

In cases of separate rather than joint possession, use the possessive form for both.

Example:

(a) Cesar's and Maribel's homes are both lovely.
(b) They don't own the homes jointly.
(c) Cesar and Maribel's homes are both lovely.
(d) The homes belong to both of them.

Rule 5: Use an apostrophe with contractions. The apostrophe is placed where a letter or letters have been removed.

Example:

doesn't, it's, 'tis, can't, you'd, should've, rock 'n' roll, etc.

Does'nt. (Incorrect)

Rule 6: There are various approaches to plurals for abbreviations, single letters, and numerals.

Many writers and editors prefer an apostrophe after single capitalized letters.

Example:

I made straight A's.

With groups of two or more capital letters, apostrophes seem less necessary.

Example:

There are two new MPs on the base.

He learned his ABCs.

She consulted with three M.D.s. OR, She consulted with three M.D.'s.

(Some write M.D.'s to give the s separation from the second period.)

Single-digit numbers are usually spelled out, but when they aren't, you are just as likely to see 2s and 3s as 2's and 3's. With double digits

Punctuations

and above, many (but not everyone) regard the apostrophe as superfluous: I scored in the high 90s.

There are different schools of thought about years and decades. The following examples are all in widespread use.

Example:

the 1990s, the 1990's, the '90s, the 90's, Awkward: the '90's

Rule 7: Amounts of time or money are sometimes used as possessive adjectives that require apostrophes.

Three days leave. (Incorrect)

Three days' leave. (Correct)

My two cents worth. (Incorrect)

My two cents' worth. (Correct)

Rule 8: The personal pronouns hers, ours, yours, theirs, its, whose, and the pronoun oneself never take an apostrophe.

Feed a horse grain. It's better for its health. (Correct)

Who's glasses are these? (Incorrect)

Whose glasses are these? (Correct)

Talking to one's self in public is odd. (Incorrect)

Talking to oneself in public is odd. (Correct)

Rule 9: When an apostrophe comes before a word or number, take care that it's truly an apostrophe (') rather than a single quotation mark (').

'Twas the night before Christmas. (Incorrect)

'Twas the night before Christmas. (Correct)

I voted in '08. (Incorrect)

I voted in '08. (Correct)

Serious writers avoid the word 'til as an alternative to until. The correct word is till, which is many centuries older than until.

Rule 10: Beware of false possessives, which often occur with nouns ending in s. Don't add apostrophes to noun-derived adjectives ending in s. Close analysis is the best guide.

Incorrect: We enjoyed the New Orleans' cuisine.

In the preceding sentence, the word the makes no sense unless New Orleans is being used as an adjective to describe cuisine. In English, nouns frequently become adjectives. Adjectives rarely if ever take apostrophes.

(a) Incorrect: I like that Beatles' song. (Incorrect)
(b) Correct: I like that Beatles song. (Correct)

Again, Beatles is an adjective, modifying song.

(c) Incorrect: He's a United States' citizen. (Incorrect)
(d) Correct: He's a United States citizen. (Correct)

Rule 11. Beware of nouns ending in y; do not show possession by changing the y to ies.

(a) The company's policy (Correct)
(b) The companies policy (Incorrect)

To show possession when a noun ending in y becomes plural, write ies'. Do not write y's.

(c) Three companies' policies (Correct)
(d) Three company's policies (Incorrect)

Exception:

Names and other proper nouns ending in y become plural simply by adding an s. They do not form their plurals with an apostrophe, or by changing the y to ies.

(a) The Flannerys are coming over. (Correct)
(b) The Flannery's are coming over. (Incorrect)
(c) The Flanneries are coming over. (Incorrect)
(d) The Flannerys' house was robbed. (Correct)
(e) The Flanneries' house was robbed. (Incorrect)

Hyphens

There are two commandments about this misunderstood punctuation mark. First, hyphens must never be used interchangeably with dashes, which are noticeably longer. Second, there should not be spaces around hyphens.

300 — 325 people (Incorrect)

300 - 325 people (Incorrect)

300-325 people (Correct)

Hyphens' main purpose is to glue words together. They notify the reader that two or more elements in a sentence are linked. Although there are rules and customs governing hyphens, there are also situations when writers must decide whether to add them for clarity.

Hyphens Between Words

Rule 1: Generally, hyphenating two or more words when they come before a noun, they modify and act as a single idea. This is called a compound adjective.

Example:

an off-campus apartment

state-of-the-art design

When a compound adjective follows a noun, a hyphen is usually not necessary.

Example:

The apartment is off campus.

However, some established compound adjectives are always hyphenated. Double-check with a dictionary or online.

Example:

The design is state-of-the-art.

See also Rule 2b in Writing Numbers

Rule 2a: A hyphen is frequently required when forming original compound verbs for vivid writing, humour, or special situations.

Example:

The slacker video-gamed his way through life.

Queen Victoria throne-sat for six decades.

Rule 2b: When writing out new, original, or unusual compound nouns, writers should hyphenate them to avoid confusion.

Example:

I changed my diet and became a no-meater.

(No-meater is too confusing without the hyphen.)

The slacker was a video gamer.

(Video gamer is clear without a hyphen, although some writers might prefer to hyphenate it.)

Writers using familiar compound verbs and nouns should consult a dictionary or look online to decide if these verbs and nouns should be hyphenated.

Rule 3: An often overlooked rule for hyphens: The adverb very and adverbs ending in -ly are not hyphenated.

The very-elegant watch (Incorrect)

The finely-tuned watch (Incorrect)

This rule applies only to adverbs. The following two examples are correct because the -ly words are not adverbs:

The friendly-looking dog (Correct)

A family-owned cafe (Correct)

Rule 4: Hyphens are often used to tell the ages of people and things. A handy rule, when writing about years, months, or any other period of time, is to use hyphens unless the period of time (years, months, weeks, days) is written in plural form.

With hyphens:

We have a two-year-old child.

We have a two-year-old.

No hyphens: The child is two years old. (Because years is plural.)

Exception: The child is one year old. (Or day, week, month, etc.)

Note:

When hyphens are used to expressing ages, two hyphens are required. Many writers forget the second hyphen:

We have a two-year old child. (Incorrect)

Without the second hyphen, the sentence is about an "old child."

Rule 5: Never hesitate to add a hyphen if it solves a possible problem. Following are two examples of well-advised hyphens:

Confusing: Springfield has little town charm.

With hyphen: Springfield has little-town charm.

Without the hyphen, the sentence seems to say that Springfield is a dreary place. With the hyphen, little-town becomes a compound adjective, making the writer's intention clear: Springfield is a charming small town.

Confusing: She had a concealed weapons permit.

With hyphen: She had a concealed-weapons permit.

With no hyphen, we can only guess: Was the weapons permit hidden from sight, or was it a permit for concealed weapons? The hyphen makes concealed-weapons a compound adjective, so the reader knows that the writer meant a permit for concealed weapons.

TRIVIA

The word "selfie" was the Oxford Dictionary's Word of the Year in 2013 because the use of the term increased 17,000% from 2012 to 2013.

Rule 6: When using numbers, hyphenate spans or estimates of time, distance, or other quantities. Remember not to use spaces around hyphens.

Example:
3:15-3:45 p.m.
1999-2016
300-325 people

Example:
3:15–3:45 p.m.
1999–2016
300–325 people

Rule 7: Hyphenate all compound numbers from twenty-one through ninety-nine.

Example:
Thirty-two children
One thousand two hundred twenty-one dollars

Rule 8a: Hyphenate all spelled-out fractions. But do not hyphenate fractions introduced with a or an.

Example:
More than one-third of registered voters oppose the measure.
More than a third of registered voters oppose the measure.

Rule 8a: When writing out numbers with fractions, hyphenate only the fractions unless the construction is a compound adjective.

The sign is five and one-half feet long. (Correct)

Correct: A five-and-one-half-foot-long sign. (Correct)

The sign is five-and-one-half feet long. (Incorrect)

Rule 9: Hyphenate most double last names.

Example:
Sir Winthrop Heinz-Eakins will attend.

Rule 10: As important as hyphens are to clear writing, they can become an annoyance if overused. Avoid adding hyphens when the meaning is clear. Many phrases are so familiar (e.g., high school, twentieth century, one hundred percent) that they can go before a noun without risk of confusing the reader.

Example:
A high school senior
A twentieth century throwback
One hundred percent correct

Rule 11: When in doubt, look it up. Some familiar phrases may require hyphens. For instance, is a book up to date or up-to-date? Don't guess; have a dictionary close by, or look it up online.

Hyphens with Prefixes and Suffixes

A prefix (a, un, de, ab, sub, post, anti, etc.) is a letter or set of letters placed before a root word. The word prefix itself contains the prefix pre. Prefixes expand or change a word's meaning, sometimes radically: the prefixes a, un, and dis, for example, change words into their opposites (e.g., political, apolitical; friendly, unfriendly; honour, dishonour).

Rule 1: Hyphenate prefixes when they come before proper nouns or proper adjectives.

Example:
Trans-American
Mid-July

Rule 2: In describing family relations, 'great' requires a hyphen, but 'grand' becomes part of the word without a hyphen.

Example:
My grandson and my granduncle never met.
My great-great-grandfather fought in the Civil War.
Do not hyphenate half brother or half sister.

Rule 3: For clarity, many writers hyphenate prefixes ending in a vowel when the root word begins with the same letter.

Example:

Ultra-ambitious

Semi-invalid

Re-elect

Rule 4: Hyphenate all words beginning with the prefixes self-, ex- (i.e., former), and all-.

Example:

Self-assured

Ex-mayor

All-knowing

Rule 5: Use a hyphen with the prefix re — omitting the hyphen would cause confusion with another word.

Example:

Will she recover from her illness?

I have re-covered the sofa twice.

(Omitting the hyphen would cause confusion with recover, which means get well.)

I must re-press the shirt.

(Omitting the hyphen would cause confusion with repress, which means subdue by force.)

The stamps have been reissued.

(A hyphen after re- is not needed because there is no confusion with another word.)

Rule 6: Writers often hyphenate prefixes when they feel a word might be distracting or confusing without the hyphen.

Example:

De-ice

(With no hyphen we get deice, which might stump readers.)

Co-worker

(With no hyphen we get coworker, which could be distracting because it starts with cow.)

A suffix (y, er, ism, able, etc.) is a letter or set of letters that follows a root word. Suffixes form new words or alter the original word to perform a different task. For example, the noun scandal can be made into the adjective scandalous by adding the suffix 'ous'. It becomes the verb sea candalise by adding the suffix ise.

Rule 1: Suffixes are not usually hyphenated. Some exceptions: -style, -elect, -free, -based.

Example:

Modernist-style paintings

Mayor-elect Smith

Sugar-free soda

Oil-based sludge

Rule 2: For clarity, writers often hyphenate when the last letter in the root word is the same as the first letter in the suffix.

Example:

Graffiti-ism

Wiretap-proof

Rule 3: Use discretion — and sometimes a dictionary — before deciding to place a hyphen before a suffix. But do not hesitate to hyphenate a rare usage if it avoids confusion.

Example:

The annual dance-athon

An eel-esque sea creature

Although the preceding hyphens help clarify unusual terms, they are optional and might not be every writer's choice. Still, many readers would scratch their heads for a moment over danceathon and eelesque.

Ellipses

An ellipsis (plural: ellipses) is a punctuation mark consisting of three dots.

Use an ellipsis when omitting a word, phrase, line, paragraph, or more from a quoted passage. Ellipses save space or remove material that is less relevant. They are useful in getting right to the point without delay or distraction:

Full quotation: "Today, after hours of careful thought, we vetoed the bill."

With ellipsis: "Today … we vetoed the bill."

Although ellipses are used in many ways, the three-dot method is the simplest. Newspapers, magazines, and books of fiction and nonfiction use various approaches that they find suitable.

Some writers and editors feel that no spaces are necessary.

Example:
I don't know…I'm not sure.

Others enclose the ellipsis with a space on each side.

Example:
I don't know … I'm not sure.

Still others put a space either directly before or directly after the ellipsis.

Example:
I don't know …I'm not sure.
I don't know… I'm not sure.

Rule 1: Many writers use an ellipsis whether the omission occurs at the beginning of a sentence, in the middle of a sentence, or between sentences.

A common way to delete the beginning of a sentence is to follow the opening quotation mark with an ellipsis, plus a bracketed capital letter:

Example:
"…[A]fter hours of careful thought, we vetoed the bill."

Other writers omit the ellipsis in such cases, feeling the bracketed capital letter gets the point across.

Rule 2: Ellipses can express hesitation, changes of mood, suspense, or thoughts trailing off. Writers also use ellipses to indicate a pause or wavering in an otherwise straightforward sentence.

Example:
I don't know … I'm not sure.
Pride is one thing, but what happens if she …?
He said, "I … really don't … understand this."

MUST REMEMBER

- Punctuation is used to create sense, clarity and stress in sentences.
- Commas customarily indicate a brief pause; they're not as final as periods.
- When starting a sentence with a dependent clause, use a comma after it.
- If something or someone is sufficiently identified, the description that follows is considered non-essential and should be surrounded by commas.
- Avoid the common mistake of using a semicolon to replace a colon.
- Avoid a semicolon when a dependent clause comes before an independent clause.
- Hyphens must never be used interchangeably with dashes, which are noticeably longer. Second, there should not be spaces around hyphens.
- An ellipsis is a punctuation mark consisting of three dots.
- Use an ellipsis when omitting a word, phrase, line, paragraph, or more from a quoted passage.

PRACTICE EXERCISE

I. Add commas wherever required in the following sentences.

1. After a hard day at the office I like to relax with a large gin.
2. The recipe needed jam flour sugar fruit eggs ketchup and baking powder.
3. "Look at this" he whispered.
4. Paulina his wife of many years had decided to go and live in Greece.
5. As the sun began to sink over the sea Karen got ready to go out.
6. She was intelligent not especially practical.
7. The thief was wearing impractical high heels so she could not run fast.
8. We go to Blackpool for the cuisine not the weather.
9. "I advise you" said the teacher "not to cross me again today."
10. Steven his head still spinning walked out of the office for the last time.

II. Decide which pairs of clauses can be connected with a semi-colon in the following sentences.

1. Which can/should be connected with a semi-colon?
   (a) I hate rice pudding _____ dairy products don't agree with me.
   (b) Spain is lovely _____ hot weather and friendly people.
   (c) Spain _____ lovely beaches, endless blue sea and great weather.
   (d) Spain is a lovely country _____ the beaches are endless and the weather is always good.

2. Which can/should be connected with a semi-colon?
   (a) Paris is a beautiful city _____ wide streets and sunshine.
   (b) Havana is a lovely city _____ rice pudding is one of my favourite foods.
   (c) I would love to go to France _____ Paris is a lovely city.
   (d) I would love to go to Greece _____ I love ancient history.

3. Which can/should be connected with a semi-colon?
   (a) Gran hates going to bed early _____ there is too much on the telly.
   (b) Gran hates doing DIY _____ too much like hard work.
   (c) Gran hates going to bed early _____ the wallpaper in her house is peeling.
   (d) Gran hates doing DIY _____ the wallpaper in her house is peeling.

4. Which can/should be connected with a semi-colon?
   (a) Understanding grammar is very important _____ despite its complexity.
   (b) Understanding grammar is very important _____ clear communication is an essential skill.
   (c) Understanding grammar is very important _____ most high level jobs require good writing skills.
   (d) Understanding grammar is very important _____ although it is not always the most fascinating subject on the planet.

5. Which can/should be connected with a semi-colon?
   (a) The stock exchange fell sharply _____ investor confidence is very low.
   (b) The stock exchange fell sharply _____ many investors decided to sell their shares.
   (c) The stock exchange fell sharply _____ a difficult day for everybody.
   (d) The stock exchange fell sharply _____ I would wait before selling your shares.

III. Select the sentence which is correctly punctuated.

1. (a) Spain is a beautiful country; the beaches are warm, sandy and spotlessly clean.
   (b) Spain is a beautiful country: the beaches are warm, sandy and spotlessly clean.
   (c) Spain is a beautiful country, the beaches are warm, sandy and spotlessly clean.
   (d) Spain is a beautiful country; the beaches are warm, sandy and spotlessly clean.

2. (a) The children's books were all left in the following places: Mrs. Smith's room, Mr. Powell's office and the caretaker's cupboard.
   (b) The children's books were all left in the following places; Mrs. Smith's room, Mr. Powell's office and the caretaker's cupboard.
   (c) The children's books were all left in the following places: Mrs. Smiths room, Mr. Powell's office and the caretakers cupboard.
   (d) The children's books were all left in the following places, Mrs. Smith's room, Mr. Powell's office and the caretaker's cupboard.

3. (a) She always enjoyed sweets, chocolate, marshmallows and toffee apples.
   (b) She always enjoyed: sweets, chocolate, marshmallows and toffee apples.
   (c) She always enjoyed sweets chocolate marshmallows and toffee apples.
   (d) She always enjoyed sweet's, chocolate, marshmallow's and toffee apple's.

4. (a) Sarah's uncle's car was found without its wheels in that old derelict warehouse.
   (b) Sarah's uncle's car was found without its wheels in that old, derelict warehouse.
   (c) Sarah's uncles car was found without its wheels in that old, derelict warehouse.
   (d) Sarah's uncle's car was found without its wheel's in that old, derelict warehouse.

5. (a) I can't see Tim's car, there must have been an accident.
   (b) I can't see Tims car; there must have been an accident.
   (c) I can't see Tim's car there must have been an accident.
   (d) I can't see Tim's car; there must have been an accident.

6. (a) Paul's neighbours were terrible; so his brother's friends went round to have a word.
   (b) Paul's neighbours were terrible: so his brother's friends went round to have a word.
   (c) Paul's neighbours were terrible, so his brother's friends went round to have a word.
   (d) Paul's neighbours were terrible so his brother's friends went round to have a word.

7. (a) Tim's gran, a formidable woman, always bought him chocolate, cakes, sweets and a nice fresh apple.
   (b) Tim's gran a formidable woman always bought him chocolate, cakes, sweets, and a nice fresh apple.
   (c) Tim's gran, a formidable woman, always bought him chocolate cakes sweets and a nice fresh apple.
   (d) Tim's gran, a formidable woman, always bought him chocolate, cakes, sweets and a nice fresh apple.

8. (a) After stealing Tims car, the thief lost his way and ended up the chief constable's garage.
   (b) After stealing Tim's car the thief lost his way and ended up the chief constable's garage.
   (c) After stealing Tim's car, the thief lost his way and ended up the chief constable's garage.
   (d) After stealing Tim's car, the thief lost his' way and ended up the chief constable's garage.

9. (a) We decided to visit: Spain, Greece, Portugal and Italy's mountains.
   (b) We decided to visit Spain, Greece, Portugal and Italys mountains.
   (c) We decided to visit Spain, Greece, Portugal and Italy's mountains.
   (d) We decided to visit Spain Greece Portugal and Italy's mountains.
10. (a) That tall man, Paul's grandad, is this month's winner.
    (b) That tall man Paul's grandad is this month's winner.
    (c) That tall man, Paul's grandad, is this months winner.
    (d) That tall man, Pauls grandad, is this month's winner.

IV. **Use appropriate punctuation marks in the following sentences.**
1. We had a great time in France the kids really enjoyed it
2. Some people work best in the mornings others do better in the evenings
3. What are you doing next weekend
4. Mother had to go into hospital she had heart problems
5. Did you understand why I was upset
6. It is a fine idea let us hope that it is going to work
7. We will be arriving on Monday morning at least I think so
8. A textbook can be a wall between teacher and class

HOTS

Direction 1-2: Select options for correctly ending the given sentences.
1. If you have any doubts could you please speak now
   (a) Comma
   (b) full stop
   (c) Exclamation mark
   (d) question mark
2. Khan was angry and shouted at his son, "Go to your room now!
   (a) Comma
   (b) Double quotation
   (c) Full stop
   (d) Question mark

Direction 3-5: Select the option correctly showing the number of exclamation marks/commas required in the following sentence.
3. "Help" she cried. "I can't swim"
   (a) One   (b) two
   (b) Three   (d) None
4. I am taking English Maths and Science at A level and my teacher Ms. Roja believes I should get 3As.
   (a) None   (b) two
   (c) Four   (d) three
5. She bought milk eggs and bread.
   (a) Two   (b) three
   (c) One   (d) none

Tenses

Learning Objectives: In this chapter, students will learn about:
- ✓ Tenses and its various types
- ✓ Uses of different type of tenses

CHAPTER SUMMARY

A form of a verb that is used to indicate if an action happened in the past, present or future.

Example:
I went to school yesterday. (Past tense)
I go to school everyday. (Present tense)
I will go to school tomorrow. (Future tense)

Kinds of Tenses

In English, there are three kinds of tenses: Present, Past, and Future.

Present Simple Tense

Form
☞ Positive statement:
   Example:
   I play.
   He plays.
☞ Negative statement:
   Example:
   I do not play./I don't play.
   He does not play/He doesn't play.
☞ Question form:
   Example:
   Do you play?
   Does he play?
☞ Negative question:
   Example:
   Do you not play?/Don't you play?
   Does he not play?/Doesn't he play?

☞ The passive voice:
   Example:
   The game is played.
   The letters are written.

Spelling
We add only -s ending (plays) in the third person singular. We add -es to the verbs that end in ss, sh, ch, x, z and o: misses, finishes, watches, mixes, buzzes, goes.
- If the verb ends with a consonant followed by -y, we change -y into -i and use the -es ending: carry - carries, try -tries.
- But, if the verb ends with a vowel and –y, only –s ending is used: play - plays, stay - stays
- The auxiliary verb do is not in questions and negative statements with modal verbs and the verb to be.
   Example:
   Are you a student?
   Is he in London?
   I am not at home.
   He is not happy.
   Can you sing?
   Must I come?
   He mustn't stay.

If the wh-word (who/which), introducing a question, is the subject of the question, we do not use the auxiliary verb do. Compare the following sentences:

Who knows you? (who is the subject)

Which cars belong to you? (which cars is the subject)

But, in the following sentence, do is used as the wh-word is not the subject here:

Who do you know? (who is the object here)

The negative question normally expresses a surprise.

Example:

Doesn't he work?

Uses of Present Simple Tense

☞ We use the present simple tense for activities that happen again and again (with adverbs like everyday, sometimes, ever, never).

Example:

(i) I sometimes go to school by bike.

(ii) You don't speak Greek.

(iii) Do they get up early?

(iv) He often travels.

(v) She doesn't work.

(vi) Does she ever help you?

☞ We use it for facts that are universally accepted to be true.

Example:

Our planet moves round the sun.

Lions eat meat.

☞ With a future time expression (tomorrow, next week), the present simple is used for planned future actions (timetables).

Example:

The train leaves at 8.15. They return tonight.

Present Continuous Tense

Form

☞ Positive statement:

Example:

(i) I am playing.

(ii) You are playing.

(iii) He is playing.

☞ Negative statement:

Example:

(i) I am not playing/I'm not playing.

(ii) You are not playing/You aren't playing.

(iii) He is not playing/He isn't playing.

☞ Question:

Example:

Are you playing?

Is he playing?

☞ Negative question:

Example:

Are you not playing?/ Aren't you playing?

Is he not playing?/ Isn't he playing?

The negative question normally expresses a surprise: Isn't he working?

Spelling

The present continuous tense is formed with the verb to be and the present participle (-ing ending).

Uses of Present Continuous Tense

The present continuous tense is used:

☞ If we want to say that something is happening at the time of speaking. We often use it with time expressions, such as, now or at the moment.

Example:

(i) I am doing housework at the moment.

(ii) You aren't listening to me now!

(iii) Look at him! What is he doing?

(iv) I am learning English at the moment.

(v) You aren't listening!

(vi) Why is he sitting here?

☞ For temporary activities that are true now, but may not be happening at the time of speaking. Time expressions such as today, this week or these days are typical of this use.

Example:

(i) I am in London. I am staying at the hotel. (But just now you can be somewhere else.)

(ii) She can't go out. She is writing her essay today. (But she can be having lunch at the moment.)

(iii) You can't borrow this book today. Mary is reading it. (But not right now.)

(iv) You can't meet him this week. He is working in Bath. (But he may not be working at the moment)

☞ For planned future arrangements. The time of the action must be given in the sentence (soon, tomorrow, on Monday, next week), otherwise it is not clear if we are talking about the future.
Example:
(i) I am coming soon.
(ii) We are leaving on Monday.
(iii) She is starting next week.

☞ With always to express the idea that something happens too often and might be annoying to the speaker.
Example:
(i) I am always forgetting my keys.
(ii) He is always playing in the living room!

We do not normally use the following groups of verbs (so called state verbs) in the continuous form:

☞ Of senses: feel, hear, see, smell, taste. On the other hand, look, watch or listen are action verbs and can be used in the continuous.
Example:
(i) I can hear you. - I am listening to you.
(ii) Can you see the bird? - Are you looking at the bird?

☞ Of likes and dislikes: like, love, hate, fear, detest, want, wish.
Example:
(i) I like animals.
(ii) I hate snakes.

☞ Of mental states: agree, believe, forget, know, remember, suppose, think.
Example:
(i) I agree with you.
(ii) I suppose you are right.

☞ Of permanent states: be, have, belong, contain, owe, own, possess.
Example:
(i) This pen belongs to me.
(ii) I have a new pet.

☞ Of appearance: seem, appear, look, sound.
Example:
(i) It seems that it will rain.
(ii) Your new haircut looks really good.

If some of these verbs are used in the present continuous, they assume a different meaning. In such cases, they become action verbs.

I think he is my best friend. (mental state) - I'm thinking of giving him a present. (mental activity)

He has a new bathroom. (possess) - He is having a bath. (take a bath)

I see what you mean. (know) - I am seeing a doctor as I am ill. (visit)

The flower smells beautiful. (scent) - The dog is smelling the sausage. (sniff)

This wine tastes sour. (It has a sour taste.) - She is tasting the soup to check if it is warm enough. (Act of tasting)

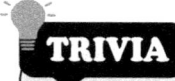

TRIVIA

Swims will be Swims even when turned upside down. Such words are usually called ambigrams.

Past Simple

Form (with Regular Verb)
☞ Positive statement:
Example:
I watched.
He watched.

☞ Negative statement:
Example:
I did not watch./ I didn't watch.
He did not watch/He didn't watch.

☞ Question:
Example:
Did you watch?

☞ Negative question:
Example:
Did you not watch?/ Didn't you watch?

It is formed by -ed ending. It is the same for all persons, singular and plural.

Spelling
We add -d (not -ed) to the verbs that end with -e: like - liked. If the verb ends with a consonant

followed by -y, we change -y into -i: carry - carried, try - tried.

But, if the verb ends with a vowel and -y, we use -ed ending.

Example:

stay - stayed, play - played

If the verb has only one syllable and ends with a vowel followed by a consonant, we double the consonant to keep the same pronunciation: stop - stopped. The same rule applies to the verbs that end with -

l: travel - travelled.

Form (with Irregular Verb)

All the irregular verbs have different forms: go - went, buy - bought, cut - cut, etc.

But, the question and negative are made in the same way: I went - Did you go? No, I did not go.

> **Notes:**
> We do not use the auxiliary verb did with the verb to be and modal verbs.

Example:

(i)   Were you a student?
(ii) Was he in London?
(iii) I was not at home.
(iv) He was not happy.
(v)   Could you sing?
(vi) Could he come?
(vii) I could not swim.
(viii) He could not stay.

The auxiliary verb did is not used in questions, beginning with wh-word (who/which) in case it happens to be the subject of the question.

Example:

Who met you? (who is the subject)

Which train arrived on time? (which train is the subject)

But, if the wh-word assumes the position of an object in a sentence, did is used.

Example:

Who did you meet? (who is the object)

Which train did you miss? (which train is the object)

The negative question normally shows a surprise.

Didn't you know it?

Uses of Past Simple Tense

☞ We use the past simple for activities or situations that were completed in the past at a definite time.

   Example:
   (i) I came home at 6 o'clock.
   (ii) When he was a child, he didn't live in a house.
   (b) The time is asked about:
       When did they get married?
   (c) The time is not mentioned in the sentence, but it is clear from the context that the action or situation finished in the past.

   Example:
   He is 20 years old. He was born in Canada.
   I've been to Iceland. (present perfect) - Did you enjoy it? (past simple)

☞ We use it for repeated actions in the past.
   We walked to school every day. - And did you ever go by bus?

☞ It is used in stories to describe events that follow each other.
   Charles entered the hall and looked around. He took off his coat and put it on a chair. He was at home.

Past Continuous

Form

☞ Positive statement:
   Example:
   I was watching.
   You were watching.

☞ Negative statement:
   Example:
   I was not watching./I wasn't watching.
   You were not watching./You weren't watching.

☞ Question:
   Example:
   Were you watching?
   Was he watching?

Tenses

☞ Negative question:
Example:
Were you not watching?/ Weren't you watching?
Was he not watching?/Wasn't he watching?

Spelling

The past continuous tense is formed with the past tense of the verb to be and the present participle (-ing form).

Uses of Past Continuous Tense

☞ We use the continuous tense for actions or situations in the past that were not completed and were in progress for a certain duration.

Example:
(i) From 10 am to 12 pm, I was washing my car. I was in the garage.
(I did not finish my work. It was in progress. I started before 10 and finished after 12.)
(ii) The sun was setting. The beach was changing its colours.
(The sun was still in the sky when I was watching it.)

☞ Compare these sentences with their past simple forms, which are used for completed activities:

Example:
(i) From 10 am to 12 pm, I washed my car. (I finished my work. I started at 10 and finished at 12.)
(ii) Finally, the sun set. It was dark and we did not see the beach anymore.
(The sun completely disappeared.)

☞ We use it for continuous, uninterrupted activities. If the action is interrupted (something is done in more intervals or we did more things one after another, we must use the past simple.

Example:
(i) Tom was watching TV on Sunday.
(ii) Tom watched TV in the morning and in the evening.
(iii) Yesterday, I was working in the garden.
(iv) Yesterday, I worked in the garden and in my house.

☞ The past continuous tense is typically used:
- In combination with the past simple tense to describe the idea that the action in the past continuous started before the action in the past simple and continued after it.

  Example:
  When she saw me, I was looking at the trees. (These two activities happened at the same time. I was looking at the trees for some time and she saw me in the middle of it.)
  Compare this sentence with the past simple:
  When she saw me, I looked at the trees.
  (These two activities happened one after another. First she saw me and then I looked at the trees.)

- With a point in time to express an action that started before that time and continued after it.

  Example:
  At 8 o'clock, Jane was having a bath.
  (At 8 o'clock, she was in the middle of the activity. She had not finished it.)
  Compare this sentence with the past simple tense:
  At 8 o'clock, Jane had a bath.
  (She started the activity at 8 o'clock and finished it.)

- To describe a situation, while the past simple is used to tell a story.
  The sun was shining. Jack and Jill were lying on the beach. Jack was reading a book and Jill was sleeping. All of a sudden, Jack raised his head. Jill woke up. Something happened.

- For incomplete activities in contrast with the past simple, which is used for completed activities.

  Example:
  I was reading a book yesterday. And today, I am going to continue.
  I read the book yesterday. I can lend it to you now.

- To show a more casual action, which is not the case when we use the past simple :

Example:
(i) I was talking to my neighbour yesterday. We had a nice chat.
(I did not do it on purpose. We just met in the street.)
(ii) I talked to my neighbour yesterday. And he promised to help me.
(I did it on purpose. I needed to ask him for help.)

Future Simple – will

Form

☞ Positive statement:
Example:
(i) I will learn/I'll learn
(ii) He will learn/He'll learn

☞ Negative statement:
Example:
(i) I will not learn/I won't learn
(ii) He will not learn/He won't learn

☞ Question:
Example:
Will you learn?

☞ Negative question:
Example:
Will you not learn?/ Won't you learn?

We can also use shall in the first person singular and plural (I, we). But this form is quite formal in modern English and is not very common.

Example:
(i) I shall do it for you.
(ii) We shall come soon.

Uses of Future Simple Tense

☞ Will is used as a modal auxiliary verb to show a general intention. He will change his job.
We'll travel abroad. (short form of will)
Example:
(i) I will not need it.
(ii) They won't change the telephone number. (short form of will not)
(iii) Will you take the exam?

☞ Will is used for predictions or opinions. It will snow in winter.
Example:
(i) The horse will not win.
We can use the following verbs or adverbs to express if we assume something, but we are not sure: think, be sure, hope, believe, suppose, perhaps, possibly, probably, surely.
(ii) They'll probably study art.
(iii) I don't think she'll accept it.

☞ Will is used to express a decision or offer made at the moment of speaking. Can I walk you home? - No, thank you. I'll take a taxi.
Please, tell Peter about it. - O.K. I'll call him.
But, we use going to in order to express our decision made before the moment of speaking: I am going to call Peter. Do you want me to say hello to him?

Future Continuous

Form

☞ Positive statement:
Example:
I will be sitting./ I'll be sitting.

☞ Negative statement:
Example:
I will not be sitting./ I won't be sitting.

☞ Question:
Example:
Will you be sitting?

☞ Negative question:
Example:
Will you not be sitting?/ Won't you be sitting?

Uses of Future Continuous Tense

☞ This tense is used for an action that will be in progress at a point of time in the future. It will start before that point of time and will continue after it. The point in time can be given by a time expression or by another action in the future simple (will). This usage is very similar to the past continuous in this aspect.

Tenses

Example:
(i) At 8 o'clock, I will be travelling to Dorset.
(ii) This time tomorrow, we'll be lying on the beach.

In these two sentences, the point of time that we refer to is given by a time expression.

(i) The shop will be closed. Will you be working?
(ii) I'll be sleeping when you come back.

In these two sentences, the point of time that we refer to is given by another activity.

☞ The future continuous describes the idea that something will happen in the normal course of events. It refers to a routine activity, not an intention, decision or plan.

Example:
(i) I'll be writing to you again. (I always write to you, so I'll do it again as usual.)
(ii) They'll be leaving on Friday. You can join them. (They normally leave on Fridays.)
(iii) Everybody will be working on a computer sooner or later. (If nothing special happens.)

Future Continuous vs. Present Continuous

Both these tense forms may be used to refer to an action/event in the future; but, present continuous imparts a tone of greater possibility to the statement than future continuous.

Example:
(i) We are going to the cinema next weekend.
(The present tense means that we have already arranged it. We know the time and place and probably have the tickets.)
(ii) We'll be going to the cinema next weekend.
(The future continuous only tells us how we will spend the weekend. But we have not arranged anything and, probably, we do not even know which film we want to see.)
(iii) I am seeing Susan tomorrow.
(I have some reason. Susan and I have arranged the time and place.)
(iv) I'll be seeing Susan tomorrow.
(Susan is my classmate and because I will go to school tomorrow, I will see her as usual.)

Future Simple vs. Continuous

Both these tense form can be used to refer to an action/event in the future. While future simple states a prediction mostly, future continuous states a habit that is in place already and will continue in future.

Example:
(i) Bill won't play football tomorrow.
(The fact is that Bill cannot play or does not want to play for some reason.)
(ii) Bill won't be playing football tomorrow.
(Bill will not play, because it will be Friday and he never plays on Fridays.)
(iii) I'll call Mimi tonight. I'll ask her.(I will do it because I need to talk to her.)
(iv) I'll be calling Mimi tonight. I can ask her.
(I call her every night, that is why I will call her tonight too.)

In these examples, the future simple shows intentions, while in the continuous there is no intention, it expresses routine actions.

Notes:

In some cases, we can use several forms for future events. But every form will have a slightly different meaning.

Example:
(i) I'll be meeting Jim next week.
(I meet Jim every week and it will be the same next week.)
(ii) I'll meet Jim next week.
(I intend to meet Jim next week or I suppose that I will meet him.)
(iii) I'm going to meet Jim next week.
(I decided to meet Jim some time ago and now I am expressing my intention.)
(iv) I'm meeting Jim next week.
(We have arranged the time and place because we have some reason to meet.)
(v) It will rain, I'm afraid.

(I assume it will rain, it is my opinion. But who knows!)

(vi) It's going to rain.

(I am sure it will rain because I can see the dark clouds in the sky. My opinion is based on clear evidence.)

The present tense (I am meeting) is more definite than be going to (I am going to meet) and will is the least definite (I will meet)

Present Perfect Simple
Form
☞ Positive statement:

Example:

(i) I have cooked./I've cooked.

(ii) I have written./I've written.

(iii) He has cooked./He's cooked.

(iv) He has written./He's written.

☞ Negative statement:

Example:

I have not worked./ I haven't worked.

He has not worked./ He hasn't worked.

☞ Question:

Example:

Have you worked?

☞ Negative question:

Example:

Have you not worked?/ Haven't you worked?

Uses of Present Perfect Tense
The present perfect combines the past and present.

☞ We use the present perfect simple for actions or states that started in the past and still continue.

Example:

(i) We have lived here since 2001.

(ii) She has known me for more than two years.

(iii) I haven't seen her since Christmas.

(iv) How long have they been here?

It is often used with expressions indicating that the activity began in the past and continues even in the present, such as: for 10 years, since 1995, all week, all the time, always, lately, recently ...

We have always worked in York. We still work in York.

It has been quite cold lately. It is still cold.

If the activity started in the past and ended in the past, we cannot use the present perfect. Compare the following two sentence:

I have played piano for five years. (present perfect - I still play piano.)

I played piano for five years. (past simple - I played piano from 2000 to 2005, then I stopped.)

☞ We use it to describe an experience that happened in the past (the time is not given), but the effects are important now.

Example:

She has been to London. And so she knows London.

Compare the following sentences:

I have already been to Greece. (experience-And I want to go somewhere else now.)

I have been in Greece for two weeks. (state - I am still in Greece.)

When we use this tense to express some experience, we can use following adverbs: ever, never, already, often, occasionally, yet, before etc.

(i) Have you ever tried it?

(ii) She has never read this book.

(iii) We haven't seen it yet.

(iv) Have you fallen off a bike yet?

(v) I haven't met her before.

☞ The present perfect simple is used for past activities that have a present result.

Example:

(i) The bus hasn't arrived.

(It did not arrive on time and we are still waiting now.)

(ii) I have bought a new house.

(I did it last month and it means that now I have a new address.)

For such activities, we often use these adverbs: yet, already, just...

(iii) They haven't finished their homework yet. They can't go out now.

(iv) Has she signed it yet? Can I take the document?

(v) I've already sent the letter. There is no need to go to the post-office.

(v) We have just heard the news. We know about it.

Present Perfect vs Past Simple

With the present perfect, we do not specify when the action happened. If we provide the time or it is clear from the context that there is a mention of a certain time in the past, we must use the past simple.

Example:
(i) Have you had breakfast? (Present Perfect)
(ii) Did you have breakfast at the hotel? (Past simple)
(iii) I've read your letter. (Present Perfect)
(iv) I read your letter last night. (Past simple)
(v) They have told me. (Present Perfect)
(vi) They told me when we met. (Past simple)
(vii) Have you had the operation? (Present Perfect)
(viii) When did you have the operation? (Past simple)

In the present perfect, we express that something happened in the past which is important now. The time is not relevant. In the past tense, the time of the action is relevant.

Present Perfect vs. Present Simple

The present perfect is used for actions that began in the past and continue at present. It expresses how long the action has been for.

The present simple is used for actions that are repeated at present. It expresses how often the action happens.

Example:
(i) She has worked here for a long time. (Present Perfect)
(ii) She works here every day. (Present Simple)
(iii) How long have you worked here? (Present Perfect)
(iv) How often do you work here? (Present Simple)

Present Perfect Continuous
Form
☞ Positive statement:
Example:
I have been cooking./I've been cooking.
He has been cooking./He's been cooking.

☞ Negative statement:
Example:
I have not been cooking./ I haven't been cooking.
He has not been cooking./He's not been cooking.

☞ Question:
Example:
Have you been cooking?

☞ Negative question:
Example:
Have you not been cooking?/Haven't you been cooking?

Uses of Present Perfect Continuous
☞ We use the present perfect continuous for events that began in the past, are continuing now and will probably continue in the future.
Example:
(i) I have been playing tennis since I was 6 years old.
(ii) She has been working here for 15 years.

☞ We use it for actions that began in the past and have only just finished.
Example:
(i) I've been skiing all day. I'm so tired.
(ii) Hello! We've been waiting for you since 5 o'clock.

Present Perfect Simple vs. Present Perfect Continuous
☞ In some situations, we can use both tenses and there is practically no difference in meaning. The continuous is more usual in the English language.
Example:
(i) It has rained for a long time.
(ii) It has been raining for a long time.

Verbs which can be used in this way include - learn, live, sleep, rain, sit, work, wait, stay...

☞ Sometimes the simple form can describe a permanent state, while the continuous form a temporary activity.

Example:

I have lived here for ten years. It is my permanent address.

I have been living here for ten years. And now I am going to move.

Some verbs cannot express this difference, because they are not normally used in the continuous tenses (verbs of senses - feel, hear, see; verbs expressing emotions - like, love, admire, wish; verbs of mental state - know, remember, mean, recognize; verbs of possession - belong, own, owe; auxiliaries - can, must and be, have in some cases; others - appear, concern, seem, sound ...). They must be used in the simple form.

(i) We have always had a dog.

(ii) I've known him since 1997.

☞ Verbs that express a single action (find, start, stop, lose, break ...) are not used in the continuous form.

Example:

(i) I've lost my purse.

(ii) They've started the fight.

☞ There is a difference between a single action in the present perfect simple and continuous.

Example:

I have painted the hall. (I have completed my work.)

I have been painting the hall. (That is how I have spent the day, but it does not mean that I have finished my job.)

☞ A single action in the present perfect continuous continues up until the time of speaking. But it is different with the simple tense.

Example:

She's been cooking dinner. (She is still in the kitchen. She has just finished or she will continue cooking.)

She has cooked dinner. (We do not know when. Yesterday or very recently? The result is important.)

☞ We can only use the present perfect continuous for uninterrupted actions.

Example:

(i) I've been visiting New York for a couple of years.

(ii) She has been writing letters since she got up.

In the above sentences, we've described uninterrupted incomplete activities. If the action is repeated or interrupted or we intend to describe a number of completed individual actions, we must use the simple form. (See also the past tense rules).

(i) I have visited New York three times.

(ii) She has written four letters since she got up.

(iii) There are two past perfect tenses in the English language:

Past Perfect Simple

Form

It is formed with the auxiliary verb "had" + past participle (-ed ending for regular verbs, e.g. worked, travelled, tried, different forms for irregular verbs, e.g. written, made, sung):

I had done.

I had not done./I hadn't done

Had I done?

Had I not done?/Hadn't I done?

Uses of Past Perfect Tense

☞ We use the past perfect to make it clear that an action was completed before another action in the past.

Example:

The doorbell rang at last. I had been in the room since breakfast.

(The bell rang at noon. I came in the morning - before that.)

When I arrived there, Sarah had already left.

(I arrived after lunch. Sara went before lunch.)

☞ It is used to refer to an activity that was completed before a point of time in the past.

Example:

In 2005, I had lived in the same place for ten years.

Had you ever travelled by plane before your holiday in Spain?

Past Perfect vs. Present Perfect Simple

☞ The past perfect is often used with expressions indicating that the activity took some time, such as: for 10 years, since 1995, all week, all the time, always, ...

Example:

When the plane landed, Tim had travelled all day.

My parents moved away from Leeds. They had lived there since they got married.

In 2005, Derek started to work in Berlin. He had always planned it. These expressions are also used with the present perfect. The difference is, however, that the present perfect refers to events that started in the past and still continue whereas the past perfect expresses events that began before a point of time (or another action) in the past and continued to that point of time in the past.

I have been in Paris for a week. (present perfect - I came a week ago and I am still in Paris.)

When I met Annie I had been in Paris for a week. (past perfect - I came to Paris a week before I met Annie and I am not there anymore.)

☞ If we use the past perfect simple, it does not always mean that an activity continued up to a point of time in the past. The event can end a long time before the point of time in the past that we refer to.

Example:

In 2001, Angie worked in Glasgow. In 1980's, she had worked in Wales. (Angie left her job in Glasgow in 1989. In 2001, she worked in Glasgow. But we do not know what she did in the meantime.)

Past Perfect vs. Past Simple

☞ The past simple is used for actions that happened some time ago. The past perfect is used for actions that happened before a point of time in the past.

Example:

Jim returned at 4 o'clock. He had called Jane on the way back home and now she appeared at the door.

Here, the sentences are in a reversed order, because in reality, first Jim called Jane and then he returned. If we want to keep this sentence order, we must use the past perfect to make it clear that Jim called Jane first.

☞ If the sentence order is the same as the order of the events, we can use the past tense. Jim called Jane on the way back home. He returned at 4 o'clock and then she appeared at the door.

Example:

This difference is important. In some situations, these two tenses have a completely different meaning.

I arrived at the garage. They told me to pay in cash. But I only had my credit card. I couldn't pay.

I arrived at the garage. They had told me to pay in cash. I paid and left immediately.

In the first case, I did not know that I had to pay in cash. They told me after my arrival.

In the second case, I was informed before my arrival and had no problems.

Past Perfect in Time Clauses

In time clauses, such as, after or when, we can use either the past tense or the past perfect tense.

We use the past tense if we want to express that the first action led to the second and that the second followed the first very closely.

Example:

When the film ended, he switched off the television.

When she washed the dishes, she put the plates in the cupboard. The past perfect is used when we want to make it clear that the first action was completed before the second started and that there is no relation between them. When she had washed the dishes, she had a cup of tea.

If we use after in a time clause, the past perfect is much more usual. After Zidane had scored the goal, the fans went wild.

We use the past perfect similarly with: as soon as, until, before, by the time. He got up as soon as he had heard the alarm clock.

We did not stop until we had reached the coast. Maria had finished her meal by the time I arrived.

Before she cut her hair, she had consulted it.

Past Perfect Continuous

Form

It is formed with the auxiliaries "had been" + present participle (-ing ending, e.g., working, trying, writing, singing): I had been doing, I had not been doing, Had I been doing? Had I not been doing?

Uses of Past Perfect Continuous Tense

The past perfect continuous is used for activities that began before a point of time in the past and were still continuing at that point of time.

Example:

Last summer, Josh had been renovating his house for two years.

(He started three years ago and last summer he was still renovating his house.)

Past Perfect Continuous vs. Present Perfect Continuous

The past perfect and present perfect continuous are basically very similar. The difference is, however, that in the past perfect, we refer to the point of time in the past while in the present perfect, we refer to the present times.

Example:

I have been practising since the morning. (present perfect - I am still practising.)

At 11 o'clock, I had been practising for two hours. (past perfect - I began at 9 o'clock and at 11 o'clock I was still practising.)

Past Perfect Simple vs. Continuous

For an action that can continue for a long time we can use both the simple and continuous forms (work, run, study, travel, sleep ...). There is practically no difference in meaning, but the continuous form is more usual in English.

Example:

Stephen was pretty tired. He had worked all day.

Stephen was pretty tired. He had been working all day.

In other cases, these two forms may have completely different meanings.

Before midnight, Paul had translated the article. (He finished his work.)

Before midnight, Paul had been translating the article. (He did not finish it. He was still translating at that moment.)

If we refer to a number of individual actions or actions that were repeated, we must use the past perfect simple.

Before the lesson ended, they had written three tests. (three individual completed activities)

But, the use of past perfect continuous in such a scenario indicates one uninterrupted incomplete activity:

It was exhausting. They had been writing tests since the lessons started.

Future Perfect Simple

Form

☞ Positive statement:

Example:

(i) I will have painted/I'll have painted.
(ii) I will have written/I'll have written.
(iii) He will have painted/He'll have painted.
(iv) He will have written/He'll have written.

☞ Negative statement:
Example:
I will not have painted/I won't have painted
He will not have painted/He won't have painted
☞ Question:
Example:
Will you have painted?
☞ Negative question:
Example:
Will you not have painted?/Won't you have painted?

Use of Future Perfect Simple Tense

We use the future perfect simple for events that will be completed before or at a certain time. It is often used with a time expression beginning with by: by then, by that time, by midnight, by the end of the year. The time can also be given by other time expressions (on Sunday, before 31 June) or other activities expressed in different future tenses.

Example:
(i) I will have sent the project by Friday.
(ii) On 11 August this year, we will have been married for five years.
(iii) When the mountaineers get back to the base, they'll have been in the snowstorm for two days.
(iv) We'll have reached the top before noon.
(v) How long will she have worked here by the end of this year?

In all these examples, at a given time the future perfect actions will be in the past.

Future Perfect Continuous

Form

☞ Positive statement:
Example:
I will have been meeting/I'll have been meeting.
☞ Negative statement:
Example:
I will not have been meeting/I won't have been meeting.
☞ Question:
Example:
Will you have been meeting?
☞ Negative question:
Example:
Will you not have been meeting?/Won't you have been meeting?

Uses of Future Perfect Continuous

We use the future perfect continuous tense for activities that will continue until a point of time in the future and will not be completed. Like the simple tense, it is normally used with by or other time expressions and future actions.

Example:
(i) I'll go home on 20 June. By then, I'll have been staying at this hotel for a fortnight.
(ii) At six o'clock, we'll have been waiting here for three hours.
(iii) When you arrive, we'll have been sitting in the classroom all day.

Future Perfect Simple vs. Continuous

It is used for incomplete, uninterrupted activities. If we refer to a number of individual actions or actions that were repeated, we must use the future perfect simple.

Example:
When I am sixty, I'll have been building houses for thirty years. (one incomplete activity)

When I am sixty, I'll have built more than fifty houses. (fifty individual actions)

By 5 o'clock, I'll have been washing this car for an hour and a half. (one uninterrupted activity)

By 5 o'clock, I'll have washed this car and replaced the tyres. (two completed activities that will be done one after another)

In this respect, the simple and continuous aspects are similar to the other tenses (the past tense, present perfect, past perfect).

Present Tenses and Going to for Future

There are several grammatical structures in the English language to describe future activities. Three of them are the present simple tense, present continuous tense and be going to + verb.

Present Tenses for Future

With the future time expressions (next Friday, tomorrow), both the present simple and present continuous are used for definite plans and arrangements in the near future. The future time must be mentioned, otherwise the sentence would have a present meaning.

Example:

I am watching TV. (a present activity: I am doing it just now.)

I am watching TV tonight. (a future activity - I will do it tonight, it is my plan.)

The present continuous for future is more personal and informal.

I am leaving on Sunday. (I have decided to leave on Sunday, it is my plan.)

I leave on Sunday. (Someone else has decided it, it is someone's plan for me.)

The present simple for future is typically used in official statements and timetables.

The new shopping centre opens on 1 March.

The bus arrives at 6.55.

The present continuous is the most usual way of expressing one's personal plans in the near future.

We are going on holiday to Italy in summer.

'Be going to'

1. 'Be going to' + verb is used to show intentions. We use this structure for decisions that we made before the moment of speaking.

    I am going to clean the car and you can pack the suitcase.

    We are going to reconstruct our house.

2. 'Be going to' is also used to express opinion that something is certain to happen. There is evidence for your prediction.

Our team is going to win. (It is 4:0 and two minutes left. I am sure we will win the match.)

The planes are going to land. (They are coming closer and closer to the airport.)

Sometimes we can use either the present continuous or 'be going to' with a little difference in meaning.

Example:

I am travelling to France in May. (my personal plan)

I am going to travel to France in May. (my personal intention)

MUST REMEMBER

- We use the present simple tense for activities that happen again and again.
- The present continuous tense is formed with the verb to be and the present participle (-ing ending).
- We use the continuous tense for actions or situations in the past that were not completed and were in progress for a certain duration.
- Will is used to express a decision or offer made at the moment of speaking.
- While future simple states a prediction mostly, future continuous states a habit that is in place already and will continue in future.
- The present perfect simple is used for past activities that have a present result.
- The present perfect is used for actions that began in the past and continue at present. It expresses how long the action has been for.
- We use the past perfect to make it clear that an action was completed before another action in the past.
- The past simple is used for actions that happened some time ago. The past perfect is used for actions that happened before a point of time in the past.
- The past perfect continuous is used for activities that began before a point of time in the past and were still continuing at that point of time.
- The past perfect and present perfect continuous are basically very similar. The difference is, however, that in the past perfect, we refer to the point of time in the past while in the present perfect, we refer to the present times.
- We use the future perfect simple for events that will be completed before or at a certain time. It is often used with a time expression beginning with by: by then, by that time, by midnight, by the end of the year.
- We use the future perfect continuous tense for activities that will continue until a point of time in the future and will not be completed.

PRACTICE EXERCISE

I. Fill in the blanks with the correct option.

1. What _____ for breakfast?
   (a) do you usually have
   (b) are you usually having
   (c) have you usually
   (d) do usually you have

2. My brother _____ very hard at the moment, because some of his colleagues are off sick.
   (a) works   (b) work
   (c) is working   (d) working

3. What _____ ?
   (a) mean this word
   (b) means this word
   (c) is this word meaning
   (d) does this word mean

4. Ouch! _____ on my foot!
   (a) You stand   (b) You're standing
   (c) You are stand (d) You'll stand

5. What _____ this weekend?
   (a) are you doing (b) do you do
   (c) are you do   (d) are doing

6. What _____ at the weekend?
   (a) are you normally do
   (b) are you normally doing
   (c) do you normally do
   (d) do you normally doing

7. A: What _____ ? B: She's an architect.
   (a) is your sister doing
   (b) does your sister do
   (c) does your sister
   (d) is your sister do

8. A: How's your brother? B: He's fine. He _____ hard at the moment, because he's got his final exams next month.
   (a) studies   (b) is studying
   (c) is study   (d) studys

9. I _____ your new coat!
   (a) like   (b) am liking
   (c) likes   (d) will like

10. I _____ this film very much. Can we leave?
    (a) don't enjoy   (b) 'm not enjoying
    (c) do enjoy   (d) enjoying

11. A: Where are my keys? Have you seen them? B: No. You _____ ! Why don't you keep them in a safe place?
    (a) always lose your keys
    (b) are always losing your keys

12. A: The coffee machine _____ so we'll have to go to a bar. B: Haven't they fixed it yet?
    (a) isn't working
    (b) doesn't work

13. A: Rachel's a vegetarian, so we'll have to ask the restaurant to provide a vegetarian menu. B: _____ fish? A: I don't think so.
    (a) Does she eat   (b) Is she eating
    (c) Is she eat   (d) Eats she

14. A: _____ a tie to work? B: No, but we've got an inspection from Head Office today!
    (a) Are you always wearing
    (b) Do you always wear
    (c) Wear you always

15. _____ a coffee?
    (a) Do you want   (b) Are you want
    (c) Are you wanting (d) None of these

16. I _____ tennis every Sunday morning.
    (a) playing   (b) play
    (c) am playing   (c) am play

17. Don't make so much noise. Noriko _____ to study for her ESL test!
    (a) try   (b) tries
    (c) tried   (d) is trying

Tenses

18. Jun-Sik _____ his teeth before breakfast every morning.
    (a) will cleaned   (b) is cleaning
    (c) cleans   (d) clean

19. Sorry, she can't come to the phone. She _____ a bath!
    (a) is having   (b) having
    (c) have   (d) has

20. _____ many times every winter in Frankfurt.
    (a) It snows   (b) It snowed
    (c) It is snowing (d) It is snow

21. How many students in your class _____ from Korea?
    (a) comes   (b) come
    (c) came   (d) are coming

22. Weather report: "It's seven o'clock in Frankfurt and _____."
    (a) there is snow   (b) it`s snowing
    (c) it snows   (d) it snowed

23. Babies _____ when they are hungry.
    (a) cry   (b) cries
    (c) cried   (d) are crying

24. Jane: "What _____ in the evenings?"
    Mary: "Usually I watch TV or read a book."
    (a) you doing   (b) you do
    (c) do you do   (d) are you doing

25. Jane: "What _____?"
    Mary: "I'm trying to fix my calculator."
    (a) you doing   (b) you do
    (c) do you do   (d) are you doing

26. Jane _____ her blue jeans today, but usually she wears a skirt or a dress.
    (a) wears   (b) wearing
    (c) wear   (d) is wearing

27. I think I _____ a new calculator. This one does not work properly any more.
    (a) needs
    (b) need
    (a) needed
    (c) am needing

28. Sorry, you can't borrow my pencil. I _____ it myself.
    (a) was using   (b) using
    (c) use   (d) am using

29. At a school dance:
    Jane: " _____ yourself?"
    Mary: "Yes, I'm having a great time!"
    (a) You enjoying
    (b) Enjoy you
    (c) Do you enjoy
    (d) Are you enjoying

30. I've just finished reading a story called Dangerous Game. It's about a man who _____ his wife because he doesn't want to lose her.
    (a) kills   (b) killed
    (c) kill   (d) is killing

31. What time _____
    (a) the train leaves?
    (b) leaves the train?
    (c) is the train leaving?
    (d) does the train leave?

32. Jane: "Are you going to the dance on Friday?"
    Mary: "No, I'm not. I _____ school dances; they're loud, hot and crowded!"
    (a) not enjoy   (b) don`t enjoy
    (c) doesn`t enjoy   (d) am not enjoying

33. I _____ for my pen. Have you seen it?
    (a) will look   (b) looking
    (c) look   (d) am looking

34. You can keep my iPod if you like. I _____ it any more.
    (a) don`t use     (b) doesn`t use
    (c) didn`t use   (d) am not using

35. The phone _____ Can you answer it, please?
    (a) rings   (b) ring
    (c) rang   (d) is ringing

II. **For each sentence, choose the best word or phrase to fill in the blanks.**

1. The school usually _____ at six o'clock each day, but on Monday it stayed open later.
   (a) close   (b) closes
   (c) is closing   (d) has closed

2. Last week we _____ some snow in our city, but it didn't stay on the ground for a long time.
   (a) have   (b) are having
   (c) have had   (d) had

3. There _____ two accidents on this road so far this year and the one last night was quite serious.
   (a) are   (b) were
   (c) have been   (d) are going to be

4. He is a very active child. Probably, when he grows up he _____ very good at sports.
   (a) is   (b) was
   (c) has been   (d) is going to be

5. Please call me back later. I can't speak right now because I _____ an English lesson.
   (a) have
   (b) have had
   (c) am having
   (d) am going to have

6. I bought this car in July, so now I _____ it for six months.
   (a) have   (b) have had
   (c) am having   (d) had

7. Jane isn't at work today. She's very sick so I don't think _____ tomorrow.
   (a) she comes
   (b) she has come
   (c) she's coming
   (d) she's going to come

8. Two days ago, I ____ my keys in my local supermarket.
   (a) lose   (b) lost
   (c) have lost   (d) am losing

9. This is the third time this week you _____ late for your class. Please don't do it again.
   (a) arrive   (b) are arriving
   (c) arrived   (d) have arrived

10. Every week, we ____ a spelling test on Friday morning with words we have learned in the week.
    (a) have   (b) had
    (c) are having (d) have had

11. Emrah _____ Hazim for two months since he started studying in the same class last November.
    (a) knows   (b) knew
    (c) has known   (d) is knowing

12. When I was on holiday in the USA, every night we _____ in a different city.
    (a) stay   (b) have stayed
    (c) stayed   (d) are staying

HOTS

Direction 1-10: Fill in the blanks in the given passage using appropriate tense forms from the option that follow:

The old man ____1____ his eyes and for a moment, it looked as if he___2___back from a long way away. Then he____3____.

"What____4____he asked.

"Supper," said the boy. "We____5____to have supper."

"I____6____very hungry."

"Come on and____7____ You can't fish and not eat."

"I already had it," the old man____8____ getting up and____9____the newspaper and folding it. Then he____10____ to fold the blanket.

1.
   (a) was opening   (b) opened
   (c) opens   (d) had opened

2.
   (a) was coming   (b) will be coming
   (c) is coming   (d) is going to come

3.
   (a) smile   (b) smiled
   (c) has smiled   (d) will smile

4.
   (a) you have got   (b) had you got
   (c) you had got   (d) have you got

5.
   (a) are going   (b) were going
   (c) shall   (d) are

6.
   (a) am   (b) was
   (c) am not   (d) was not

7.
   (a) eat   (b) have eaten
   (c) eats   (d) ate

8.
   (a) says   (b) was saying
   (c) had said   (d) said

9.
   (a) was taking   (b) taking
   (c) is taking   (d) took

10.
   (a) was started   (b) was starting
   (c) started   (d) had started

Conditionals   8

Learning Objectives : In this chapter, students will learn about:
- ✓ Conditional Sentences and their usage

CHAPTER SUMMARY

Conditional sentences are sentences, expressing factual implications or hypothetical situations and their consequences. They are so called because the validity of the main clause of the sentence is conditional on the existence of certain circumstances, which may be expressed in a dependent clause or may be understood from the context.

A full conditional sentence (one which expresses the condition as well as its consequences), therefore, contains two clauses: the dependent clause expressing the condition; and the main clause expressing the consequence.

Example:

If it does not rain, the crops will wither.

If-Clauses (Conditional Clauses)

Conditional sentences are also known as 'Conditional Clauses' or 'If Clauses.' They are used to express that the action in the main clause (without if) can only take place if a certain condition (in the clause with if) is fulfilled. There are three types of conditional sentences.

Conditional Sentence Type 1

☞ It is possible and also very likely that the condition will be fulfilled.

Form: if + Simple Present, will-Future

Example:

If I find her address, I'll send her an invitation.

Conditional Sentence Type 2

☞ It is possible but very unlikely, that the condition will be fulfilled.

Form: if + Simple Past, Conditional I (= would + Infinitive)

Example:

If I found her address, I would send her an invitation.

> **TRIVIA**
>
> If you were to write out every number name in full (one, two, three, four…), you wouldn't use a single letter B until you reached one billion.

Conditional Sentence Type 3

☞ It is impossible that the condition will be fulfilled because it refers to the past.

Form: if + Past Perfect, Conditional II (= would + have + Past Participle)

Example:

If I had found her address, I would have sent her an invitation.

Exceptions:

Sometimes Conditional Sentences Type I, II and III can also be used with other tenses.

MUST REMEMBER

- Conditional sentences are sentences, expressing factual implications or hypothetical situations and their consequences.
- A full conditional sentence ontains two clauses: the dependent clause expressing the condition; and the main clause expressing the consequence.

PRACTICE EXERCISE

I. Fill in the blanks with the correct option:

1. If I had had enough money, I _____ that radio.
   (a) bought
   (b) would buy
   (c) would have bought
   (d) had bought

2. If it rains, you _____ wet.
   (a) will get
   (b) would get
   (c) get
   (d) had got

3. She would go to the Job Centre if she _____ a job.
   (a) had wanted
   (b) will want
   (c) wanted
   (d) wants

4. The dog _____ you if it hadn't been tied up.
   (a) would bite
   (b) will bite
   (c) would have bitten
   (d) bites

5. It _____ easy to paint pictures if you knew how to.
   (a) would be
   (b) had been
   (c) would have been
   (d) be

6. If I come, I _____ you.
   (a) saw
   (b) would see
   (c) will see
   (d) sees

7. She _____ pleased if you came.
   (a) would be
   (b) would have been
   (c) would has been
   (d) was

8. If it _____ I would stay at home.
   (a) rains
   (b) rained
   (c) has rained
   (d) had rained

9. You will catch the train if you _____ earlier.
   (a) left
   (b) leaves
   (c) leave
   (d) would leave

10. If he _____ thirsty, he would have drunk some water.
    (a) was
    (b) had been
    (c) is
    (d) would drink

II. Fill in the blanks with suitable conditional verb forms:

1. If you _____ to learn a musical instrument, you have to practise.
   (a) want
   (b) wanted
   (c) would want
   (d) have wanted

2. If you _____ maths at school, you would find commerce difficult to understand
   (a) learned
   (b) didn't learn
   (c) doesn't learn
   (d) won't learn

3. If that was John, why _____ he stop and say hello?
   (a) do
   (b) did
   (c) don't
   (d) didn't

4. If I _____ enough time tomorrow, I will come and see you.
   (a) get
   (b) will get
   (c) had got
   (d) have got

5. If I _____ her name, I would tell you.
   (a) know
   (b) knew
   (c) have known
   (d) had known

6. If I marry you, we both _____ be happy.
   (a) will
   (b) would
   (c) would have
   (d) would been

7. Oil _____ if you pour it on water.
   (a) float
   (b) floats
   (c) would float
   (d) floated

8. She would have come if you _____ her.
   (a) would invite
   (b) had invited
   (c) invited
   (d) invite

9. If he _____ well, he would have passed the examination.
   (a) studied
   (b) study
   (c) had studied
   (d) has studied

10. If you asked him nicely, he _____ you.
    (a) would have helped
    (b) will have helped
    (c) would help
    (d) will help

III. **Fill in the blanks with the suitable pairs:**

1. Michael is a banker and he enjoys his work very much. However, if he _____ back to college next year, he _____ a teacher so he could help children more.
    (a) goes, will become
    (b) went, would become
    (c) had gone, would have become

2. Harry is a serious criminal. If he _____ one more crime, he _____ to jail.
    (a) commits, will be sent
    (b) committed, would be sent
    (c) had committed, would have been sent

3. There is a lot of evidence against your client. If she _____ to the crime, I _____ sure that her sentence is lenient.
    (a) admits, will make
    (b) admitted, would make
    (c) had admitted, would have made

4. I am sure she didn't do it, so if my client _____ to the crime she _____ lying.
    (a) admits, will be
    (b) admitted, would be
    (c) had admitted, would have been

5. It is her decision, so I _____ her if she _____ to accept your offer.
    (a) will ask, wants
    (b) would ask, wanted
    (c) would have asked, had wanted

6. If the police _____ the murder weapon, she _____ put in prison last year.
    (a) find, will be
    (b) found, would be
    (c) had found, would have been

7. If they _____ to arrest until last month, she _____ the country.
    (a) wait, will leave
    (b) waited, would leave
    (c) had waited, would have left

8. When the jury _____ into the courtroom, they _____ straight at the accused
    (a) comes, will look
    (b) came, would look
    (c) had come, would have looked

9. I believe that mankind is generally honest. Most people _____ the truth if they _____ to do so.
    (a) will tell, swear
    (b) would tell, swore
    (c) would have told, had sworn

10. I know it's not likely, but if she _____ her plea to guilty she _____ less than five years in prison.
    (a) changes, will get
    (b) changed, would get
    (c) had changed, would have gotten

IV. **Fill in the blanks with the most suitable option:**

1. I will go to the cinema if I _____ well in my English test.
    (a) will do   (b) doing
    (c) do   (d) did

2. What _____ if you don't do well in the test?
    (a) will happen (b) happened
    (c) happens   (d) is happen

3. If it _____ a comedy, I won't watch the film.
    (a) doesn't
    (b) isn't
    (c) won't / doesn't be
    (d) isn't / won't be

4. If you _____ carefully, you _____ have an accident.
    (a) will drive / don't (b) drive / aren't
    (c) will drive / not   (d) drive / won't

5. If I _____ clean the garage, my father _____ give me any money.
    (a) don't / won't   (b) am / will
    (c) won't / doesn't (d) am not / isn't

6. If your dad's old games _____ work on your new computer, what _____ you do?
   (a) doesn't / will   (b) won't / do
   (c) aren't / will   (d) don't / will
7. My parents will help me if they _____ too busy.
   (a) aren't   (b) won't be
   (c) aren't be   (d) don't
8. If Jenny is free tonight, I _____ ask her to come for the cinema
   (a) am   (b) will
   (c) don't   (d) will be
9. If there _____ any milk in the fridge, I _____ and buy some.
   (a) is / go   (b) be / will go
   (c) isn't / will go   (d) isn't / don't go

V. **Choose the correct option to fill in the blanks:**

1. I wouldn't tell her if I _____ you. She can't keep a secret.
   (a) will be   (b) were
   (c) am   (d) had been
2. Paul would be a good artist if he _____ more patience.
   (a) had   (b) has
   (c) will have   (d) have
3. If they invited me to their party, I _____ absolutely delighted.
   (a) am   (b) will be
   (c) would be   (d) was
4. He _____ so many accidents if he drove more carefully.
   (a) hadn't
   (b) wouldn't have had
   (c) hasn't
   (d) won't have
5. I would help them if they _____ to me.
   (a) had listened   (b) listened
   (c) will listen   (d) would listen
6. If the weather _____ warmer, we would go out.
   (a) will be   (b) had been
   (c) were   (d) is
7. Unless you _____, you won't find out the truth.
   (a) will ask   (b) won't ask
   (c) ask   (d) don't ask
8. If you _____ me, I will bring you the book.
   (a) reminded   (b) will remind
   (c) would remind   (d) remind
9. If I _____ about your birthday, I would have bought you a present.
   (a) knew   (b) would know
   (c) know   (d) had known
10. If Anna _____ a little taller, she could become a model.
    (a) will be   (b) is
    (c) had been   (d) were
11. If I smoked a cigarette, _____ you?
    (a) would it bother   (b) will it bother
    (c) does it bother   (d) it bothers
12. If he _____ swimming in such a rough sea, he wouldn't have drowned
    (a) wouldn't have gone
    (b) didn't go
    (c) won't
    (d) hadn't gone
13. If I _____ Paul's number, I would have invite him to the party.
    (a) have   (b) had
    (c) am having   (d) had had
14. If I _____ John, I'd ask Mary for a date.
    (a) will be   (b) am
    (c) were   (d) would be
15. If I sat on the armchair, I _____ more comfortable.
    (a) would have been
    (b) had been
    (c) were
    (d) will have been
16. If it is warm, we _____ to the park.
    (a) will go   (b) went
    (c) would go   (d) are going

Conditionals

17. If they _____ so much time surfing the internet, they would get better marks in their exams.
    (a) don't spend   (b) hadn't spent
    (c) didn't spend   (d) didn't spend

18. We _____ out in the garden if it hadn't been so cold.
    (a) would had sat   (b) would sit
    (c) had sat   (d) would have sat

19. If I had bought more milk, I _____ enough for breakfast.
    (a) would have   (b) had had
    (c) would have had   (d) would had have

20. If we walk so slowly, we _____ late.
    (a) will being   (b) will be
    (c) be   (d) would be

VI. Spot the missing word and fill in at the appropriate place:

1. If I to Leipzig, I'll visit the zoo.
2. If it, we'd be in the garden.
3. If you a lighter jacket, the car driver would have seen you earlier.
4. We TV tonight if Peter hadn't bought the theatre tickets.
5. She wouldn't have had two laptops if she the contract.
6. If I was/were a millionaire, I in Beverly Hills.
7. You would save energy if you the lights more often.
8. If we had read the book, we the film.
9. My sister could score better on the test if the teacher the grammar once more.
10. They on time if they hadn't missed the train.
11. If it rains, the boys hockey.
12. If he his own vegetables, he wouldn't have to buy them.
13. Jim whisky distilleries if he travelled to Scotland.
14. Would you go out more often if you so much in the house?
15. She wouldn't have yawned the whole day if she late last night.
16. If you a minute, I'll come with you.
17. If we arrived at 10, we Tyler's presentation.
18. We John if we'd known about his problems.
19. If they new batteries, their camera would have worked correctly.
20. If I went anywhere, it New Zealand.

HOTS

Read the imaginary situations given below and complete the sentence that describes the situation in each case. One has been done for you as an example.

Example:	
You have always wanted to be the owner of a five-star hotel. What would you do if you won a million rupees?	If I won a million rupees, I would build a five-star hotel.

1. Shikha is in her farm-house. During her morning walk one day, she narrowly escapes being bitten by a snake. What do you think would happen if she was bitten by a snake?

2. I have misplaced the book Ajay gave me on my birthday. I must find it. If I lost the book, how would Ajay feel?

3. Mira might win an air ticket to Europe. She has been dreaming of going to England. Where do you think you would go if you won an air ticket?

4. Delhi Textile Mill is planning to closedown its factory. As a consequence, many workers would lose their jobs. The Workers' Union wants it to stay open and says to the management:

5. Your friend Mani parks his scooter in the lane outside: You fear that it will be stolen one day if he continues to park it there. So you ask him:

Voice and Narration

Learning Objectives: In this chapter, students will learn about:
- ✓ Active and Passive Voice
- ✓ Direct and Indirect speech

CHAPTER SUMMARY

VOICE
Voice is the form of a verb, which shows whether the subject does something or has something done to it.

Types of Voices
We have two voices in English:

(a) Active Voice

(b) Passive Voice

We've all heard this before from our English teachers: 'You should always write in the active voice.' But what exactly does this mean?

Example:

Henry threw the ball. (Active Voice)

The ball was thrown by Henry. (Passive Voice)

Let's take a look at the first sentence. The subject of the sentence is 'Henry,' and 'ball' is the object, which receives the action of the verb 'threw'.

Now, moving onto the second sentence, we can see that 'ball' is the subject of the sentence, and 'Henry' is now the object that receives the action of the verb 'was thrown'.

The grammatical term active voice refers to a sentence in which the subject performs an action indicated by the verb. The first sentence is written in active voice, because Henry is the subject and he is performing the action.

By comparison, the second sentence is written in passive voice, because Henry is no longer the subject; now, he's just the object at the end of the sentence. In grammar, the passive voice refers to sentences in which the verb acts upon a noun or subject, which receives instead of initiating it the action.

Active Voice
A verb is in the active voice when its subject does something, or in simple words the active voice indicates that the subject is performing the action.

Example:

(a) He writes good stories.

(b) We eat all the mangoes.

(c) They play cricket.

(d) I bought a new car.

In these sentences, the subjects (he, we, they, I) do something, so the verbs used are said to be in the Active Voice.

> **TRIVIA**
>
> If we place a comma before the word "and" at the end of a list, this is known as an "Oxford comma" or a "serial comma". For example: "I drink coffee, tea, and juice."

Passive Voice
A verb is in the passive voice when something is done to its subject, or in simple words the passive voice indicates that the action of the verb is being performed upon the subject.

(i) Good stories are written by him.
(ii) All the mangoes are eaten by them.
(iii) Cricket is played by them.
(iv) A new car is bought by me.

In these sentences, the subjects (letter, oranges, hockey, furniture) are acted upon; they remain inactive or passive and their verbs are, therefore, said to be in the passive voice.

Formation of Passive Voice from Active Voice

Only transitive verbs (verbs that take direct object) can be used in the passive voice.

When an active verb is changed into the passive, the direct object of the active verb becomes the subject of the passive verb.

Pooja delivered a wonderful speech. (Active Voice)

A wonderful speech was delivered by Pooja. (Passive Voice)

Rules to Change from Active to Passive Voice

(i) Change the subject into the object and the object into the subject.
(ii) Third form of verb is used in the passive voice.
(iii) Use 'by' after the third form of verb and before the object.
(iv) Change in pronouns: The subjective form of verb is changed into objective form.

Active Voice	Passive Voice
I	Me
We	Us
You	You
He	Him
She	Her
They	Them
Who	By whom

Example:
(i) I called Jimmy last night.
(ii) Deborah read the book.
(iii) Bobby dug the ditch.
(iv) Now, let's take a look at how those same sentences read in the passive voice:
(v) Jimmy was called by me last night.
(v) The book was read by Deborah.
(vi) The ditch was dug by Bobby.

Did you notice that all the sentences written in the passive voice used the verb 'to be'?

Active and Passive Voice (In different Tense forms)

S. No.	Tense/Verb	Active Voice	Passive Voice
1.	Present Simple	Raman wrote a letter.	A letter is written by Raman.
2.	Present Continuous	Right now, Sarah is writing the letter.	Right now, the letter is being written by Sarah.
3.	Simple Past	Sam repaired the car.	The car was repaired by Sam.
4.	Past Continuous	The salesman was helping the customer when the thief came into the store.	The customer was being helped by the salesman when the thief came into the store.
5.	Present Perfect	Many tourists have visited that castle.	That castle has been visited by many tourists.
6.	Present Perfect Continuous	Recently, John has been doing the work.	Recently, the work was being done by John.

Voice and Narration

7.	Past Perfect	George had repaired many cars before he received his mechanic's license.	Many cars had been repaired by George before he received his mechanic's license.
8.	Past Perfect Continuous	Chef Jones had been preparing the restaurant's fantastic dinners for two years before he moved to Paris.	The restaurant's fantastic dinners were being prepared by Chef Jones for two years before he moved to Paris.
9.	Simple Future *(will)*	Someone will finish the work by 5:00 PM.	The work will be finished by 5:00 PM.
10.	Simple Future *(be going to)*	Sally is going to make a delicious dinner tonight.	A delicious dinner is going to be made by Sally tonight.
11.	Future Continuous *(will be)*	At 8:00 PM tonight, John will be washing the dishes.	At 8:00 PM tonight, the dishes will be washed by John.
12.	Future Continuous *(be going to)*	At 8:00 PM tonight, John is going to be washing the dishes.	At 8:00 PM tonight, the dishes are going to be washed by John.
13.	Future Perfect *(will have)*	They will have completed the project before the deadline.	The project will have been completed before the deadline.
14.	Future Perfect *(be going to)*	They are going to have completed the project before the deadline.	The project is going to have been completed before the deadline.
15.	Future Perfect Continuous *(will have been)*	The famous artist will have been painting the mural for over six months by the time it is finished.	The mural will have been being painted by the famous artist for over six months by the time it is finished.
16.	Future Perfect Continuous *(be going to)*	The famous artist is going to have been painting the mural for over six months by the time it is finished.	The mural is going to have been being painted by the famous artist for over six months by the time it is finished.
17.	Used to	Jerry used to pay the bills.	The bills used to be paid by Jerry.
18.	Would Always	My mother would always make the pies.	The pies would always be made by my mother.
19.	Future in the Past *(Would)*	I knew John would finish the work by 5:00 PM.	I knew the work would be finished by John by 5:00 PM.
20.	Future in the Past *(Was Going to)*	I thought Sally was going to make a delicious dinner tonight.	I thought a delicious dinner was going to be made by Sally tonight.

In writing or speech, narration is the process of recounting a sequence of events, real or imagined. It is also called storytelling.

The person who recounts the events is called a narrator. The account itself is called a narrative. The perspective from which a speaker or writer recounts a narrative is called point of view.

There are always two ways to convey message from one to another person: direct speech and indirect speech.

Example:

Suppose your mother tells you, "I will gift you a new car on your birthday." You go to school and want to tell your friend what your mother said.

There are two ways to tell this:

My mother said "I will gift you a new car on your birthday." (Direct)

My mother said that she would give me a new car on my birthday. (Indirect)

Direct/Quoted Speech

Saying exactly what someone has said is called direct speech (sometimes called quoted speech). Here what a person says appears within quotation marks ("...") and should be same word to word.

Example:

She said, "Today's lesson is on presentations."

Some people introduce a direct quote with a colon, and not a comma.

Example:

She said: "Today's lesson is on presentations."

When you lead with the quote, you use a comma.

Example:

"Today's lesson is on presentations," she said.

Indirect/Reported Speech

Assertive Sentence

☞ Indirect speech (sometimes called reported speech) doesn't use quotation marks to enclose what the person said and it doesn't have to be word for word.

When reporting speech the tense usually changes. This is because when we use reported speech, we are usually talking about a time in the past (because obviously the person who spoke originally spoke in the past). The verbs therefore usually have to be in the past too.

Example:

Direct speech / Quoted speech	Indirect speech / Reported speech
"I'm going to the cinema," he said.	He said he was going to the cinema.
"We could go to the cinema," he thought.	He thought we could go to the cinema.

Interrogative Sentence

☞ If there is an interrogative sentence in reported speech, in that terms we join these two sentence like this

☞ If there is interrogative adverb (where, what, when, how, why how) or interrogative pronoun (whose, who, what, which), then we don't use any connective like that.

He said "what are you eating?" (Direct)

He asked what I was eating. (Indirect)

☞ Wrong expression (He asked me that what I was eating)

He said "who is you father?" (Direct)

He asked me who my father was. (Indirect)

☞ If the direct speech starts with "auxiliary verb," we use "whether" or "if" in the place of "that" to change it into indirect speech.

He asked "Is she a dancer?" (Direct)

He asked me whether she was a dancer. (Not -that whether or not she was a dancer.) (Indirect)

I said, "Do you smoke?" (Direct)

I asked whether you smoked. (Indirect)

Imperative Sentence

☞ If there is an imperative sentence (request or command), we don't use the connective "that", "whether", or "if" but we change the verb in "infinitive," for example,

He said "please give me a red pen." (Direct)

He requested to give him a red pen. (Indirect)

Voice and Narration

He said to the lady, "Close the door." (Direct)

He asked the lady to close the door. (Indirect)

Exclamatory Sentence

☞ If there is an exclamatory sentence (surprise, fear, wish), we change it into assertive sentence and we use that to join them like:

He said "May you live long!" (Direct)

He wished that she may live long. (Indirect)

She said "What a terrible scene!" (Direct)

She observed that it was a terrible scene. (Indirect)

Rules of Direct and Indirect Speech

Tense change in Direct to Indirect Speech

1. Present simple tense → Past simple
2. Present Continuous tense → Past continuous
3. Present Perfect tense → Past perfect
4. Present Perfect Continuous → Past perfect continuous
5. Past simple → Past Perfect
6. Past Continuous → Past Perfect Continuous
7. Past Perfect → Past Perfect
8. Future simple, will → would
9. Future Continuous, will be → would be
10. Future Perfect, will have → would have

Example:

She said, "It's cold." (Direct)

She said it was cold. (Indirect)

She said, "I'm teaching English online." (Direct)

She said she was teaching English online. (Indirect)

She said, "I've been on the web since 1999." (Direct)

She said she had been on the web since 1999. (Indirect)

She said, "I've been teaching English for seven years." (Direct)

She said she had been teaching English for seven years. (Indirect)

She said, "I taught online yesterday." (Direct)

She said she had taught online yesterday. (Indirect)

She said, "I was teaching earlier." (Direct)

She said she had been teaching earlier. (Indirect)

She said, "The lesson had already started when he arrived." (Direct)

She said the lesson had already started when he arrived. (Indirect) NO CHANGE

She said, "I'd already been teaching for five minutes." (Direct)

She said she'd already been teaching for five minutes. (Indirect) NO CHANGE

Change in Modal Verbs

Will → Would

Example:

She said, "I'll teach English online tomorrow." (Direct)

She said she would teach English online tomorrow. (Indirect)

Can → Could

Example:

She said, "I can teach English online." (Direct)

She said she could teach English online. (Indirect)

Must → Had to

Example:

She said, "I must have a computer to teach English online." (Direct)

She said she had to have a computer to teach English online. (Indirect)

Shall → Should

Example:

She said, "What shall we learn today?" (Direct)

She asked what we should learn today. (Indirect)

May → Might

Example:

She said, "May I open a new browser?" (Direct)

She asked if she might open a new browser. (Indirect)

Note:
- There is no change to; could, would, should, might and ought to.

  "I might go to the cinema," he said. (Direct)

  He said he might go to the cinema. (Indirect)

- You can use the present tense in reported speech if you want to say that something is still true, i.e. my name has always been and will always be Lynne so:

  "My name is Lynne," she said. (Direct)

  She said her name was Lynne./She said her name is Lynne. (Indirect)

- You can also use the present tense if you are talking about a future event.

  "Next week's lesson is on reported speech," she said. (Direct)

  She said next week's lesson will be on reported speech. (Indirect)

Time Change in Indirect Speech

If the reported sentence contains an expression of time, you must change it to fit in with the time of reporting.

For example, we need to change words like here and yesterday if they have different meanings at the time and place of reporting.

Example:

"Today's lesson is on presentations."

She said yesterday's lesson was on presentations. She said yesterday's lesson would be on presentations.

Expressions of time if reported on a different day

This (evening)	→	That (evening)
Today	→	Yesterday ...
These (days)	→	Those (days)
Now	→	Then
(a week) Ago	→	(a week) Before
Last weekend	→	The weekend before last / the previous weekend
Here	→	There
Next (week)	→	The following (week)
Tomorrow	→	The next/following day

In addition, if you report something that someone said in a different place to where you heard it you must change the place (here) to the place (there).

Example:

"How long have you worked here?" She asked me how long I'd worked there.

Pronoun Change in Indirect Speech

In reported speech, the pronoun often changes.

Example:

"I teach English online."

Direct Speech	Reported Speech
She said, "I teach English online."	She told me she teaches English online.
"I teach English online," she said.	She told me she taught English online.

Reporting Verbs in Indirect Speech

- Said, told and asked are the most common verbs used in indirect speech.

  We use 'asked' to report questions.

  Example:

  I asked Lynne what time the lesson started.

  We use 'told' with an object.

  Example:

  Lynne told me she felt tired.

  In the above sentence, 'me' is the object.

- We usually use 'said' without an object.

  Example:

  Lynne said she was going to teach online.

- If 'said' is used with an object we must include 'to';

  Example:

  Lynne said to me that she'd never been to China.

Note:

We usually use 'told'.

Example:

Lynne told me (that) she'd never been to China.

There are many other verbs we can use apart from said, told and asked. These include:

accused, admitted, advised, alleged, agreed, apologised, begged, boasted, complained, denied, explained, implied, invited, offered, ordered, promised, replied, suggested, etc. Using them properly can make what you say much more interesting and informative.

Example:

He asked me to come to the party.

He invited me to the party.

He begged me to come to the party.

He ordered me to come to the party.

He advised me to come to the party.

He suggested I should come to the party.

Uses of 'That' in reported speech

☞ In reported speech, the word 'that' is often used.

Example:

He told me that he lived in Greenwich.

☞ However, that is optional.

Example:

He told me he lived in Greenwich.

Note:

'That' is never used in questions, instead we often use 'if'.

Example:

He asked me if I would come to the party.

Indirect Speech of Assertive Sentences

1. Boys said, "It has been raining since morning and we cannot play." (Direct)
   Boys said that it had been raining since morning and they could not play. (Indirect)
2. She said to him, "I am leaving now and shall return after two hours." (Direct)
   She told him that she was leaving then and would return after two hours. (Indirect)
3. The girl said to me, "My father went to the market and brought toys for me." (Direct)
   The girl told me that her father had gone to the market and had brought toys for her. (Indirect)
4. Her husband said to her, "I shall not go to the office today as I am not feeling well." (Direct)
   Her husband told her that he would not go to the office that day as he was not feeling well. (Indirect)
5. My father said to me, "I fear that you have caught cold again." (Direct)
   My father told me that he feared that I had caught cold again. (Indirect)
6. His brother said to me, "I am not going to attend the meeting today." (Direct)
   His brother told me that he was not going to attend the meeting that day. (Indirect)
7. She said to him, "Love begets love." (Direct)
   She told him that love begets love. (Indirect)
8. The inspector said to the people, "We have caught the thief and he will be brought to book soon." (Direct)
   The inspector told the people that they had caught the thief and he would be brought to book soon. (Indirect)
9. The teacher said, "Boys, I shall give you a test in English today." (Direct)
   The teacher told the boys that he would give them a test in English that day. (Indirect)
10. My friend said to me, "I am going to my house now. I shall call on you tomorrow." (Direct)
    My friend told me that he was going to his house then and he would call on me the next day. (Indirect)

Indirect Speech of Interrogative Sentences

1. His wife said to him, "Do you know that my servant maid stole our money?" (Direct)
   His wife asked him if he knew that her servant maid had stolen their money. (Indirect)

2. Her friend said to her, "Can you spare your book for me for a week?" (Direct)
   Her friend asked her if she could spare her book for her for a week. (Indirect)
3. She said to him, "Can I do anything for you? Will you mind my extending help to you?" (Direct)
   She asked him if she could do anything for him and if he would mind her extending help to him. (Indirect)
4. His mother said to him, "Will you come home in the evening in time?" (Direct)
   His mother asked him if he would come home in the evening in time. (Indirect)
5. His friend said to him, "Did I not warn you against this beforehand?" (Direct)
   His friend asked him if he had not warned him against that beforehand. (Indirect)
6. John said to his sister, "Is it not a surprise to see your friend here today?" (Direct)
   John asked his sister if it was not a surprise to see her friend there that day. (Indirect)
7. The doctor said to his patient, "Are you taking medicine prescribed to you regularly?" (Direct)
   The doctor asked his patient if he was taking medicine prescribed to him regularly. (Indirect)
8. She said to me," Do you know how to swim?" (Direct)
   She asked me if I knew how to swim. (Indirect)
9. The captain said to the players, "Will you put your heart and soul in playing the game so that we may win the match?" (Direct)
   The captain asked the players if they would put their heart and soul in playing the game so that they might win the match. (Indirect)
10. The stranger said to the lady, "Have you ever been to Delhi?" (Direct)
    The stranger asked the lady if she had ever been to Delhi. (Indirect)

Indirect Speech of Exclamatory Sentences

1. The woman said, "What a beautiful child this is!" (Direct)
   The woman exclaimed that the child was very beautiful. (Indirect)
2. His aunt said, "What a pleasant surprise to see you here!" (Direct)
   His aunt exclaimed that it was a pleasant surprise to see him there. (Indirect)
3. Hamlet said, "How unlucky I am that I cannot find out any solution!" (Direct)
   Hamlet exclaimed that he was very unlucky that he could not find out any solution. (Indirect)
4. The captain said, "Bravo! Well done, boys!" (Direct)
   The captain applauded the boys saying that they had done well. (Indirect)
5. The leader said, "Alas! We have lost the game." (Direct)
   The leader exclaimed with sorrow that they had lost the game. (Indirect)
6. Boys said, "Hurrah! We have won the match!" (Direct)
   Boys exclaimed with joy that they had won the match. (Indirect)
7. She said, "What a beautiful weather it is!" (Direct)
   She exclaimed that it was a very beautiful weather. (Indirect)
8. Father said, "What a lazy fellow she is!" (Direct)
   Father exclaimed that she was a very lazy fellow. (Indirect)
9. The cobbler said, "How stupid I am!" (Direct)
   The cobbler exclaimed that he was very stupid. (Indirect)
10. The girl said, "What a stupid fellow I am!" (Direct)
    The girl exclaimed that she was a stupid fellow. (Indirect)

Voice and Narration

11. The captain said, "Good morning, Friends!" (Direct)
    The captain bade his friends good morning. (Indirect)
12. The leader said, "Farewell, my countrymen!" (Direct)
    The leader bade his countrymen farewell. (Indirect)
13. The boy said, "If I were a king!" (Direct)
    The boy wished that he had been a king. (Indirect)
14. The old lady said, "May you live long, my son!" (Direct)
    The old lady prayed that her son might live long. (Indirect)
15. They said, "May you live a long and prosperous life!" (Direct)
    They prayed that you might live a long and prosperous life. (Indirect)

MUST REMEMBER

- Voice is the form of a verb, which shows whether the subject does something or has something done to it.
- A verb is in the active voice when its subject does something, or in simple words the active voice indicates that the subject is performing the action.
- A verb is in the passive voice when something is done to its subject, or in simple words the passive voice indicates that the action of the verb is being performed upon the subject.
- When an active verb is changed into the passive, the direct object of the active verb becomes the subject of the passive verb.
- In writing or speech, narration is the process of recounting a sequence of events, real or imagined. It is also called storytelling.
- The person who recounts the events is called a narrator. The account itself is called a narrative.
- If the reported sentence contains an expression of time, you must change it to fit in with the time of reporting.

PRACTICE EXERCISE

I. Fill in the blanks with suitable active and passive verb forms.

1. This house _____ in 1970 by my grandfather.
   (a) built (b) was built
   (c) was build (d) has built

2. The robbers _____ by the police.
   (a) have arrested
   (b) have been arrested
   (c) was arrested
   (d) had arrested

3. We _____ for the examination.
   (a) have preparing
   (b) are preparing
   (c) had preparing
   (d) have been prepared

4. It _____ since yesterday.
   (a) is raining (b) has been raining
   (c) have been raining (d) was raining

5. I _____ for five hours.
   (a) have been working
   (b) has been working
   (c) was working
   (d) am working

6. The students _____ to submit their reports by the end of this week.
   (a) have asked (b) were asked
   (c) has asked (d) are asking

7. She _____ for a while.
   (a) are ailing
   (b) is ailing
   (c) has been ailing
   (d) have been ailing

8. The teacher _____ the student for lying.
   (a) has been punished
   (b) punished
   (c) is punished
   (d) was punished

9. I _____ to become a successful writer.
   (a) have always wanted
   (b) am always wanted
   (c) was always wanted
   (d) am always wanting

10. The inmates of the juvenile home _____ well by their caretakers.
    (a) were not being treated
    (b) were not treating
    (c) have not being treated
    (d) was not being treated

11. As the patient could not walk, he _____ home in a wheel chair.
    (a) has carried
    (b) has been carried
    (c) was carried
    (d) was carrying

12. The injured _____ to the hospital in an ambulance.
    (a) were taking (b) was taking
    (c) were taken (d) have taken

II. Fill in the blanks with the correct form of verb given in brackets.

1. Paul _____ (send) to prison. (Future tense)
2. He _____ (tell) to wait outside. (Past tense)
3. I _____ (not pay) for the work. (Past tense)
4. Policemen _____ (often ask) the way. (Present tense)
5. The lawn _____ (cut) once a week. (Present tense)
6. We _____ (ask) by the police. (Future tense)
7. They _____ (teach) French. (Present tense)
8. The fire brigade _____ (phone) soon after the fire had broken out. (Past tense)
9. All the fruits _____ (eat up) by the guests. (Past tense)
10. The letter _____ (answer) tomorrow. (Future tense)

Voice and Narration

III. Choose the most appropriate option to fill in the blanks.

1. Most of the patient visits _____ to physician assistants in the recent years all around the world.
    (a) have been made
    (b) was made
    (c) will have been made
    (d) have made
    (e) make

2. These differences between two photographs _____ with the help of Photoshop.
    (a) should remove
    (b) must have removed
    (c) have to remove
    (d) could have been removed
    (e) were able to remove

3. No clinical studies _____ in this child disease research so far.
    (a) had completed
    (b) will be completed
    (c) have completed
    (d) had to complete
    (e) have been completed

4. The government _____ that the tasks _____ with great success.
    (a) is confirming / maintained
    (b) confirms / have been maintained
    (c) was confirmed / have maintained
    (d) will confirm / had been maintained
    (e) confirmed / are maintaining

5. With this comprehensive international report, the country's position in the regional and global arena _____ with measurable criteria.
    (a) is to identify   (b) identifies
    (c) will be identified (d) identified
    (e) is going to identify

6. The critics _____ that the review _____ as a book in English and in many other languages.
    (a) are said / could be published
    (b) say / can be published
    (c) will say / had been published
    (d) said / may be published
    (e) have said / should publish

7. New legislation _____ in the congress but it _____ by many.
    (a) was introduced / wasn't accepted
    (b) introduced / didn't accept
    (c) will be introduced / isn't accepted
    (d) introduced / hadn't been accepted
    (e) is introduced / won't accept

8. If you would like to know what _____ in the project so far, you _____ the full report at our website.
    (a) has been completed / may be visited
    (b) completed / will be found
    (c) completes / should be found
    (d) was completed / had been found
    (e) will be completed / can find

9. These clothes _____ for daily use so you _____ them wherever you want.
    (a) design / should be worn
    (b) will be designed / must wear
    (c) are designed / can wear
    (d) were designed / could be worn
    (e) designed / might be worn

10. A more developed model of this car _____ in the showroom soon.
    (a) is going to show
    (b) will be shown
    (c) was shown
    (d) has been shown
    (e) had shown

HOTS

Complete the paragraph by filling in the blanks with the appropriate options.

Six bananas___1___ into a pulp. Half a litre of milk___2___and banana pulp and sugar___3___ to it. The mixture___4___and then___5___from the heat.

1.
   (a) is crushed
   (b) are crushed
   (c) should crush
   (d) should be crush

2.
   (a) is boiled
   (b) will be boiled
   (c) was boiled
   (d) should boil

3.
   (a) is added
   (b) was added
   (c) are added
   (d) should be adding

4.
   (a) is stirred
   (b) will stir
   (c) are stirred
   (d) should stir

5.
   (a) was removed
   (b) will be removed
   (c) are removed
   (d) removed

Voice and Narration

Spelling, Analogy and Collocations — 10

Learning Objectives: In this chapter, students will learn about:
- ✓ Basic concepts related to Spelling
- ✓ Concept of Analogy
- ✓ Usage of Collocations

CHAPTER SUMMARY

In written language, spelling is the choice and arrangement of letters that form words. "English spelling," says R.L. Trask, "is notoriously complex, irregular, and eccentric, more so than in almost any other written language."

Although 'good' and 'food' contain the same vowel letters (oo), in most dialects of English these two words aren't pronounced the same. English has 20 vowel sounds but just five proper vowel letters. This discrepancy, says linguist David Crystal, "underlies the complexity of English spelling."

British Spelling vs. American Spelling

"The lexicographer Noah Webster is responsible for many of the differences that distinguish American spelling from British spelling. His American Dictionary of the English Language, which came out in 1828, became the standard for US spelling. He originally wanted Americans to use much more strictly phonetic spelling, but he later compromised with only minor modifications. British spelling has also undergone reform since 1828. Most notably, terror and horror have lost their -our endings. The -ise suffix is relatively new to British spelling."

British -our and -re Endings

"Noah Webster, through the influence of his spelling book and dictionaries, was responsible for Americans settling upon -or spellings for a group of words spelled in his day with either -or or -our: armo(u)r, behavio(u)r, colo(u)r, favo(u)r, flavo(u)r, harbo(u)r, labo(u)r, neighbo(u)r, and the like. All such words were current in earlier British English without the u, though most Britons today are probably unaware of that fact; Webster was making no radical change in English spelling habits. Furthermore, the English had themselves struck the u from a great many words earlier spelled -our, alternating with -or: author, doctor, emperor, error, governor, horror, mirror, and senator, among others.

"Webster is also responsible for the American practice of using -er instead of the -re that the British came to favor in a number of words--for instance, calibre, centre, litre, manoeuvre, metre (of poetry or of the unit of length in the metric system), sepulchre, and theatre. . . . Except for litre, which did not come into English until the nineteenth century, all these words occurred in earlier British English with -er."

The c-s Difference

"The British [c] spelling of the nouns defence, licence, offence, pretence, and practice has an [s] counterpart in American spelling: defense, license, etc. The British distinction between the noun spelling (licence, practice) and verb spelling (license, practise) is lost. Rather confusingly, the form practice can also be found as an American spelling of both noun and verb. The British use of the [c]-[s] difference to mark nouns and verbs is also found to some small extent in advice-advise, device-devise, prophecy-prophesy."

Spelling rules are a bit like weather forecasts: we may use them, but we really can't depend on them to be right 100% of the time. In fact, the only foolproof rule is that all spelling rules in English have exceptions. Still, many writers find that certain rules help them remember how to spell particular types of words, especially those formed by adding suffixes (or word endings).

Spelling Rules

Rule 1: Using I Before E

Use i before e, except after c, or when sounded as "a" as in "neighbor" and "weigh."

Example:

believe, chief, piece, and thief; deceive, receive, weigh, and freight

Common Exceptions: efficient, weird, height, neither, ancient, caffeine, foreign

Rule 2: Dropping the Final E

Drop the final e before a suffix beginning with a vowel (a, e, i, o, u) but not before a suffix beginning with a consonant.

Example:

ride + ing = riding

guide + ance = guidance

hope + ing = hoping

entire + ly = entirely

like + ness = likeness

arrange + ment = arrangement

Common Exceptions: truly, noticeable

Rule 3: Changing a Final Y to I

Change a final y to i before a suffix, unless the suffix begins with i.

Example:

defy + ance = defiance

party + es = parties

pity + ful = pitiful

try + es = tries

try + ing = trying

copy + ing = copying

occupy + ing = occupying

Common Exceptions: memorize

Rule 4: Doubling a Final Consonant

Double a final single consonant before a suffix, beginning with a vowel, when both of these conditions exist:

(a) a single vowel precedes the consonant;

(b) the consonant ends an accented syllable or a one-syllable word.

Example:

stop + ing = stopping

admit + ed = admitted

occur + ence = occurrence

stoop + ing = stooping

benefit + ed = benefitted

delight + ful = delightful

Commonly Misspelt Words

absence	athlete	brilliant
accommodate	awful	business
achieve	balance	calendar
acquire	basically	careful
across	becoming	ceiling
advertise	before	cemetery
advice	beginning	certain
among	believe	chief
apparent	benefit	citizen

coming	heroes	original
competition	humorous	ought
convenience	identity	parallel
criticize	imitation	particularly
definite	immediately	peculiar
deposit	incidentally	perceive
describe	independent	permanent
desperate	interesting	persevere
difference	interfere	personally
dilemma	interpretation	persuade
disappear	interruption	picture
disappoint	invitation	piece
discipline	irrelevant	planning
does	irritable	pleasant
during	island	political
easily	jealous	possible
eight	knowledge	practical
embarrass	laboratory	prefer
environment	length	prejudice
equipped	lesson	privilege
exaggerate	license	probably
except	loneliness	professional
exercise	losing	promise
existence	lying	proof
expect	marriage	psychology
experience	mathematics	quantity
experiment	medicine	quarter
explanation	miniature	quiet
familiar	minute	quite
fascinating	naturally	realize
foreign	necessary	receive
forty	neighbor	recognize
forward	neither	reference
friend	occasion	religious
generally	occurred	repetition
government	official	restaurant
grammar	often	rhythm
guarantee	omission	ridiculous
guidance	operate	sacrifice
happiness	optimism	safety

scissors	successful	until
separate	surely	unusual
shining	surprise	using
similar	temperature	usually
sincerely	temporary	village
speech	through	weird
stopping	toward	welcome
strength	tries	whether
studying	truly	writing
succeed	twelfth	

Analogy

Analogy comes from the Greek word *analogia*, which is a combination of the prefix ana- (upon, again, or back) and the suffix –logos (ratio, word, or speech). Together, the word means something akin to "proportion."

Analogy is a comparison between two things. Analogies function to describe or explain one thing by examining its similarities with another thing. The two things may be very dissimilar and the analogy forces the reader or listener to understand the connection between them. On the other hand, the analogy could provide a comparison between two very similar things, one of which might be more obscure; the analogy provides a way for a reader or listener to understand the more obscure thing by picturing the more common thing.

Many common literary devices are examples of analogy, such as metaphor, simile, allegory, parable, and exemplification. We examine the differences between these devices below.

Understanding the meaning of an analogy is key to the success of the analogy in communication. Some analogies will be understood by most people, who speak the same language. Within small social groups of people, there are often shared analogies that bind the group together. Other analogies are only understood by people living in a certain region or country.

Types of Analogy

As the definition of analogy includes all types of comparisons, the following list qualifies as analogies:

Metaphor

A metaphor compares two subjects without any connecting words such as "like" or "as." Metaphors are considered a strong form of analogy as they assert that one thing is another.

Simile

A simile is a comparison between two things, using the connecting words "like" or "as." Not quite as strong of a comparison as metaphor, simile still requires the reader to understand the similarities between the two things and make new cognitive links. Eg:- He is like a rock.

Allegory

An allegory is a story in which the characters, images, and/or events function as symbols. These symbols can be interpreted to have deeper significance and may illustrate moral truths or a political or historical situation.

Parable

Similar to allegory, though more condensed, a parable is a simple story used to illustrate an instructive lesson or principle.

Exemplification

Exemplification is the relation between a sample and what it refers to. For example, if a sign at an arboretum said "oak" in front of an oak tree, that tree would be an exemplification of the label.

Common Analogies and Their Meanings

Analogy examples with corresponding meanings are the best way to show the meaning of the word "analogy." The following is a list of some common analogies and an explanation of their meanings:

1. The relationship between them began to thaw. (This means that the relationship was changing.)
2. I am going to be toast when I get home. (This is usually said when someone is in trouble with their significant other.)
3. He is like a rock. (This means he is steadfast and strong.)
4. She attended the celebrity roast. (The person being roasted is being honored by people making harmless jokes about him or her.)
5. I feel like a fish out of water. (This implies that you are not comfortable in your surroundings.)
6. She was offended when I said she was as flaky as a snowstorm. (This means that she is not stable and, therefore, can hardly be trusted.)
7. There are plenty of fish in the sea. (Unless you really are a fish, this encourages you to move on and find another potential mate.)
8. She was as quiet as a mouse. (It is hard to hear a mouse, so that means she was very quiet.)
9. Bing Crosby had a velvet voice. (As voices are not made of velvet, this implies that his voice was smooth and soothing.)
10. Life is like a box of chocolates. (This has many meanings and is a great analogy for life. It mostly means life is full of surprises and anything can happen next.)

TRIVIA

The chess term "checkmate" comes from a 14th century Arabic phrase, "Shah-Mat", which means "the king is helpless".

Examples of Analogy from Everyday Life

We use analogy in our everyday conversation. Some common analogy examples are given below:
1. Life is like a race. The one who keeps running wins the race and the one who stops to catch a breath loses.
2. Just as a sword is the weapon of a warrior, a pen is the weapon of a writer.
3. How a doctor diagnoses diseases is like how a detective investigates crimes.
4. Just as a caterpillar comes out of its cocoon, so we must come out of our comfort zone.
5. You are as annoying as nails on a chalkboard.

More Examples of Analogy

Here are some simple examples of analogy:
Green : Colour :: Orchid : Flower
Scientist : Einstein :: Musician : Mozart
Human : Fingernail :: Tiger : Claw
There are many other analogies that we can find in common speech. Here are some examples of simile, one of the main types of analogy:
1. Mary had a little lamb / Her fleece was *white as snow.*
2. *As light as a feather*
3. *As dead as a doornail*
4. *As busy as a bee*
5. *As quiet as a mouse*
6. *As happy as a clam*
7. *Sly like a fox*
8. *You're as sweet as sugar*
9. That would be *as difficult as finding a needle in a haystack.*
10. "We will not be satisfied until *justice rolls down like waters, and righteousness like a mighty stream*" –Martin Luther King, Jr. "I have a dream" speech".

Collocation

According to the Cambridge dictionary, 'collocation' is:
1. "a word or phrase that is often used with another word or phrase, in a way that sounds correct to people who have spoken the language all their lives, but might not be expected from the meaning."
2. "The combination of words formed when two or more words are often used together in a way that sound correct."

Types of Collocations

There are six main types of collocation; they are:

Adjective + Noun

There are many adjectives, which can gather with noun, but here are some adjectives to give you obvious examples.
Example:
(a) He has been a *heavy smoker* and drinker all his adult life.

(b) She speaks English quite well but with *strong French accent*.
(c) They have a *hard life* and worked through a *hard time*.
(d) We don't have *hard evidence* that they had used *hard drugs*.
(e) The doctor ordered him to take *regular exercise*.
(f) The Titanic sank on its *maiden voyage*.

Noun + Noun (such as collective noun)
Example:
(a) I would like to buy two *bars of soaps*.
(b) There is a *glass of water* on the table.
(c) Would you like to have a *cup of coffee*?
(d) He will give a *bar of chocolate* to his girlfriend on Valentine's Day.
(e) Her *bouquet of flower* is the best of all.

Verb + Noun
Example:
(a) I always try to *do my homework* in the morning after *making my bed*.
(b) Do you think the bank would *forgive a debt*?
(c) We are going to *have lunch* together, would you like to join?
(d) Every day, I *take a shower* at 6 o'clock.

Adverb + Adjective
Example:
(a) This test is *ridiculously easy*! I didn't even study, but I will get high score.
(b) Janet is a *highly successful* businesswoman. She owns several restaurants and hotels around the country.

(c) That is *utterly ridiculous*. She didn't steal your favourite book. She wasn't even in the office yesterday.
(d) Roger is *strongly opposed* to anything bad for health. He doesn't eat junk food at all.
(e) Are you okay? I am *deeply concerned* about you. You have been desperate since you lost your job.

Verb + Prepositional Phrase/Phrasal Verb
Example:
(a) Their behaviour was enough to *drive anybody to crime*.
(b) We had to return home because we *had run out of money*.
(c) I am going to *look up* the meaning in the dictionary.
(d) She is going to *dress up* for her first date with him.
(e) You have to *make up* your mind before doing something.

Verb + Adverb
Example:
(a) Mary *whispered softly* in John's ear.
(b) The boy *speaks politely*, and is very well-behaved.
(c) The accident happened because he was *driving dangerously*.
(d) After 2 years in London, he *speaks* English *fluently*.
(e) I *waited patiently*, but she never came.

- A metaphor compares two subjects without any connecting words such as "like" or "as."
- A simile is a comparison between two things, using the connecting words "like" or "as."
- An allegory is a story in which the characters, images, and/or events function as symbols.
- Exemplification is the relation between a sample and what it refers to.

PRACTICE EXERCISE

I. Add a letter or two to complete the spelling of each word given in parentheses others are correct as they stand.

1. Bob is (tru-ly) sorry for taking your book without informing you.
2. The minister was criticized (sever-ly) for not living up to the expectations of the people.
3. The incident shattered her (complet-ly).
4. I am (sincer-ly) grateful to her for offering me help on time.
5. That couple is (argu-ing) again.
6. He (argu-d) with his teacher for hours.
7. When are you (com-ing) back home?
8. Maya is (writ-ing) her autobiography.
9. Mr. White is (judg-ing) the essay contest.
10. Be (careful) when you cross the main road.

II. Add 'IE' OR 'EI' to some of the words wherever required in the following sentences.

1. Paint the (c--ling) before you paint the walls.
2. Arun has been (rec--ving) threatening calls.
3. A (w--rd) noise came out of the attic.
4. Can I have that (p--ce) of pie?
5. I don't (bel--ve) in coincidence.
6. All the parents have been advised to accompany (th--r) children to the event.
7. (N--ther) of us can help you today.
8. Our (n--ghbors) are very nice people.
9. The wet coat (w--ghs) less when it is dry.
10. We waited for the (fr--ght) train to pass.

III. Add 'i' OR 'y' to the words given in parenthesis wherever required.

1. Have you (tr-ed) the dessert yet?
2. The baby (cr-ed) throughout the night.
3. We compared two (theor-es) of evolution.
4. She felt (betra-ed) by her friend.
5. You should be (stud-ing) for Wednesday's exam.
6. (Lonel-ness) was never a problem for Henry.
7. The bird (fl-es) on broken wings.
8. I have always (rel-ed) on my friends.
9. She doesn't believe in (apolog-es) or regrets.
10. It was a (pit-ful) sight.

IV. Complete each word with the letter a, e, or i in the following sentences.

1. I borrowed these flowers from the (cemet-ry).
2. My bird eats huge (quant-ties) of seed.
3. The tax cuts will (ben-fit) the private sector.
4. It was a (priv-lege) to attend this meeting.
5. He has a remarkably (unpleas-nt) disposition.
6. We placed the puppies in (sep-rate) rooms.
7. She is very (independ-nt) by nature and hardly takes anyone's help.
8. I found an (excell-nt) excuse to resign from the committee.
9. There are different (cat-gories) of products listed on the website.
10. Professor Mittal made another (irrelev-nt) remark.

V. Double the consonant of the words given in parenthesis, wherever required in the following sentences.

1. The sun was (shin-ing) down like honey.
2. The experiment was (control-ed) by a restricted group of scientists.
3. The patient is slowly (begin-ing) to recover.
4. I (pour-ed) sugar over my oatmeal.
5. She keeps (forget-ing) to call me.
6. I've (admit-ed) my mistake.
7. They were (sweat-ing) outside.
8. That idea never (occur-ed) to me.
9. The bunny went (hop-ing) down to the hole.
10. His doctor (refer-ed) him to a skin specialist.

VI. Add one or more letters to the words given in parenthesis wherever required in the following sentences.

1. Most of the things in life come without a (g-arantee).
2. Rita (su-prised) me.
3. It's (prob-ly) going to rain.
4. Does she (reali-e) that she is looking awful?
5. (D-scribe) the man who hit you.
6. We waited (until-) the priest arrived.
7. Mary (recom-ended) a psychiatrist.
8. Take two (asp-rin) and go to bed.
9. She loves to watch (ath-letic) programs.
10. The (tem-rature) reached 50 degrees in Delhi.

VII. Add one or more letters to the words given in parenthesis wherever required in the following sentences.

1. Facebook recently (a-quired) an Israeli company called Pebbles Interfaces.
2. He is (basic-ly) lazy.
3. We must work together to improve the (envir-ment).
4. I wish my tutor would just (dis-pear).
5. He should attend to his (bus-ness).
6. Mary wrote a story (sim-lar) to yours.
7. She (fin-ly) agreed to participate in the match.
8. I was (dis-appointed) by the salesman's behavior.
9. You can find test-tubes in the school (lab-ratory).
10. My father works in a (gover-ment) firm.

VIII. Select the correct option in order to complete the analogy.

1. Doctor : Nurse :: ? : Follower
   (a) Employer (b) Leader
   (c) Worker   (d) Manager
2. Moon : Satellite :: Earth : ?
   (a) Sun   (b) Planet
   (c) Solar System (d) Asteroid
3. Fear : Threat :: Anger : ?
   (a) Compulsion (b) Panic
   (c) Provocation (d) Force
4. Clock : Time :: Thermometer : ?
   (a) Heat   (b) Radiation
   (c) Energy   (d) Temperature
5. Cup : Lip :: Bird : ?
   (a) Bush   (b) Grass
   (c) Forest   (d) Beak
6. Tractor : Trailer :: Horse : ?
   (a) Stable   (b) Cart
   (c) Saddle   (d) Engine
7. Flower : Bud :: Plant : ?
   (a) Twig   (b) Seed
   (c) Taste   (d) Flower
8. Flow : River :: Stagnant : ?
   (a) Rain   (b) Stream
   (c) Pool   (d) Canal
9. Paw : Cat :: Hoof : ?
   (a) Lamb   (b) Horse
   (c) Elephant (d) Lion
10. Car : Garage :: Aeroplane : ?
    (a) Port   (b) Depot
    (c) Hangar   (d) Harbour
11. Venerate : Worship :: Extol : ?
    (a) Glorify (b) Homage
    (c) Compliment (d) Recommend
12. Nurture : Neglect :: Denigrate : ?
    (a) Reveal   (b) Extol
    (c) Recognise (d) Caluminate
13. Hong Kong : China :: Vatican : ?
    (a) Rome   (b) Mexico
    (c) Canada   (d) Australia
14. Illiteracy : Education :: Flood : ?
    (a) Rain   (b) Bridge
    (c) Dam   (d) River
15. Hill : Mountain :: Stream : ?
    (a) River   (b) Canal
    (c) Glacier (d) Avalanche
16. Fruit : Banana :: Mammal : ?
    (a) Cow   (b) Snake
    (c) Fish   (d) Sparrow
17. Fire : Ashes :: Explosion : ?
    (a) Flame   (b) Debris
    (c) Sound   (d) Death
18. Drama : Stage :: Tennis : ?
    (a) Net   (b) Tournament
    (c) Racket   (d) Court

19. Sculptor : Statue :: Poet : ?
    (a) Canvas   (b) Pen
    (c) Verse   (d) Chisel
20. Malaria : Disease :: Spear : ?
    (a) Wound   (b) Sword
    (c) Weapon   (d) Death
21. Reading : Knowledge :: Work : ?
    (a) Experience (b) Engagement
    (c) Employment (d) Experiment
22. Cricket : Bat :: Hockey : ?
    (a) Field   (b) Stick
    (c) Player   (d) Ball
23. Enough : Excess :: Sufficiency : ?
    (a) Adequacy   (b) Surplus
    (c) Competency (d) Import
24. Skeleton : Body :: Grammar : ?
    (a) Language   (b) Sentence
    (c) Meaning   (d) Education
25. Mature : Regressed :: Varied : ?
    (a) Rhythmic   (b) Monotonous
    (c) Decorous   (d) Obsolete
26. Ship : Sea :: Camel : ?
    (a) Forest   (b) Land
    (c) Mountain   (d) Desert
27. Dilatory : Expeditious :: Direct : ?
    (a) Tortuous   (b) Circumlocutory
    (c) Straight   (d) Curved
28. Wrist : Elbow :: Ankle : ?
    (a) Heel   (b) Fingers
    (c) Foot   (d) Knee
29. Amber : Yellow :: Caramine : ?
    (a) Red   (b) Green
    (c) Violet   (d) Blue
30. Wax : Wane :: Zenith : ?
    (a) Nadir   (b) Bottom
    (c) Fall   (d) Height
31. Foundation : Edifice :: Constitution: ?
    (a) Government (b) State
    (c) Nation   (d) Cabinet
32. Video : Cassette :: Computer : ?
    (a) Reels   (b) Recordings
    (c) Files   (d) Floppy
33. Produce : Waste :: Contrast : ?
    (a) Match   (b) Correct
    (c) Oppose   (d) Contradict
34. Palaeography : Writings :: Ichthyology : ?
    (a) Fishes   (b) Whales
    (c) Oysters   (d) Mammals
35. Painting : Artist :: Symphony : ?
    (a) Novelist   (b) Poet
    (c) Essayist   (d) Composer

IX. Fill in the blanks with the correct option.
1. I'd like to stop smoking but I just can't _____ it up.
    (a) give   (b) turn
    (c) put   (d) hurry
2. I'm getting really unfit. I think I should _____ up a sport.
    (a) speak   (b) take
    (c) put   (d) hurry
3. I'm fed up of hearing you talk all the time. Why don't you just _____ up and listen for once?
    (a) cheer   (b) move
    (c) put   (d) shut
4. He's a really irritating person. I don't see how you _____ up with him.
    (a) speak   (b) move
    (c) put   (d) hurry
5. If you don't put any oil in the motor when the warning light comes on, it's likely to _____ up.
    (a) send   (b) seize
    (c) put   (d) set
6. There's not enough room for all my papers. I'm going to ask maintenance to _____ up some more shelves.
    (a) cheer   (b) move
    (c) put   (d) hurry
7. If you ever come to my city you must _____ me up and we'll have dinner together.
    (a) speak   (b) move
    (c) put   (d) look
8. Let's ask Andrew and see if he can _____ up with any good ideas.
    (a) come   (b) set
    (c) put   (d) turn
9. It was really embarrassing. I'd had too much to drink and when we left the bar I was sure I was going to _____ up.
    (a) cheer   (b) sign
    (c) throw   (d) hurry

10. It's a difficult market to enter but we intend to _____ up a small subsidiary anyway.
    (a) cheer   (b) turn
    (c) throw   (d) set
11. When I saw that this course was available, I rushed to _____ up for it.
    (a) cheer   (b) sign
    (c) gee   (d) feel
12. That was a complete surprise - a total _____ up for the books.
    (a) speak   (b) move
    (c) turn   (d) throw
13. Stop acting so childishly. _____ up.
    (a) cheer   (b) move
    (c) grow   (d) hurry
14. I couldn't afford to buy it but my parents _____ up the money for me.
    (a) cheer   (b) move
    (c) put   (d) throw
15. He's always making fun of me. I wish he wouldn't _____ me up like that.
    (a) send   (b) move
    (c) gee   (d) hurry
16. I knew he would get promoted. It's good to see him _____ up the ladder.
    (a) speak   (b) move
    (c) gee   (d) throw
17. They badly need motivating. Perhaps you can _____ them up?
    (a) cheer   (b) grow
    (c) gee   (d) throw
18. They're so miserable. Perhaps you can _____ them up?
    (a) cheer   (b) grow
    (c) put   (d) give
19. What's taking them so long? Perhaps you can _____ them up?
    (a) speak   (b) grow
    (c) give   (d) hurry
20. We can't hear you at the back. Perhaps you could _____ up a bit?
    (a) speak   (b) seize
    (c) put   (d) throw

HOTS

Direction 1-5: Select the pair among the given choices which is related in the same way as the words given in CAPITAL letters.

1. REPROACH : APPROVAL :: ?
   (a) Sorcery : Black magic
   (b) Disapprove : Disgrace
   (c) Stupendous : Gigantic
   (d) Svelte : Obese
   (e) None of these
2. AUGUR : FUTURE :: ?
   (a) Knight : Medieval
   (b) Poet : Century
   (c) Vanguard : Pack
   (d) Historian : Past
   (e) None of these
3. GARBAGE : SQUALOR :: ?
   (a) Colour : Brush
   (b) Dirt : Cleanliness
   (c) Diamond : Magnificence
   (d) Poor : Hunger
   (e) None of these
4. IRK : APPEASE :: ?
   (a) Appreciate : Deprave
   (b) Quibble : Clarify
   (c) Ridicule : Decorate
   (d) Stupefy : Debilitate
5. WIND : GALE :: ?
   (a) Disaster : Calamity
   (b) Storm : Sea
   (c) Love : Passion
   (d) Disgust : Infatuation

Synonyms, Antonyms, Homophones and Homonyms

11

Learning Objectives : In this chapter, students will learn about:
- ✓ Synonyms and Antonyms
- ✓ Homophones and Homonyms

CHAPTER SUMMARY

A synonym is a word or phrase that means exactly or nearly the same as another word or phrase in the same language. Words that are synonyms are said to be synonymous, and the state of being a synonym is called synonymy. The word comes from Ancient Greek syn ('with') and onoma ('name').

An example of synonym of the word 'begin' are 'start' and 'commence'. Words can be synonymous when meant in certain senses, even if they are not synonymous in all of their senses.

Antonyms

An antonym is a word that means the opposite of a particular word. For instance, the antonym of 'hot' is 'cold.' The root words for the word 'antonym' are the words 'anti,' meaning 'against' or 'opposite,' and 'onym,' meaning 'name.'

In order to better understand antonyms, let's revise what the word 'synonym' means. A synonym is a word that has a similar meaning to or exactly the same meaning as another word. Synonyms and antonyms are exactly the opposite.

Words related to weather

There are a lot of weather words in English. It is difficult for someone to remember them all at a go. Nonetheless, you come across words related to weather during a conversation, or while watching a TV show, or while going through books or study materials. You must know the meaning of the words to have proper communication. So here is a list of weather vocabulary that will help you increase your knowledge and add a few words to your everyday use.

Name of Weather Vocabulary words

Weather describes the state of the atmosphere, such as how hot or cold it is, how wet or dry it is, and how clear or foggy it is. This list consists of weather-related words and definitions of the same so that you can understand them well. These words related to sky and weather will help you with an effective way to communicate or understand things better.

List of Weather Vocabulary

- Balmy
- Blustery
- Breeze
- Cloudy
- Cold
- Cold Front
- Dew
- Downpour
- Drizzle
- Easterlies
- Fog

- Frost
- Gale
- Gust
- Icicle
- Lightning
- Mist
- Muggy
- Overcast
- Permafrost
- Rain
- Rainbow
- Sleet
- Smog
- Snow
- Snowfall
- Tropical
- Warm
- Westerlies
- Whirlwind
- Wind
- Wind Chill

Description of the Weather Vocabulary words.

- Balmy- Balmy weather is mild and pleasant and is characterized by warm weather.
- Blustery- Blustery is the weather that is characterized by strong winds.
- Breeze- It is a light, pleasant wind that can either be warm or cold.
- Cloudy- Cloudy weather occurs when the sky is obscured by clouds.
- Cold- We call it cold weatherwhen the weather is at a relatively lower temperature than our human body.
- Cold Front- A cold front is the extreme end of a cooler air mass at ground level that replaces a warmer mass of air and is located within a deep surface low pressure trough.
- Dew- Dew is droplets of water that form on thin, exposed objects in the morning or evening owing to condensation. As the exposed surface cools by radiating heat, air moisture condenses faster than it can evaporate, resulting in water droplets.
- Downpour- A downpour is characterized by heavy rainfall.
- Drizzle- Drizzle is a type of light liquid precipitation consisting of liquid water drops smaller than raindrops – typically less than 0.5 mm in diameter. Stratocumulus clouds and low stratiform clouds typically create drizzle.
- Easterlies- The trade winds, also known as easterlies, are the persistent east-to-west winds that blow in the Earth's equatorial region.
- Fog- Fog is a visible aerosol made up of microscopic water droplets or ice crystals floating in the air near or on the Earth's surface. Fog is a low-lying cloud that resembles stratus and is significantly impacted by neighboring bodies of water, geography, and wind conditions. Fog, in turn, has an impact on many human activities, including shipping, travel, and warfare.
- Frost- Frost is the thin layer of ice formed on a solid surface when water vapor in an above-freezing atmosphere comes into contact with a solid surface below freezing, resulting in a phase shift from water vapor to ice as the water vapor approaches the freezing point. It most typically appears on surfaces near the ground as delicate white crystals in temperate regions; in frigid climates, it appears in a broader range of forms.
- Gale- A gale is a violent wind that is commonly used in nautical contexts as a descriptive. When winds of 34–47 knots are forecasted, forecasters often issue gale warnings.
- Gust- A gust, also known as a wind gust, is a transient increase in wind speed that lasts less than 20 seconds. It is more fleeting than a storm, which lasts minutes and is followed by a lull or a wind slowing. Winds are generally least gusty over big bodies of water and most gusty over rocky terrain and near tall buildings.
- Icicle- An icicle is a spike of ice generated when waterfalls from a frozen object.
- Lightning- Lightning is a naturally occurring electrostatic discharge in which

two electrically charged regions, either in the atmosphere or on the ground, temporarily equalize, resulting in the sudden release of up to one gigatonne of energy. This discharge can produce a wide range of electromagnetic radiation, from heat generated by the rapid flow of electrons to dazzling bursts of visible light in the form of black-body radiation.

- Mist– Mist is a natural occurrence generated by microscopic droplets of water floating in the air. It is a physical example of dispersion. It is most typically observed where warm, moist air meets quick cooling, as in exhaled air in the cold or splashing water into a hot sauna stove.
- Muggy– Muggy refers to a combination of humidity and heat that causes you to sweat and feel uncomfortable, making you desire air conditioning.
- Overcast– Overcast, often known as overcast weather, is a meteorological situation in which clouds obscure at least 95 percent of the sky. On the other hand, the overall cloud cover cannot be attributed to obscuring phenomena near the surface, such as fog.
- Permafrost– Permafrost is defined as ground that has consistently remained below 0 °C (32 °F) for two or more years and can be found on land or under the sea. Permafrost does not have to be the ground's first layer. It can range in depth from one inch to several miles beneath the Earth's surface.
- Rain– Rain is liquid water in droplets condensate from air-water vapor and becomes heavy enough to fall due to gravity. Rain is an integral part of the water cycle since it is responsible for depositing the majority of the fresh water on Earth.
- Rainbow - A rainbow is a meteorological phenomenon created by the reflection, refraction, and dispersion of light in water droplets collide, causing a spectrum of light to appear in the sky. It resembles a multicolored circular arc. Sunlight-induced rainbows always appear in the part of the sky directly opposite the Sun.
- Sleet - Sleet is a different type of precipitation than snow, hail, and freezing rain. It is formed when a temperature inversion causes snow to melt and then refreeze in particular weather circumstances.
- Smog– Smog is a type of air pollution named from the combination of smoke and fog in the air. Classic smog is formed by a mixture of smoke and Sulphur dioxide caused by significant amounts of coal burning in a region.
- Snow– Snow is composed of individual ice crystals that form while hanging in the atmosphere (typically within clouds) and then fall to the ground, where they undergo additional modifications. Throughout its life cycle, it is made up of frozen crystalline water.
- Snowfall– Snowfall is what we term a snowfall, namely the amount of snow that falls in a single storm or over a specific period.
- Tropical– A tropical climate is found in the tropics. It has a humid environment with typical temperatures exceeding 18°C (64.4 °F) throughout the year. Rainfall occurs throughout the year in some tropical places, mainly in the afternoon. Others, for example, have a rainy season and a dry season as a result of the monsoon.
- Warm– Warm weather is characterized by a moderate degree of heat when the weather is moderately hot.
- Westerlies– The westerlies, also known as anti-trades or prevailing westerlies, are prevailing winds that blow from the west to the east in the middle latitudes between 30 and 60 degrees latitude. They form in high-pressure regions in the horse latitudes, move towards the poles, and drive extratropical cyclones in this general direction.
- Whirlwind– A whirlwind is a weather phenomenon that occurs when a vortex of wind emerges due to instabilities and turbulence caused by heating and flow gradients. Whirlwinds can occur at any time of year and in any location on the planet.
- Wind– Wind can be defined as the natural movement of air or other gases on the surface of a planet. Wind occurs on various

scales, from thunderstorm flows lasting tens of minutes to local breezes formed by heating land surfaces and lasting a few hours to global winds caused by differences in solar energy absorption between Earth's temperate zones.

- Wind Chill– The wind chill is a word that meteorologists use during the colder months of the year. Forecasters may also refer to this as the "feels-like" temperature because the wind chill is essentially how cold it feels on your skin when the wind is factored in.

Words related to countries
1. Agrarian
2. Georgic
3. Bucolic
4. Countrified
5. Homey

Words related to languages
1. Dialect
2. Expression
3. Utterance
4. Conversation
5. Discourse

Words related to people
1. Body politic
2. Folks
3. Persons
4. Tribe
5. Clan

Homonyms and Homophones

Homonyms are words that share the same spelling and the same pronunciation but have different meanings.

For example, bear.

A bear (the animal) can bear (tolerate) very cold temperatures.

The driver turned left (opposite of right) and left (departed from) the main road.

Homophones, also known as sound-alike words, are words that are pronounced identically although they have different meanings and often have different spellings as well. These words cause confusion when being written.

TRIVIA

A word formed by joining together parts of existing words is called a "blend" Many new words enter the English language in this way. Examples are "brunch" (breakfast + lunch); "motel" (motorcar + hotel); and "guesstimate" (guess + estimate). Note that blends are not the same as compounds or compound nouns, which form when two whole words join together, for example: website, blackboard, darkroom.

Common examples of sets of homophones include: *to, too,* and *two; they're* and *their; bee* and *be; sun* and *son; which* and *witch;* and *plain* and *plane.*

Some common homophones include:

ad / add	board / bored	cell / sell
allowed / aloud	boy / buoy	cent / scent / sent
ant / aunt	brake / break	census / senses
ate / eight	by / bye / buy	cereal / serial
ball / bawl	beach / beech	chews / choose
band / banned	bolder / boulder	choral / coral
bear / bare	bread / bred	chute / shoot
be / bee	browse / brows	clothes / close
billed / build	capital / capitol	colonel / kernel
blew / blue	caret / carrot / carat / karat	creak / creek

crews / cruise
cymbal / symbol
days / daze
dear / deer
dew / do / due
die / dye
disc / disk
discreet / discrete
discussed / disgust
doe / dough
doughs / doze
earn / urn
ewe / you
eye / I
fare / fair
feat / feet
find / fined
fir / fur
flea / flee
flew / flu / flue
flower / flour
for / four / fore
forth / fourth
foul / fowl
frees / freeze
gneiss / nice
gnu / knew / new
gored / gourd
gorilla / guerrilla
grays / graze
grate / great
guessed / guest
hale / hail
hall / haul
hare / hair
heal / heel / he'll
heard / herd
hew / hue

hi / high
higher / hire
him / hymn
hair / hare
hoarse / horse
hole / whole
hour / our
idle / idol
idle / idol / idyll
in / inn
incite / insight
its / it's
jam / jamb
jeans / genes
knead / need / kneed
knight / night
knows / nose / no's
lead / led
leased / least
lessen / lesson
lie / lye
links / lynx
load / lode / lowed
loan / lone
locks / lox
loot / lute
maid / made
mail / male
maize / maze
meet / meat
medal / meddle
mince / mints
miner / minor
missed / mist
mooed / mood
morning / mourning
muscle / mussel
mussed / must

nays / neighs
no / know
none / nun
nose / knows / no's
not / knot / naught
one / won
or / oar / ore
overdo / overdue
paced / paste
pail / pale
pain / pane
pair / pare / pear
passed / past
patience / patients
pause / paws
peace / piece
peak / peek / pique
peal / peel
pedal / peddle
peer / pier
pi / pie
plain / plane
plum / plumb
praise / prays / preys
presence / presents
principal / principle
prince / prints
quarts / quartz
rain / reign / rein
raise / rays / raze
rap / wrap
read / reed
read / red
real / reel
reek / wreak
rest / wrest
right / rite / write
ring / wring

road / rode / rowed
roe / row
role / roll
root / route
rose / rows
rote / wrote
roux / rue
rye / wry
sacks / sax
sail / sale
sawed / sod
scene / seen
sea / see
seam / seem
seas / sees / seize
serf / surf
serge / surge
sew / so / sow
shoe / shoo
side / sighed
sighs / size
sign / sine
sight / site / cite
slay / sleigh
soar / sore
soared / sword
sole / soul
son / sun
some / sum
spade / spayed
staid / stayed
stair / stare
stake / steak
stationary / stationery
steal / steel
straight / strait
suede / swayed
summary / summery

sundae / Sunday
tacks / tax
tail / tale
taut / taught
tea / tee
teas / tease / tees
tents / tense
tern / turn
there / their / they're
threw / through
throne / thrown
thyme / time
tide / tied
tighten / titan
to / too / two
toad / toed / towed
toe / tow
told / tolled
tracked / tract
trussed / trust
use / ewes
vein / vane
verses / versus
vial / vile
vice / vies
wade / weighed
wail / whale
waist / waste
wait / weight
waive / wave
Wales / whales
war / wore
ware / wear / where
warn / worn
wax / whacks
way / weigh / whey
we / wee
weather / whether

we'd / weed
weld / welled
we'll / wheel
wen / when
we've / weave
weak / week
which / witch
whirled / world
whirred / word
whine / wine
whoa / woe
who's / whose
wood / would
worst / warts
yoke / yolk
you'll / yule
your / you're / yore
ail / ale
airs / heirs
aisle / I'll
ascent / assent
aural / oral
auricle / oracle
berth / birth
boy / buoy
cached / cashed
carrot / karat
cede / seed
censor / sensor
chased / chaste
choirs / quires
chords / cords
chute / shoot
coax / cokes
cocks / cox
coffer / cougher
colonel / kernel
cops / copse

Synonyms, Antonyms, Homophones and Homonyms

core / corps	key / quay	rest / wrest
cygnet / signet	knap / nap	review / revue
cymbal / symbol	knead / need	rex / wrecks
dew / due	knit / nit	ring / wring
done / dun	knob / nob	rite / write
draft / draught	lichens / likens	rote / wrote
earns / urns	licker / liquor	rude / rued
ewes / use	lieu / loo	rye / wry
eyelet / islet	links / lynx	taught / taut
gnu / knew	loon / lune	tear / tier
halls / hauls	marshal / martial	vail / veil
heed / he'd	metal / mettle	vain / vein
hertz / hurts	oohs / ooze	variance / variants
him / hymn	racks / wracks	vial / vile
hoarse / horse	rapt / wrapped	wade / weighed
holy / wholly	recede / reseed	watts / what's
instance / instants	receipt / reseat	wright / write
intense / intents	reek / wreak	
jewels / joules	reign / rein	

- A synonym is a word or phrase that means exactly or nearly the same as another word or phrase in the same language.
- Words can be synonymous when meant in certain senses, even if they are not synonymous in all of their senses.
- An antonym is a word that means the opposite of a particular word.
- Synonyms and antonyms are exactly the opposite.
- Homonyms are words that share the same spelling and the same pronunciation but have different meanings.
- Homophones, also known as sound-alike words, are words that are pronounced identically although they have different meanings and often have different spellings as well.

PRACTICE EXERCISE

I. Choose the correct option to mark the synonym of the words given in the questions.

1. Sage
   (a) Wise man   (b) Era
   (c) Tropical tree   (d) Fool
2. Admonish
   (a) Polish   (b) Distribute
   (c) Escape   (d) Caution
3. Beset
   (a) Plead   (b) Deny
   (c) Perplex   (d) Deprive
4. Figment
   (a) Ornamental openwork
   (b) Perfume
   (c) Invention
   (d) Undeveloped
5. Glib
   (a) Dull   (b) Fluent
   (c) Thin   (d) Sharp
6. Coalesce
   (a) Associate   (b) Conspire
   (c) Combine   (d) Cover
7. Quack
   (a) Clown   (b) Dressmaker
   (c) Philanthropist   (d) Charlatan
8. Gauche
   (a) Clumsy   (b) Impudent
   (c) Stupid   (d) Foreign
9. Redundant
   (a) Necessary   (b) Diminishing
   (c) Plentiful   (d) Superfluous
10. Atrophy
    (a) Wither   (b) Grow
    (c) Soften   (d) Spread
11. Vehement
    (a) Thorough
    (b) Smooth-running
    (c) Airy
    (d) Forceful
12. Remuneration
    (a) Understanding   (b) Protest
    (c) Finality   (d) Compensation
13. Frivolity
    (a) Lightness   (b) Ornamentation
    (c) Irritability   (d) Impurity
14. Aura
    (a) Bitterness
    (b) Prophet
    (c) Delight
    (d) Distinctive atmosphere
15. Personable
    (a) Self-centred   (b) Intimate
    (c) Attractive   (d) Sensitive
16. Resilience
    (a) Submission   (b) Determination
    (c) Elasticity   (d) Recovery
17. Analogy
    (a) Similarity   (b) Distinction
    (c) Transposition   (d) Variety
18. Facetious
    (a) Obscene   (b) Complimentary
    (c) Shrewd   (d) Witty
19. Diatribe
    (a) Debate   (b) Tirade
    (c) Monologue   (d) Oration
20. Malediction
    (a) Curse
    (b) Tactless remark
    (c) Epitaph
    (d) Grammatical error
21. Turbulence
    (a) Treachery   (b) Triumph
    (c) Commotion   (d) Overflow
22. Defer
    (a) Discourage   (b) Minimize
    (c) Postpone   (d) Estimate
23. Adage
    (a) Proverb   (b) Youth
    (c) Supplement   (d) Hardness
24. Ensue
    (a) Compel   (b) Plead
    (c) Remain   (d) Follow
25. Zenith
    (a) Lowest Point   (b) Middle
    (c) Compass   (d) Summit

Synonyms, Antonyms, Homophones and Homonyms

26. Hypothetical
    (a) Magical (b) Theoretical
    (c) Visual (d) Two-faced
27. Superficial
    (a) Shallow (b) Aged
    (c) Unusually fine (d) Proud
28. Disparage
    (a) Separate (b) Belittle
    (c) Compare (d) Imitate
29. Protagonist
    (a) Prophet (b) Convert
    (c) Explorer (d) Champion
30. Impromptu
    (a) Offhand (b) Rehearsed
    (c) Laughable (d) Deceptive
31. Chivalrous
    (a) Crude (b) Foreign
    (c) Military (d) Handsome
32. Havoc
    (a) Festival (b) Sea battle
    (c) Disease (d) Ruin
33. Rejuvenate
    (a) Reply (b) Judge
    (c) Renew (d) Age
34. Obnoxious
    (a) Dreamy (b) Daring
    (c) Offensive (d) Visible
35. Verbatim
    (a) Word for word (b) In secret
    (c) At will (d) In summary

II. Choose the correct option to mark the antonym of the words given in the questions.

1. Awe
    (a) borrow (b) shallow
    (c) low (d) contempt
2. Pit
    (a) group (b) peak
    (c) select (d) marry
3. Rotund
    (a) round (b) unimportant
    (c) thin (d) dull
4. Talent
    (a) ungrateful (b) silent
    (c) show (d) inability
5. Common
    (a) strange (b) uneasy
    (c) quick (d) fast
6. Brazen
    (a) bashful (b) boisterous
    (c) noisy (d) heated
7. Expect
    (a) attend (b) regret
    (c) despair (d) loathe
8. Malodorous
    (a) acrid (b) pungent
    (c) fragrant (d) delicious
9. Expound
    (a) besmirch (b) confuse
    (c) confine (d) condemn
10. Pique
    (a) value (b) gully
    (c) smooth (d) soothe
11. Abate
    (a) free (b) augment
    (c) provoke (d) wane
12. Dearth
    (a) lack (b) poverty
    (c) abundance (d) foreign
13. Peaked
    (a) tired (b) arrogant
    (c) pointy (d) ruddy
14. Abridge
    (a) shorten (b) extend
    (c) stress (d) easy
15. Kindle
    (a) smother (b) detest
    (c) enemy (d) discourage
16. Meagre
    (a) kind (b) generous
    (c) thoughtful (d) copious
17. Philistine
    (a) novice (b) intellectual
    (c) pious (d) debutante
18. Zenith
    (a) worst (b) apex
    (c) nadir (d) past
19. Germane
    (a) irrelevant (b) indifferent
    (c) impartial (d) improvident

20. Irascible
    (a) determined (b) placid
    (c) reasonable (d) pliant
21. Approbate
    (a) ingratitude (b) condemn
    (c) dissatisfaction (d) master
22. Supercilious
    (a) unimportant (b) relevant
    (c) serious (d) meek
23. Improvident
    (a) cautious (b) fortunate
    (c) proven (d) intelligent
24. Demur
    (a) embrace (b) crude
    (c) boisterous (d) falter
25. Fatuous
    (a) crafty (b) frugal
    (c) sensible (d) inane
26. Quiescent
    (a) lackadaisical (b) active
    (c) dull (d) prescient
27. Sartorial
    (a) cheerful (b) sincere
    (c) inelegant (d) homespun
28. Sapient
    (a) hunched (b) strong
    (c) simple (d) simian
29. Matutinal
    (a) paternal (b) crepuscular
    (c) maritime (d) marsupial
30. Impecunious
    (a) wealthy (b) cautious
    (c) hungry (d) tardy
31. Blooming
    (a) fading (b) flowering
    (c) quiet (d) mild
32. Bliss
    (a) merge (b) disseminate
    (c) dull (d) suffering
33. Bewitch
    (a) disenchant (b) rapture
    (c) profit (d) avail
34. Bauble
    (a) plaything (b) valuable
    (c) modest (d) besiege
35. Busy
    (a) bully (b) curb
    (c) indolence (d) occupied
36. Celebrity
    (a) celebration (b) solemnity
    (c) obscurity (d) hazy
37. Cataclysm
    (a) peace (b) deluge
    (c) quibble (d) conjecture
38. Concord
    (a) consolidate (b) bestow
    (c) outline (d) discord
39. Compliance
    (a) condone (b) clamour
    (c) resistance (d) condense
40. Circumlocution
    (a) amass (b) ambiguity
    (c) effusion (d) simplicity

III. Fill in the blanks with the correct option to make each sentence complete.

1. We _____ several trucks on the highway.
   (a) passed (b) past
2. The trail goes _____ the mountains.
   (a) threw (b) through
3. _____ your history teacher?
   (a) Who's (b) Whose
4. Is that _____ book?
   (a) you're (b) your
5. The TV has lost _____ picture.
   (a) it's (b) its
6. My grandfather has a great deal of common _____.
   (a) sense (b) since
7. Returning students can enrol early for _____ classes.
   (a) their (b) there
   (c) they're
8. Your answer is _____!
   (a) right (b) rite
   (c) write
9. _____ going to have a wonderful vacation!
   (a) You're (b) Your

10. Did you _____ that sound?
    (a) hear   (b) here
11. The quarterback _____ the ball to the wide receiver.
    (a) threw   (b) through
12. Put your backpack _____, on the table in the corner.
    (a) their   (b) there
    (c) they're
13. Is it _____ late to sign up for the golf tournament?
    (a) to   (b) too
    (c) two
14. Tom has been collecting comic books _____ he was ten years old.
    (a) sense   (b) since
15. Baptisms, weddings, and funerals are examples of _____.
    (a) rights   (b) rites

IV. Fill in the blanks with the correct option to make each sentence complete.

1. Street signs are written with _____ letters.
   (a) capital   (b) capitol
2. The healthiest drink is _____ water.
   (a) plain   (b) plane
3. Both countries signed the _____ treaty.
   (a) peace   (b) piece
4. Maria has just completed her _____ semester of college.
   (a) forth   (b) fourth
5. Thank you for the birthday _____!
   (a) presence   (b) presents
6. Aspirin can _____ some types of pain.
   (a) lessen   (b) lesson
7. Wine and cheese _____ each other.
   (a) complement
   (b) compliment
8. The park ranger _____ the lost hikers to safety.
   (a) lead   (b) led
9. _____ did you put my car keys?
   (a) Wear   (b) Where
10. Telling my grandmother she is a good cook is the _____ she loves best.
    (a) complement
    (b) compliment
11. The public water supply is tested to be sure it contains no _____.
    (a) lead   (b) led
12. We felt honoured by the governor's _____ at our graduation ceremony.
    (a) presence
    (b) presents
13. During our tour of the _____, we saw the chamber in which the legislature meets.
    (a) capital   (b) Capitol
14. Would you like a _____ of cake?
    (a) peace
    (b) piece
15. The mountain search and rescue team _____ the lost hikers to safety.
    (a) lead   (b) led

V. Choose the correct option to make the following sentences meaningful.

1. Is that their/they're car?
2. I'm going to see a movie tonight. Would you like to go along two/too?
3. We should turn right/write at the corner.
4. We saw him/hymn at the restaurant last week.
5. The bride will walk down the isle/aisle with her father.
6. Your next assignment is due/do on Friday.
7. The wind blew/blue her hat right off her head.
8. Don't ever try to feed a bare/bear when you are camping in the woods.
9. Queen Elizabeth is the raining/reigning monarch in England.
10. Eight/Ate boys will play softball together on a team this summer.

VI. Choose the correct homophones:
Example: Please try not to (waste, waist) paper.

1. Can I go (to, too, two) the party?

2. This is my favourite (pare, pair, pear) of jeans.
3. I (sent, scent, cent) a letter to my aunt in Vietnam.
4. The children got (bored, board) during the lecture.
5. Mr. and Mrs. Rodriguez like to work in (there, they're, their) garden.
6. Alec is going to (wear, ware) his work boots today.
7. Do you think it is going to (rein, rain, reign) this afternoon?
8. I saw a restaurant just off the (rode, road) about a mile back.
9. David's brother is in a (band, banned) which plays Russian music.
10. Juana wants her socks because her (tows, toes) are cold.
11. The teacher walked down the (aisle, isle) between the rows of desks.
12. Hadil has a (pane, pain) in her shoulder.
13. The school (principal, principle) spoke to a group of parents.
14. The clerk wants to (sell, cell) as many TVs as possible.
15. I don't want to talk about the (passed, past) anymore.
16. Nobody (knows, nose) what you are thinking.
17. I have (for, four, fore) dollars in my pocket.
18. I need to take a (break, brake) from this exercise!
19. Humans have hands. Dogs have (paws, pause).
20. (He'll, Heel, Heal) be here in a few minutes.

HOTS

Select a suitable synonym from the given options.

1. Entice
   (a) Inform
   (b) Attract
   (c) Observe
   (d) Disobey
2. Acclaim
   (a) Discharge
   (b) Divide
   (c) Excel
   (d) Applaud
3. Stilted
   (a) Artificial
   (b) Fashionable
   (c) Canonical
   (d) Senseless
4. Soliloquy
   (a) Figure of speech
   (b) Isolated position
   (c) Historical Incident
   (d) Monologue

Direction for 5-10: Fill in the blanks with the words opposite in meaning to those underlined.

5. What looks like a convenient shortcut may prove to be very _____ in the long run.
6. No one wants to listen to an ignorant man but everybody listens to a _____ man.
7. Gold in an expensive metal while iron is _____
8. My application was accepted but his was _____
9. The teacher tried to make the student confident but he still looked very _____
10. He failed to qualify in the first two attempts but _____ in the third one.

Synonyms, Antonyms, Homophones and Homonyms   143

One Word 12

Learning Objectives: In this chapter, students will learn about:
- Concept of One Word substitution

CHAPTER SUMMARY

One Word Substitution
One Word Substitutions help express the idea of a phrase or a clause in a single word and, thereby, make communication and writing precise. Your knowledge of 'one word substitutions' depends on how much you read and remember. Below are lists of one word substitutes for people, general objects, groups, places, fields of science and arts, etc. to help you improve your vocabulary.

TRIVIA

About 100 languages uses the same alphabet like in English.

Kinds of One Words Substitute
(i) One word substitution for people
   Example:
   One who is not sure about God's existence: Agnostic

(ii) One word substitution for general objects
   Example:
   A formal resignation and renunciation of powers: Abdication

(iii) One word substitution for places
   Example:
   A place where animals are slaughtered: Abattoir

(iv) One word substitution for groups
   Example:
   A published collection of poems: Anthology

(v) One word substitution for science and arts
   Example:
   The study of sound is called: Acoustics

(vi) Some general one word substitutions
   Example:
   One who studies the pattern of voting in election: Psephologist

MUST REMEMBER

➡ One Word Substitutions help express the idea of a phrase or a clause in a single word and, thereby, make communication and writing precise.

PRACTICE EXERCISE

I. Choose the correct option that best explains the given word.

1. Altruist
   (a) One who is lover of beauty.
   (b) One who never stops.
   (c) A lover of mankind.
   (d) A person who hates mankind.
2. Amateur
   (a) One who is not having experience.
   (b) One who does a thing for pleasure and not as a profession.
   (c) One who have all happiness.
   (d) One who remains sad.
3. Ambidextrous
   (a) Person who can eat veg and non veg.
   (b) One who feeds on flesh
   (c) One who can use either hand with ease.
   (d) None of the above.
4. Anarchist
   (a) Religious person.
   (b) Person against a particular religion.
   (c) Person who always suspects.
   (d) One who is out to destroy all governments, peace and order
5. Arbitrator
   (a) A person appointed by two parties to solve a dispute
   (b) A person who is appointed to give punishment
   (c) A person who is always aggressive
   (d) A person who always give blessings
6. Ascetic
   (a) One who is in confusion
   (b) One who make paintings
   (c) One who leads an austere life
   (d) One who is lover of beauty
7. Bohemian
   (a) Waves in the sea
   (b) Fresh mood
   (c) Irritation
   (d) An unconventional style of living
8. Cacographist
   (a) One who is having ego
   (b) One who has unique style
   (c) One who is bad in spelling
   (d) One who is good in spelling
9. Chauvinist
   (a) A person displaying aggressive or exaggerated patriotism
   (b) A person showing disappointment
   (c) A person feeling low
   (d) A person feeling very excited
10. Connoisseur
    (a) An ideal
    (b) A participant
    (c) An expert judge
    (d) A beautiful girl
11. Contemporaries
    (a) A type dance.
    (b) A person or thing, living or existing at the same time.
    (c) Angry mob.
    (d) A type of protest.
12. Convalescent
    (a) One who is always obeyed.
    (b) One who gets whatever he desires.
    (c) One who have lost his loved one.
    (d) Recovering from an illness or operation.
13. Coquette
    (a) A motivational lady.
    (b) A woman who flirts.
    (c) A woman who can protect herself.
    (d) None of the above.
14. Cosmopolitan
    (a) A person who can speak all languages.
    (b) A person who regards the whole world as his country.
    (c) A person who is having knowledge of all topics.
    (d) None of the above.
15. Cynosure
    (a) One who always remains happy.
    (b) One who is not present.
    (c) One who is hated by everyone.
    (d) One who is centre of attraction.

16. Cynic
    (a) One who sneers at the beliefs of others.
    (b) One who appreciates.
    (c) One who is confused.
    (d) One who is candidate for something.
17. Debonair
    (a) Suave.
    (b) Irritated.
    (c) Calm.
    (d) None of the above.
18. Demagogue
    (a) A leader who is not true to people.
    (b) A leader or orator who espoused the cause of the common people.
    (c) A leader who has good skills of speaking.
    (d) A leader who does not deserve to be.
19. Dilettante
    (a) Very intelligent.
    (b) Eager to learn.
    (c) An amateur who engages in an activity without serious intentions and who pretends to have knowledge.
    (d) Person who do not want to learn.
20. Effeminate
    (a) Having or showing characteristics regarded as typical of a woman.
    (b) Having or showing characteristics regarded as typical of a strong man.
    (c) Having a habit of sharing secrets.
    (d) None of the above.
21. Almanac
    (a) A modern calendar.
    (b) An annual calendar with position of stars.
    (c) A calendar only with holidays list.
    (d) A calendar with historical information.
22. Amphibian
    (a) Animal that lives in both land and sea.
    (b) Animal that lives in sea.
    (c) Animal that lives in land.
    (d) Animal that lives at trees.
23. Allegory
    (a) A story told by elders to younger ones.
    (b) A story with no moral.
    (c) A story that express ideas through language.
    (d) A story that express ideas through symbols.
24. Axiom
    (a) A statement that required proofs to get it established.
    (b) A statement or proposition that is regarded as being established.
    (c) A statement which is not relevant.
    (d) A statement which is relevant to current situation.
25. Belligerent
    (a) A nation or person thinking of itself.
    (b) A nation or person talking of peace.
    (c) A nation or person engaged in war.
    (d) A nation or person helping unconditional.
26. Biopsy
    (a) An examination of tissue removed from a living body.
    (b) An examination of tissue removed from a dead body.
    (c) An examination of old bones.
    (d) An examination of old civilization.
27. Blasphemy
    (a) An act of speaking for ruler.
    (b) An act of speaking against ruler.
    (c) An act of speaking for religion.
    (d) An act of speaking against religion.
28. Chronology
    (a) The arrangement of events on the basis of even odd.
    (b) The arrangement of events in some algorithmic way.
    (c) The arrangement of events in the order of their occurrence.
    (d) The arrangement of events in random order.
29. Crusade
    (a) A war going to happen in near future.
    (b) A religious war.
    (c) A never ending war.
    (d) A war of past.

30. Ephemeral
    (a) Lasting for a very short time.
    (b) Everlasting.
    (c) Lasting till we wish.
    (d) Lasting till certain event.
31. Extempore
    (a) Spoken or done with proper preparation.
    (b) Spoken or done without preparation.
    (c) Spoken or done in alone.
    (d) Spoken or done in front of public.
32. Gregarious
    (a) Living with an aim.
    (b) Living without any aim.
    (c) Living alone.
    (d) Living in flocks.
33. Indelible
    (a) A mark that can be erased.
    (b) A mark that cannot be erased.
    (c) A mark which we can see from long distance.
    (d) None of the above.
34. Venial
    (a) A big fault that is forgiven
    (b) A slight fault that cannot be forgiven.
    (c) A big fault that cannot be forgiven.
    (d) A slight fault that can be forgiven.
35. Nostalgia
    (a) A sort of joyful moment.
    (b) A sort of horror.
    (c) A sentimental longing for the past.
    (d) Excitement for the coming future.
36. Red-tapism
    (a) Rude ruler.
    (b) Nice ruler.
    (c) Official formality resulting in delay.
    (d) Official formality helping in a quick action.
37. Utopia
    (a) An imagined place or state of things in which everything is perfect.
    (b) An imagined place which is worst for human beings to live.
    (c) An imagined place where two lovers want to go.
    (d) An imagined place where everything is free.
38. Apiary
    (a) Where bees are kept.
    (b) Where dogs are kept.
    (c) Where cats are kept.
    (d) Where rabbits are kept.
39. Arena
    (a) A place for hockey.
    (b) A place for indoor games.
    (c) A place for racing.
    (d) A place for wrestling.
40. Arsenal
    (a) A place where garments for military are stored or made.
    (b) A place where weapons and military equipment are stored or made.
    (c) A place where army do practice.
    (d) A place won by army in a war.
41. Asylum
    (a) A place where joint meeting is held.
    (b) A place where political refugees are given shelter.
    (c) A place where refugees are given prosecuted.
    (d) A place which is having boundary issues between two countries.
42. Aviary
    (a) Place where birds are kept.
    (b) Place where animals are kept.
    (c) Place where children are kept.
    (d) Place for old people.
43. Burrow
    (a) Safety places made by army.
    (b) A hole or tunnel dug by a small animal.
    (c) Specific locations which are important in war.
    (d) None of the above.
44. Cache
    (a) Destroyed place.
    (b) A rehabilitated place.
    (c) A place where ammunition is hidden.
    (d) A place where large number of animals are kept.

One Word

45. Cemetery
    (a) A place related to birds.
    (b) A place related to animals.
    (c) A place where post-mortem of dead bodies is done.
    (d) A graveyard where dead are buried.
46. Creche
    (a) Where children are cared for.
    (b) Where old people are cared for.
    (c) Where flowers are cared for.
    (d) Where bees are cared for.
47. Decanter
    (a) A bottle having unique design on it.
    (b) A bottle which is made by different metals.
    (c) A bottle with a stopper for serving wine or water.
    (d) A very old bottle.
48. Dormitory
    (a) Inner part of the city.
    (b) Outskirts of a city.
    (c) Sleeping rooms in an institution.
    (d) Exercise rooms in an institution.
49. Drey
    (a) The place to hide near water.
    (b) The place where animals live.
    (c) The nest of a sparrow.
    (d) The nest of a squirrel.
50. Elysium
    (a) A place where no happiness is there.
    (b) A place or state of perfect happiness.
    (c) A place where you can meditate.
    (d) A place where you can fulfil all desires.
51. Granary
    (a) Where treasures are kept.
    (b) Where woods are kept.
    (c) Where clothes are kept.
    (d) Where grains are kept.
52. Hangar
    (a) A place for housing aeroplanes.
    (b) A place for housing cars.
    (c) A place for housing trucks.
    (d) A place for housing cycles.
53. Hive
    (a) A place for peococks.
    (b) A place for dogs.
    (c) A place for bees.
    (d) A place for monkeys.
54. Hutch
    (a) A cage for parrot.
    (b) A cage for rabbits.
    (c) A cage for tiger.
    (d) A cage for lion.
55. Infirmary
    (a) A hospital.
    (b) A picnic spot.
    (c) A wonder place.
    (d) A historical place.
56. Kennel
    (a) Shelter for elephant.
    (b) Shelter for hen.
    (c) Shelter for dog.
    (d) Shelter for lion.
57. Mint
    (a) A place where beverages are made.
    (b) A place to display things.
    (c) A place where garments are made.
    (d) A place where money is coined.
58. Battery
    (a) A group of official documents.
    (b) A group of secret agents.
    (c) A group of heavy guns.
    (d) A bunch of clothes.
59. Bale
    (a) A group of fishes.
    (b) A bundle of paper, cotton, etc. tightly wrapped.
    (c) A container.
    (d) None of the above.
60. Bevy
    (a) Collection of stamps.
    (b) Collection of coins.
    (c) Envoy of tanks.
    (d) A large group of people or things of a particular kind.

61. Bouquet
    (a) A collection of goods.
    (b) An arranged bunch of flowers.
    (c) A bunch of corns.
    (d) A bunch of birds.
62. Brood
    (a) A collection of notebooks.
    (b) A family of young animals.
    (c) A family of old animals.
    (d) A family of young and old animals.
63. Brace
    (a) A pair of pigeons.
    (b) Collection of makeup.
    (c) Sort of feeling.
    (d) None of the above.
64. Cache
    (a) Collection at a hidden place.
    (b) Collection at a open place.
    (c) A type of weapon.
    (d) A type of instrument.
65. Caravan
    (a) A group of people, typically with vehicles or animals travelling together.
    (b) A group of animals going together.
    (c) A group of birds flying back to their nests, especially in the evening.
    (d) None of the above.
66. Caucus
    (a) A group of people taking part in a procession.
    (b) A group of people making noise.
    (c) A closed political meeting.
    (d) A group of people dancing.
67. Clique
    (a) A small group of people serving community.
    (b) A small group of people with shared interests.
    (c) A small group of people with opposite interests.
    (d) A small group of people doing wrong.
68. Claque
    (a) A group of people at a meeting.
    (b) A group of people with evil intentions.
    (c) A group of people, applauding at a performance.
    (d) A group paid to applaud.
69. Constellation
    (a) A collection of notebooks.
    (b) A collection of goods.
    (c) A series of islands.
    (d) A series of stars.
70. Cortege
    (a) A funeral procession.
    (b) A wining procession.
    (c) Uncontrolled crowd.
    (d) A systematically managed crowd.

One Word

HOTS

Choose the correct option that best explains the given word.

1. Chemistry in ancient times is called
    (a) Anatomy (b) Alchemy
    (c) Bibliography (d) Anthropology
2. The study of plants is called
    (a) Bacteriology (b) Astrology
    (c) Arboriculture (d) Botany
3. The study of human population with the help of the records of the number of births and deaths is called
    (a) Ecology (b) Demography
    (c) Entomology (d) Epigraphy
4. The study of duration of life is called
    (a) Calligraphy (b) Ceramics
    (c) Chronobiology (d) Chronology
5. The art of making fireworks is called
    (a) Chromatics (b) Cosmogony
    (c) Cosmography (d) Cosmology
6. The art of secret writings is called
    (a) Dactylography (b) Cytology
    (c) Cryogenics (d) Cypher
7. The technique of communication by signs made with the fingers is called
    (a) Ethnology (b) Ethology
    (c) Dactylology (d) Etymology
8. The study and tracing of lines of descent or development is called
    (a) Genealogy (b) Ergonomy
    (c) Eugenics (d) Genetics
9. The therapeutic use of sunlight is called
    (a) Gymnastics (b) Heliotherapy
    (c) Geology (d) Histology
10. The art or practice of garden cultivation and management is called
    (a) Iconography (b) Hagiology
    (c) Horticulture (d) Hydropathy
11. The study of animal life is called
    (a) Telepathy (b) Spelelogy
    (c) Zoology (d) Seismology
12. The science of law is called
    (a) Iconology (b) Jurisprudence
    (c) Lexicography (d) Numismatics
13. The scientific study of teeth is called
    (a) Odontology (b) Ornithology
    (c) Orthoepy (d) Pedagogy
14. Absence of the government
    (a) Anarchy (b) Aristocracy
    (c) Autocracy (d) Autonomy
15. Government run by officials is called
    (a) Democracy (b) Bureaucracy
    (c) Gerontocracy (d) Kakistocracy
16. Government by inexperienced persons is called
    (a) Panarchy (b) Oligarchy
    (c) Neocracy (d) Ochlocracy
17. Government by the rich is called
    (a) Theocracy (b) Thearchy
    (c) Monarchy (d) Plutocracy
18. Murder of one's own children is called
    (a) Foeticide (b) Filicide
    (c) Fratricide (d) Homicide
19. Murder of king or queen is called
    (a) Matricide (b) Parricide
    (c) Regicide (d) Uxoricide
20. The practice of having two wives or husbands at a time is called
    (a) Adultery (b) Alimony
    (c) Bigamy (d) Celibacy
21. The sound of apes is called
    (a) Gibber (b) Clang
    (c) Bray (d) Moan
22. Sound made by brakes is called
    (a) Drone (b) Jingle
    (c) Chirp (d) Screech
23. Sound made by the camels is called:
    (a) Mew (b) Grunt
    (c) Clank (d) Low
24. Creak is the sound of:
    (a) Crows (b) Doors
    (c) Dogs (d) Coins
25. Replace the underlined person with right substitute

    Hardly had she finished her dinner than the phone rang.
    (a) when (b) while
    (c) then (d) since

Idioms 13

Learning Objectives: In this chapter, students will learn about:
- Basic of Idioms
- Some common Idioms and their meanings

CHAPTER SUMMARY

Idiom is a manner of speaking that is natural to native speakers of a language.

Every language has its own collection of wise sayings. They offer advice about how to live and also transfer some underlying ideas, principles and values of a given culture/society. These sayings are called "idioms" - or proverbs if they are longer. These combinations of words have (rarely complete sentences) a "figurative meaning"; they basically work with "pictures".

TRIVIA

Can you believe that there is a word in the English language for "Day after tomorrow"? It was "Overmorrow" and was never used.

Some commonly used idioms and sayings can help to speak English by learning English idiomatic expressions. The following list contains most commonly used idioms and their meanings.

1. **A hot potato**
   Meaning: Speak of an issue (mostly current) which many people are talking about and which is usually disputed.

2. **A penny for your thoughts**
   Meaning: A way of asking what someone is thinking.

3. **Actions speak louder than words**
   Meaning: People's intentions can be judged better by what they do than what they say.

4. **Add insult to injury**
   Meaning: To further a loss with mockery or indignity; to worsen an unfavourable situation.

5. **An arm and a leg**
   Meaning: Very expensive or costly. A large amount of money.

6. **At the drop of a hat**
   Meaning: Without any hesitation; instantly.

7. **Back to the drawing board**
   Meaning: When an attempt fails and it's time to start all over.

8. **Ball is in your court**
   Meaning: It is up to you to make the next decision or step.

9. **Barking up the wrong tree**
   Meaning: Looking in the wrong place. Accusing the wrong person.

10. **Be glad to see the back of**
    Meaning: Be happy when a person leaves.

11. **Beat around the bush**
    Meaning: Avoiding the main topic. Not speaking directly about the issue.

12. **Best of both worlds**
    Meaning: All the advantages.

13. **Best thing since sliced bread**
    Meaning: A good invention or innovation. A good idea or plan.

14. **Bite off more than you can chew**
    Meaning: To take on a task that is way too big.

15. **Blessing in disguise**
    Meaning: Something good that isn't recognized at first.
16. **Burn the midnight oil**
    Meaning: To work late into the night, alluding to the time before electric lighting.
17. **Can't judge a book by its cover**
    Meaning: Cannot judge something primarily on appearance.
18. **Caught between two stools**
    Meaning: When someone finds it difficult to choose between two alternatives.
19. **Costs an arm and a leg**
    Meaning: This idiom is used when something is very expensive.
20. **Cross that bridge when you come to it**
    Meaning: Deal with a problem if and when it becomes necessary, not before.
21. **Cry over spilt milk**
    Meaning: When you complain about a loss from the past.
22. **Curiosity killed the cat**
    Meaning: Being inquisitive can lead you into an unpleasant situation.
23. **Cut corners**
    Meaning: When something is done badly to save money.
24. **Cut the mustard**
    Meaning: To succeed; to come up to expectations; adequate enough to compete or participate
25. **Devil's Advocate**
    Meaning: To present a counter argument
26. **Don't count your chickens before the eggs have hatched**
    Meaning: This idiom is used to express "Don't make plans for something that might not happen".
27. **Don't give up the day job**
    Meaning: You are not very good at something. You could definitely not do it professionally.
28. **Don't put all your eggs in one basket**
    Meaning: Do not put all your resources in one possibility.
29. **Drastic times call for drastic measures**
    Meaning: When you are extremely desperate you need to take drastic actions.
30. **Elvis has left the building**
    Meaning: The show has come to an end. It's all over.
31. **Every cloud has a silver lining**
    Meaning: Be optimistic, even difficult times will lead to better days.
32. **Far cry from**
    Meaning: Very different from.
33. **Feel a bit under the weather**
    Meaning: Feeling slightly ill.
34. **Give the benefit of the doubt**
    Meaning: Believe someone's statement, without proof.
35. **Hear it on the grapevine**
    Meaning: This idiom means 'to hear rumours' about something or someone.
36. **Hit the nail on the head**
    Meaning: Do or say something exactly right
37. **Hit the sack / sheets / hay**
    Meaning: To go to bed.
38. **In the heat of the moment**
    Meaning: Overwhelmed by what is happening in the moment.
39. **It takes two to tango**
    Meaning: Actions or communications need more than one person
40. **Jump on the bandwagon**
    Meaning: Join a popular trend or activity.
41. **Keep something at bay**
    Meaning: Keep something away.
42. **Kill two birds with one stone**
    Meaning: This idiom means, to accomplish two different things at the same time.
43. **Last straw**
    Meaning: The final problem in a series of problems.
44. **Let sleeping dogs lie**
    Meaning: do not disturb a situation as it is - since it would result in trouble or complications.
45. **Let the cat out of the bag**
    Meaning: To share information that was previously concealed.
46. **Make a long story short**
    Meaning: Come to the point - leave out details.

47. **Method to my madness**
    Meaning: An assertion that, despite one's approach seeming random, there actually is structure to it.
48. **Miss the boat**
    Meaning: This idiom is used to say that someone missed his or her chance.
49. **Not a spark of decency**
    Meaning: No manners
50. **Not playing with a full deck**
    Meaning: Someone who lacks intelligence.
51. **Off one's rocker**
    Meaning: Crazy, demented, out of one's mind, in a confused or befuddled state of mind, senile.
52. **On the ball**
    Meaning: When someone understands the situation well.
53. **Once in a blue moon**
    Meaning: Happens very rarely.
54. **Picture paints a thousand words**
    Meaning: A visual presentation is far more descriptive than words.
55. **Piece of cake**
    Meaning: A job, task or other activity that is easy or simple.
56. **Put wool over other people's eyes**
    Meaning: This means to deceive someone into thinking well of them.
57. **See eye to eye**
    Meaning: This idiom is used to say that two (or more people) agree on something.
58. **Sit on the fence**
    Meaning: This is used when someone does not want to choose or make a decision.
59. **Speak of the devil**
    Meaning: This expression is used when the person you have just been talking about arrives.
60. **Steal someone's thunder**
    Meaning: To take the credit for something someone else did.
61. **Take with a grain of salt**
    Meaning: This means not to take what someone says too seriously.
62. **Taste of your own medicine**
    Meaning: Something happens to you, or is done to you, that you have done to someone else.
63. **To hear something straight from the horse's mouth**
    Meaning: To hear something from the authoritative source.
64. **Whole nine yards**
    Meaning: Everything. All of it.
65. **Wouldn't be caught dead**
    Meaning: Would never like to do something.
66. **Your guess is as good as mine**
    Meaning: To have no idea; do not know the answer to a question.

MUST REMEMBER

→ Idiom is a manner of speaking that is natural to native speakers of a language.
→ Every language has its own collection of wise sayings. They offer advice about how to live and also transfer some underlying ideas, principles and values of a given culture/society. These sayings are called "idioms" - or proverbs if they are longer.

PRACTICE EXERCISE

I. Choose the correct meaning of the given proverb/idiom. If there is no correct meaning given, i.e. 'None of these' will be the answer.

1. To make clean breast of
   (a) To gain prominence
   (b) To praise oneself
   (c) To confess without of reserve
   (d) To destroy before it blooms
   (e) None of these

2. To keep one's temper
   (a) To become hungry
   (b) To be in good mood
   (c) To preserve ones energy
   (d) To be aloof from
   (e) None of these

3. To catch a tartar
   (a) To trap wanted criminal with great difficulty
   (b) To catch a dangerous person
   (c) To meet with disaster
   (d) To deal with a person who is more than one's match
   (e) None of these

4. To drive home
   (a) To find one's roots
   (b) To return to place of rest
   (c) Back to original position
   (d) To emphasise
   (e) None of these

5. To have an axe to grind
   (a) A private end to serve
   (b) To fail to arouse interest
   (c) To have no result
   (d) To work for both sides
   (e) None of these

6. To cry wolf
   (a) To listen eagerly
   (b) To give false alarm
   (c) To turn pale
   (d) To keep off starvation
   (e) None of these

7. To end in smoke
   (a) To make completely understand
   (b) To ruin oneself
   (c) To excite great applause
   (d) To overcome someone
   (e) None of these

8. To be above board
   (a) To have a good height
   (b) To be honest in any business deal
   (c) They have no debts
   (d) To try to be beautiful
   (e) None of these

9. To put one's hand to plough
   (a) To take up agricultural farming
   (b) To take a difficult task
   (c) To get entangled into unnecessary things
   (d) Take interest in technical work
   (e) None of these

10. To pick holes
    (a) To find some reason to quarrel
    (b) To destroy something
    (c) To criticise someone
    (d) To cut some part of an item
    (e) None of these

11. To smell a rat
    (a) To see signs of plague epidemic
    (b) To get bad small of a bad dead rat
    (c) To suspect foul dealings
    (d) To be in a bad mood
    (e) None of these

12. To hit the nail right on the head
    (a) To do the right thing
    (b) To destroy one's reputation
    (c) To announce one's fixed views
    (d) To teach someone a lesson
    (e) None of these

13. To set one's face against
    (a) To oppose with determination
    (b) To judge by appearance
    (c) To get out of difficulty
    (d) To look at one steadily
    (e) None of these

II. **Choose the alternative which best expresses the meaning of underlined idiom/phrase.**

1. Sobhraj could be easily arrested because the police were <u>tipped off</u> in advance
   (a) Toppled over
   (b) Bribed
   (c) Given advance information
   (d) Threatened

2. I met him after a long time, but he gave me <u>the cold shoulder</u>.
   (a) Scolded me
   (b) Insulted me
   (c) Abused me
   (d) Ignored me

3. He <u>passed himself off</u> as a noble man.
   (a) Was regarded as
   (b) Pretended to be
   (c) Was thought to be
   (d) Was looked upon

4. This matter has been <u>hanging fire</u> for the last many months and must, therefore, be decided one way or the other.
   (a) Going on slowly
   (b) Hotly debated
   (c) Stuck up
   (d) Ignored

5. In the armed forces, it is considered a great privilege to <u>die in harness</u>.
   (a) Die on a horse back
   (b) Die in the battlefield
   (c) Die while still working
   (d) Die with honour

6. The cricket match proved to be a <u>big draw</u>.
   (a) A keen contest
   (b) A huge attraction
   (c) A lovely spectacle
   (d) A game without any result

7. When he heard that he had once again not been selected, he <u>lost heart</u>.
   (a) Became desperate
   (b) Felt sad
   (c) Became angry
   (d) Became discouraged

8. He was undecided. He <u>let the grass grow under his feet</u>.
   (a) Loitered around
   (b) Stayed out
   (c) Sat unmoving
   (d) Moved away

9. Although he has failed in the written examination, he is using <u>backstairs influence</u> to get the job.
   (a) Political influence
   (b) Backing influence
   (c) Deserving and proper influence
   (d) Secret and unfair influence

III. **Choose the alternative which best expresses the meaning of the underlined idiom/phrase.**

1. He is an interesting speaker but tends to <u>go off at a tangent</u>.
   (a) Change the subject immediately
   (b) Forget things in between
   (c) Go on at great length
   (d) Become boisterous

2. He sold his house for a <u>song</u>.
   (a) At a reasonable price
   (b) At a discount
   (c) Very cheaply
   (d) At a premium

3. Despite the trust bestowed on the minister, he turned out to be <u>a snake in the grass</u> during the revolution.
   (a) A secret enemy
   (b) A treacherous person
   (c) An unforeseen danger
   (d) An unexpected misfortune

4. Women should be paid the same as men when they do the same job, for, surely <u>what is sauce for the goose is sauce for the gander</u>.
   (a) What is thought suitable pay for a man should also be for a woman.
   (b) Goose and the gander eat the same sauce.
   (c) Both goose and gander should be equally treated.
   (d) The principle of equal treatment should be implemented.

Idioms

5. The party stalwarts have advised the President <u>to take it lying down</u> for a while.
   (a) To be cautious
   (b) To be on the defensive
   (c) To take rest
   (d) To show no reaction

6. The thief <u>took to his heels</u> when he saw a policeman on the beat.
   (a) Had some pain in his heels
   (b) Ran away from the scene
   (c) Confronted the policeman
   (d) Could not decide what to do

7. He <u>struck several bad patches</u> before he made good.
   (a) Came across bad soil
   (b) Had a bad time
   (c) Went through many illness
   (d) Had many professional difficulties

8. The accounts of the murder <u>made her flesh creep</u>.
   (a) Made her sad
   (b) Surprised her
   (c) Made her cry bitterly
   (d) Fill her with horror

HOTS

Select the option with the correct usage/meaning of the word/phrase.

1.

	Dictionary definition		Usage
A	Adequately and properly aged so as to be free of harshness	E	He has mellowed with age
B	Freed from the rashness of youth	F	The tones of the old violin were mellow
C	Of soft and loamy consistency	G	Some wines are mellow.
D	Rich and pleasant	H	Mellow soil is found in the Gangetic plains.

A. A-E, B-G, C-F, D-H
B. A-E, B F, C-G, D-H
C. A G, B E, C-H, D-F
D. A-H, B-G, C-F, D-E

2.

	Dictionary definition		Usage
A	Remove a stigma from the name of	E	The opposition was purged after the coup.
B	Make clean by removing whatever is superfluous, foreign	F	The committee heard his attempt to purge himself of a charge of heresy
C	Get rid of	G	Drugs that purge the bowels are often bad for the brain.
D	To cause evacuation of	H	It is recommended to purge water by distillation

A. A-E, B-G, C-F, D-H
B. A-F, B-E, C-G, D-H
C. A-H, B-F, C-G, D-E
D. A-F, B-H, C-E, D-G

3.

	Dictionary definition		Usage
A	To extend outside of or enlarge beyond	E	The mercy of God exceeds our finite minds
B	To be greater than or superior to	F	Their accomplishments exceeded our expectation.
C	Be beyond the comprehension of	G	He exceeded his authority when he paid his brother's gambling debts with money from the trust.
D	To go beyond a limit set by (as an authority or privilege)	H	If this rain keeps up, the river will exceed its banks by morning.

Idioms

A. A-H, B-F, C-E, D-G
B. A-H, B-E, C-F, D-G
C. A-G, B-F, C-E, D-H
D. A-F, B-G, C-H, D-E

4.

	Dictionary definition		Usage
A	Removal or lightening of something distressing	E	A ceremony fellows the relief of a sentry after the morning shift.
B	Aid in the form of necessities for the indigent	F	It was relief to take off the tight shoes
C	Diversion	G	The only relief I get is by playing cards.
D	Release from the performance of duty	H	Disaster relief was offered to the victims

A. A-F, B-H, C-E, D-G
B. A-F, B-H, C-G, D-E
C. A-H, B-F, C-G, D-E
D. A-G, B-E, C-H, D-F

5.

	Dictionary definition		Usage
A	To derive by reasoning or implication	E	We see smoke and then infer fire
B	To surmise	F	Given some utterance, a listener may infer from it all sorts of things which neither the utterance nor the uttered implied
C	To point out	G	I waited all day to meet him; from this you can infer my zeal to see him
D	To hint	H	She did not take part in the debate except to ask and question inferring that she was not interested in the debate.

A. A-G, B-E, C-F, D-H
B. A-F, B-H, C-E, D-G
C. A-H, B-G, C-F, D-E
D. A-E, B-F, C-G, D-H

Question Tags   14

 **Learning Objectives :** In this chapter, students will learn about:
- ✓ Usage of Question Tags

CHAPTER SUMMARY

Question tags are short questions at the end of statements.

They are mainly used in speech when we want to:

- **confirm that something is true or not**, or
- **to encourage a reply** from the person we are speaking to.

Question tags are formed with the auxiliary or modal verb from the statement and the appropriate subject.

A **positive** statement is followed by a **negative** question tag.

- Jack **is** from Spain, **isn't** he?
- Mary **can** speak English, **can't** she?

A **negative** statement is followed by a **positive** question tag.

- They **aren't** funny, **are** they?
- He **shouldn't** say things like that, **should** he?

When the verb in the main sentence is in the present simple we form the question tag with **do/does**.

- You *play* the guitar, **don't** you?
- Alison *likes* tennis, **doesn't** she?

If the verb is in the past simple we use **did**.

- They *went* to the cinema, **didn't** they?
- She *studied* in New Zealand, **didn't** she?

When the statement contains a word with a **negative** meaning, the question tag needs to be **positive**.

- He **hardly ever** speaks, **does** he?
- They **rarely** eat in restaurants, **do** they?

TRIVIA
The word nice was originally used for describing something foolish, stupid or senseless.

Exceptions

Some verbs / expressions have different question tags. For example:

I am: I am attractive, **aren't** I?

Positive imperative: Stop daydreaming, **will / won't** you?

Negative imperative: Don't stop singing, **will** you?

Let's - Let's go to the beach, shall we?

Have got (possession)" He has got a car, **hasn't** he?

There is / are: There aren't any spiders in the bedroom, **are there**?

This / that is: This is Paul's pen, **isn't it**?

Intonation

When we are sure of the answer and we are simply encouraging a response, the intonation in the question tag goes down:

- This is your car, **isn't it**?

    (Your voice goes down when you say isn't it.)

When we are not sure and want to check information, the intonation in the question tag goes up:

- He is from France, **isn't he**?

    (Your voice goes up when you say isn't he.)

MUST REMEMBER

- Question tags are short questions at the end of statements.
- Question tags are formed with the auxiliary or modal verb from the statement and the appropriate subject.
- When the statement contains a word with a negative meaning, the question tag needs to be positive.

PRACTICE EXERCISE

I. Add appropriate question tags to the following sentences.

1. It is not very hot today, _____ (is it / isn't it / does it)
2. They haven't paid their dues, _____? (have they / haven't they / hadn't they)
3. That is your book, _____? (is it / isn't it / doesn't it)
4. The sun does not shine at night, _____? (is it / isn't it / does it)
5. He studies very well, _____? (does he / doesn't he / don't he)
6. These shirts are very expensive, _____? (are they / aren't they / don't they)
7. Raju works hard, _____? (does he / doesn't he / don't he)
8. Earth goes round the sun, _____? (does it / doesn't it / didn't it)
9. Children rush about, _____? (do they / don't they / didn't they)
10. You received the parcel in the morning, _____? (did you / didn't you / hadn't you)

II. Select correct options (question tags) to fill the blanks.

1. They haven't come, ____?
    (a) has they   (b) have they
    (c) had they   (d) haven't they
2. You are free, ____?
    (a) were you   (b) weren't you
    (c) aren't you   (d) are you
3. Your sister is cooking well, ____?
    (a) has she   (b) will she
    (c) hasn't she   (a) isn't she
4. She hasn't come yet, ____?
    (a) has she   (b) had she
    (c) hasn't she   (d) isn't she
5. Gopal has broken the glass, ____?
    (a) has he   (b) has Gopal
    (c) hasn't he   (d) isn't he

HOTS

Choose the proper question tag:

1. These shoes are not very costly, _____
    (a) were they?   (b) aren't they?
    (c) is it?   (d) are they?
2. We could easily come earlier, _____
    (a) should we?   (b) could we?
    (c) couldn't we?   (d) wouldn't we?
3. Jaspal Rana won the gold medal _____
    (a) did he?   (b) does he?
    (c) hasn't he?   (d) didn't he?
4. Jaspal Rana has not won the gold medal _____
    (a) didn't he?   (b) has he?
    (c) did he?   (d) doesn't he?
5. Nobody won the match, _____
    (a) does they?   (b) didn't they?
    (c) did they?   (d) isn't it?
6. Dogs are most faithful, _____
    (a) isn't it?   (b) aren't they?
    (c) are they?   (d) weren't they?
7. The children did not trouble you, _____
    (a) didn't they?   (b) did they?
    (c) haven't they?   (d) have they?
8. You have got the required baskets, _____
    (a) have you?   (b) hasn't you?
    (c) hadn't you?   (d) haven't you?
9. That was not my meaning, _____
    (a) is it?   (b) was it?
    (c) wasn't it?   (d) weren't it?

Question Tags

10. The girls performed quite well, _____
    (a) hadn't they?   (b) didn't they?
    (c) didn't she?   (d) doesn't she?

11. That man is your uncle, ____
    (a) isn't he?   (b) wasn't he?
    (c) aren't he?   (d) is he?

12. All the boys are very tall, _____
    (a) isn't they?   (b) aren't they?
    (c) weren't they?   (d) are they?

13. That article was very interesting, _____
    (a) was it?   (b) wasn't it?
    (c) weren't it?   (d) hadn't it?

14. This ship is not very big, ____
    (a) is it?   (b) isn't it?
    (c) aren't it?   (d) wasn't it?

15. You will call me, ____
    (a) will you?   (b) won't you?
    (c) don't you?   (d) shall you?

SECTION 2
READING COMPREHENSION

Comprehension

Reading comprehension is the ability to read text, process it and understand its meaning. An individual's ability to comprehend text is influenced by their traits and skills, one of which is the ability to make inferences. If word recognition is difficult, students use too much of their processing capacity to read individual words, which interferes with their ability to comprehend what is read. There are a number of approaches to improve reading comprehension, including improving one's vocabulary and reading strategies.

Comprehension is the act of or capacity for grasping with the intellect. It is the last step of the reading process taught to children, after they've learned phonics, fluency, and vocabulary. The term is most often used in connection with tests of reading skills and language abilities, though other abilities (e.g., mathematical reasoning) may also be examined.

Types of Reading Comprehension

Five types of reading comprehension can be taught to children:

- Lexical Comprehension
- Literal Comprehension
- Interpretive Comprehension
- Applied Comprehension
- Affective Comprehension

To really understand these different levels, let's take a familiar text and see how different types of questions probe different understandings of the same story.

The fairy tale Cinderella tells the story of a young girl, whose evil stepmother won't let her go to the ball. Cinderella's fairy godmother, however, magically whisks her off for the night and Cinderella eventually marries her Prince Charming.

5 Types of Reading Comprehension

Lexical Comprehension
Understand key vocabulary in the text

> Preview vocabulary before reading the story or text.
> Review new vocabulary during or after the text.
> **Example Lexical Compression Question:**
> What does 'enchanted' mean?
> What words are most like 'enchanted': Magical of funny? Scary or special?

Literal Comprehension
Answer Who, What, When, and Where questions

> Look in the text to find the answers in the story.
> Ask questions from the beginning, middle, and end of the story.
> **Example Literal Comprehension Questions:**
> Who was the girl who lost the glass slipper?
> Where did Cinderella go to live at the end of the story?

Interpretive Comprehension
Answer What if, Why, and How questions

> Understand 'facts' that are not explicitly stated in the story.
> Illustrations may help to infer meaning.
> **Example Interpretive Comprehension Questions:**
> How did the pumpkin turn into a carriage?
> What would have happened to Cinderella if she hadn't lost her slipper?

Applied Comprehension
Relate story to existing knowledge or opinion

> Not a simple question that can be marked right or wrong.
> Challenge children to support their answer with logic or reason.
> **Example Applied Comprehension Question:**
> Do you think Cinderella was wrong for going to the ball after her stepmother told her she couldn't go?

Affective Comprehension
Understand social and emotional aspect

> Preview social scripts to ensure understanding of plot development.
> Connect motive to plot and character development.
> **Example Applied Comprehension Question:**
> What do you do when you're disappointed because you cannot do something fun? Is that how Cinderella reacted?

Types of Comprehension Strategies

There are six main comprehension strategies:

1. **Make Connections**: Readers connect the topic or information to what they already know about themselves, about other texts, and about the world.
2. **Ask Questions**: Readers ask themselves questions about the text, their reactions to it, and the author's purpose for writing it.
3. **Visualize**: Readers make the printed word real and concrete by creating a 'movie' of the text in their minds.
4. **Determine Text Importance**: Readers:
   (a) distinguish between what's essential versus what's interesting
   (b) distinguish between fact and opinion
   (c) determine cause-and-effect relationships
   (d) compare and contrast ideas or information
   (e) discern themes, opinions, or perspectives
   (f) pinpoint problems and solutions
   (g) name steps in a process
   (h) locate information that answers specific questions
   (i) summarize.
5. **Make Inferences**: Readers merge text clues with their prior knowledge and determine answers to questions that lead to conclusions about underlying themes or ideas.

Comprehension

6. **Synthesize**: Readers combine new information with existing knowledge to form original ideas, new lines of thinking, or new creations.

Note:
Students quickly grasp how to make connections, ask questions, and visualize. However, they often struggle with the way to identify what is most important in the text, identify clues and evidence to make inferences, and combine information into new thoughts. All these strategies should be modelled in isolation many times so that students get a firm grasp of what the strategy is and how it helps them comprehend text.

However, students must understand that good readers use a variety of these strategies every time they read. Simply knowing the individual strategies is not enough, nor is it enough to know them in isolation. Students must know when and how to collectively use these strategies.

Tips to Improve Reading Comprehension Skills

Below is a description of think-aloud as a way to improve reading comprehension skills. There are many ways to conduct think-alouds:
1. The teacher models the think-aloud while she reads aloud, and the students listen.
2. The teacher thinks aloud during shared reading, and the students help out.
3. Students think aloud during shared reading, and the teacher and other students monitor and help.
4. The teacher or students think aloud during shared reading while writing on an overhead, on self-stick notes, or in a journal.
5. Students think aloud in small-group reading, and the teacher monitors and helps.
6. Students individually think aloud during independent reading using self-stick notes or a journal. Then students compare their thoughts with others.

When you introduce a new comprehension strategy, model during read-aloud and shared reading:
1. Decide on a strategy to model.
2. Choose a short text or section of text.
3. Read the text ahead of time. Mark locations where you will stop and model the strategy.
4. State your purpose—name the strategy and explain the focus of your think-alouds.
5. Read the text aloud to students and think aloud at the designated points.
6. If you conduct a shared reading experience, have students highlight words and phrases that show evidence of your thinking by placing self-stick notes in the book.
7. Reinforce the think-alouds with follow-up lessons in the same text or with others.

Use the above-listed comprehension strategies to model the chosen strategy :

Make Connections
A few expressions for making connection are:

This reminds me of a time when I ...

I know about this topic because I ...

The setting of this book is just like ...

This book is something like ...

What's going on in this book is just like what's happening in ...

Ask Questions
A few expressions for asking questions are:

Before I read this text, I wonder about ...

While I'm reading, I try to figure out ...

After I read, I ask myself ...

I wonder why...

What does this word mean?

Why did _____ do that?

What is going to happen next?

Why did the author put that part in there?

I have questions about this part because it doesn't make sense. I need to make sure I read it right. If I reread and fix a mistake, that might answer my question.

Visualize

A few expressions for showing visualization are:

The author gives me a picture in my mind when he or she describes …

I can really see what the author talks about when he or she …

I can draw a picture of what the author describes.

Determine Importance of Text

A few expressions for determining important of text are:

I know these parts of the story are important because they match my purpose for reading, which was …

I believe the author thinks _____ is important because …

I think the author's opinion about _____ is _____ because …

This text uses the (cause/effect, problem/solution, description, compare/contrast, sequence/steps in a process) text structure. I can use a graphic organizer to help me understand it.

I see lots of information right here. I need to identify which parts are important and which parts are just interesting.

All these ideas are important, but I think some are more important than others. I need to determine which ideas are the most important.

This (chart, table, graph, time line) helps me understand that …

These (boldfaced words, font changes, bullets, captions) help me locate what is important.

Let me take the big ideas and summarize the text.

Make Inferences

A few expression for making inferences are:

The author says this, but means …

If I read between the lines, the author tells me that …

The clues to prove my inference are …

Because of what the author said, I know that …

From the clues or information the author gives, I can conclude that …

I think that _____ will happen next because the author says _____.

Synthesize

A few expressions for showing synthesis are:

This story or passage is really about… My views on this are…

My opinion of _____ is …

I first thought _____ about the topic. Now I think …

I've read a lot of information. Let me stop and think about this for a minute.

My judgment of this information is …

From this information, I can generalize that …

PRACTICE EXERCISE

Exercise 1
Read the passages and choose the correct option to answer the questions that follow:

At this stage of civilisation, when many nations are brought in to close and vital contact for good and evil, it is essential, as never before, that their gross ignorance of one another should be diminished, that they should begin to understand a little of one another's historical experience and resulting mentality. It is the fault of the English to expect the people of other countries to react as they do to political and international situations. Our genuine goodwill and good intentions are often brought to nothing, because we expect other people to be like us. This would be corrected if we knew the history, not necessarily in detail but in broad outlines, of the social and political conditions which have given to each nation its present character.

1. According to the author, 'Mentality' of a nation is mainly a product of its
   (a) history
   (b) international position
   (c) politics
   (d) present character

2. The need for a greater understanding between nations
   (a) was always there
   (b) is no longer there
   (c) is more today than ever before
   (d) will always be there

3. The character of a nation is the result of its
   (a) mentality
   (b) cultural heritage
   (c) gross ignorance
   (d) socio-political conditions

4. According to the author, his countrymen should
   (a) read the story of other nations
   (b) have a better understanding of other nations
   (c) not react to other actions
   (d) have vital contacts with other nations

5. Englishmen like others to react to political situations like
   (a) us
   (b) themselves
   (c) others
   (d) each others

Exercise 2

Male lions are rather reticent about expending their energy in hunting; more than three quarters of kills are made by lionesses, who stay in front, tensely scanning ahead, the cubs lag playfully behind and the males bring up the rear, walking slowly, their massive heads nodding with each step as if they were bored with the whole matter. But slothfulness may have survival value. With lionesses busy hunting, the males function as guard for the cubs, protecting them particularly from hyenas.

1. According to the passage, male lions generally do not go for hunting because
   (a) they do not like it
   (b) they want lioness to get training
   (c) they wish to save their vigour for other things
   (d) they are very lazy

2. Male lions protect their cubs
   (a) from the members of their own species
   (b) from hyenas only
   (c) from hyenas as much as from other enemies
   (d) more from hyenas than from other animals

3. Lioness go for hunting
   (a) all alone
   (b) with their male partners only
   (c) with their cubs and male partners
   (d) with their cubs only

4. When the lionesses go in search for their prey, they are very
   (a) serious
   (b) cautious
   (c) playful
   (d) sluggish

5. Which word is the passage means "hesitant"?

(a) slothfulness (b) Reticent
(c) Lay (d) Expend

Exercise 3

What needs to be set right is our approach to work. It is a common sight in our country of employees reporting for duty on time and at the same time doing little work. If an assessment is made of time they spend in gossiping, drinking tea, eating "pan" and smoking cigarettes, it will be shocking to know that the time devoted to actual work is negligible. The problem is the standard, which the leader in administration sets for the staff. Forget the ministers because they mix politics and administration. What do top bureaucrats do? What do the below down officials do? The administration set up remains weak mainly because the employees do not have the right example to follow and they are more concerned about being in the good books of the bosses than doing work.

1. The employees in our country
   (a) are quite punctual but not duty conscious
   (b) are not punctual, but somehow manage to complete their work
   (c) are somewhat lazy but good natured
   (d) are not very highly qualified
2. According to the writer, the administration in India
   (a) is by and large effective
   (b) is very strict and firm
   (c) is affected by red tape
   (d) is more or less ineffective
3. The word 'assessment' means
   (a) enquiry
   (b) report
   (c) evaluation
   (d) summary
4. The leadership in administration
   (a) sets a fine example to the employees
   (b) is of a reasonably high standard
   (c) is composed of idealists
   (d) is of a very poor standard
5. The central idea of passage could be best expressed by the following

(a) The employee outlook towards work is justified
(b) The employee must change their outlook towards work
(c) The employees would never change their work culture
(d) The employer-employee relationship is far from healthy

Exercise 4

Speech is a great blessing but it can also be a great curse. While it helps us to make our intentions and desires known to our fellows, it can also if we use it carelessly, make our attitude completely misunderstood. A slip of the tongue, the use an of unusual word, or of an ambiguous word, and so on, may create an enemy where we had hoped to win a friend. Again, different classes of people use different vocabularies, and the ordinary speech of an educated may strike an uneducated listener as pompous. Unwillingly, we may use a word which bears a different meaning to our listener from what it does to men of our own class. Thus, speech is not a gift to use lightly without thought, but one which demands careful handling. Only a fool will express himself alike to all kinds of men.

1. The best way to win a friend is to avoid
   (a) irony in speech
   (b) pomposity in speech
   (c) verbosity in speech
   (d) ambiguity in speech
2. While talking to an uneducated person, we should use
   (a) ordinary speech (b) his vocabulary
   (c) simple words (d) polite language
3. If one used the same style of language with everyone, one would sound
   (a) flat (b) boring
   (c) foolish (d) democratic
4. A 'slip of the tongue' means something said
   (a) wrongly by choice
   (b) unintentionally
   (c) without giving proper thought
   (d) to hurt another person

5. Speech can be curse, because it can
   (a) hurt others
   (b) lead to carelessness
   (c) create misunderstanding
   (d) reveal our intentions

Exercise 5

Mahatma Gandhi believed that industrialisation was no answer to the problems that plague the mass of India's poor and that villagers should be taught to be self-sufficient in food, weave their own cloth from cotton and eschew the glittering prizes that the 20th century so temptingly offers. Such an idyllic and rural paradise did not appear to those who inherited the reins of political power.

1. The meaning of 'glittering prizes that the 20th century so temptingly offers' is
   (a) pursuit of a commercialised material culture
   (b) replacement of rural by urban interests
   (c) complete removal of poverty
   (d) absence of violence and corruption
2. The basis of 'an idyllic and rural paradise' is
   (a) rapid industrialisation of villages
   (b) self sufficiency in food clothes and simplicity of the lifestyle
   (c) bringing to the villages the glittering prizes of the 20th century
   (d) supporting those holdings powerful political positions
3. Which one of the following best illustrates the relationship between the phrases:
   (i) 'eschew the glittering prizes' and
   (ii) 'idyllic and rural paradise'?
   (a) unless you do (i), you cannot have (ii)
   (b) (i) and (ii) are identical in meaning
   (c) first of all you must have (ii) in order to do (i)
   (d) the meaning of (i) is directly opposite to (ii)
4. Mahatma Gandhi's views opposed industrialisation of villages because
   (a) it would help the poor and not the rich
   (b) it would take away the skill of the villagers
   (c) it would affect the culture of the Indians
   (d) it would undermine self-sufficiency and destroy the beauty of life of the villager
5. Mahatma Gandhi's dream of 'an idyllic and rural paradise' was not shared by
   (a) those who did not believe in the industrialisation of the country
   (b) those who called him the Father of Nation
   (c) those who inherited political powers after independence
   (d) those who believed that villages should be self-sufficient in food and cloth

Exercise 6

Organisations are institutions in which members compete for status and power. They compete for resource of the organisation, for example, finance to expand their own departments, for career advancement and for power to control the activities of others. In pursuit of these aims, groups are formed and sectional interests emerge. As a result, policy decisions may serve the ends of political and career systems rather than those of the concern. In this way, the goals of the organisation may be displaced in favour of sectional interests and individual ambition. These preoccupations sometimes prevent the emergence of organic systems. Many of the electronic firms in a study had recently created research and development departments employing highly qualified and well paid scientists and technicians. Their high pay and expert knowledge were sometimes seen as a threat to the established order of rank, power and privilege. Many senior managers had little knowledge of technicality and possibilities of new developments and electronics. Some felt that close cooperation with the experts in an organic system would reveal their ignorance and show their experience was now redundant.

1. The theme of the passage is
   (a) groupism in organizations
   (b) individual ambitions in organizations
   (c) frustration of senior managers
   (d) emergence of sectional interests in organizations

2. "Organic system" as related to the organization implies its
   (a) growth with the help of expert knowledge
   (b) growth with input from science and technology
   (c) steady all around development
   (d) natural and unimpeded growth

3. Policy decision in organization would involve
   (a) cooperation at all levels in the organization
   (b) modernization of the organization
   (c) attracting highly qualified personnel
   (d) keeping in view the larger objectives of the organizations

4. The author makes out a case for
   (a) organic system
   (b) Research and Development in organisations
   (c) an understanding between senior and middle level executives
   (d) a refresher course for senior managers

5. The author tends to the senior managers as
   (a) ignorant and incompetent
   (b) a little out of step with their work environment
   (c) jealous of their younger colleagues
   (d) robbed of their rank, power and privilege

SECTION 3
SPOKEN AND WRITTEN EXPRESSIONS

Giving and Accepting Compliments

Giving and Accepting Compliments

Compliments are an expression of praise or admiration and an act of civility and respect. They boost another's morale when given sincerely and when received graciously can bring happiness to the giver. There are socially acceptable ways to give and receive compliments.

A striking aspect of compliments is that despite being a positive thing, they can be difficult to give and especially accept. There can be many reasons for this. Perhaps, a person has low self-esteem, or they don't feel that they have done anything special to deserve it. Giving compliments can also be tricky and sometimes people just shy away from saying anything at all.

When giving a compliment, there are a few things to remember. Instead of giving a general compliment, say something specific. For example, instead of saying "Great job!" say, "I think the topic you presented in your report was very interesting and newsworthy." Or perhaps, instead of "You look very nice," say "I really like your hair today; it's very pretty."

Receiving compliments is one of the hardest things for some to do. Most people when given a compliment will actually argue with the giver of it. They will say, "Oh no, that's not true!" "Or you really think so? I don't see it!" Sometimes, they will make a joke of it or try to sound confident and overly agree. This can sound arrogant or can feel as if the gift was thrown back in the face of the complimenter. This is just painful to hear.

When receiving a compliment, whether you agree with it or not, simply smile and just say, "Thank you." Practise giving compliments to others. Look for something nice to say to those around you and mean it. In doing this, you are not only learning to see the goodness in others, but also the goodness in yourself.

Deflecting compliments is a well strengthened reflex for a surprising number of people. Someone speaks kind of us and we brush it off, change the subject or fail to find the truth in what has been said. Inability to receive a compliment mirrors our own feelings of not being good enough. It prevents us from experiencing the gift of someone's kind words, and it stops the other person from experiencing the gift of making someone else feel good.

So why is the gift of receiving a compliment so hard to accept?

We listen and believe our negative thoughts all day long that hearing positive words are alien and unknown. Maybe we don't trust the person who has given us the compliment and believe they have an ulterior motive. We think if we accept the compliment we will appear arrogant or vain.

How to Accept a Compliment

1. Start looking for your strengths and positive characteristics and when somebody else notices what you have already recognised, it won't feel so alien.
2. Develop your self confidence and integrity so the other person's motives become unimportant to you, as you trust your own reactions and behaviour.
3. As opposed to reacting to a compliment in a way that you think other people will approve of, react with sincere appreciation for that person's time and kind words.
4. Start replying to compliments with a simple and honest 'thank you'. This will become a habit once you start.
5. When we see the value in who we are, we won't need to receive compliments and yet we can still smile when we do.

Why is it difficult to give a compliment or say 'thank you'?

1. We may find it difficult to give a compliment if it is laced with envy for something that person has, is or does.
2. We find it difficult to compliment someone if we feel as if we are complimenting them for something they 'should' be doing anyway. Our lack of self esteem and fear of losing someone may stop us from giving compliments and thus feeding their confidence.

Why giving compliments helps ourselves and those closest to us?

1. If we feel envious our emotions are telling us that another person has something that we would like to have, be or experience. Give the compliment and make the other person feel good while affirming to yourself and the universe that it is you want. Start to take the necessary steps to achieve it.
2. When you feel appreciated by a person, you want to do more for that person. Show your gratitude and watch as the number of things you have to be grateful for multiplies.
3. Ironically, giving compliments develops our confidence. We feel good as we help other people to feel good. If you want to develop your self-esteem, the fastest way to do it, is, to help improve someone else's.
4. Any negative comments you hear about yourself slide off the non-sticky side, and all of those positive compliments that you are given stick onto the velcro and stay with you.

SECTION 4
ACHIEVERS' SECTION

Some Thoughtful Questions

1. **There are many ideas about how the world will 'end'. Do you think the world will end someday? Have you ever thought what would happen if the sun got so hot that it 'burst', or grew colder and colder?**

   Answer:
   There are multiple theories about how the world will 'end'. Yes, I do believe that the world will end someday as we all know that every particular thing which begins also has an end to it. This holds true for the world too, that if the Sun got so hot and it bursts, the entire life on Earth would perish immediately as the planet would not be able to tolerate the intensity of heat. On the contrary, if the Sun grew colder and colder, it is obvious that life will come to an end without sunlight. We are aware of the fact that sunlight is a rich source of energy to all the planets in the solar system.

2. **Have you ever lost something or someone you liked very much? Write a paragraph describing how you felt then and saying whether — and how — you got over your loss.**

   Answer:
   Yes, I had lost my pet dog in a road accident when he was just five years old. One day, I was playing with my puppy with a ball in my garden. I threw the ball in the air while playing with him, my dog jumped to catch it, but it bounced back and rolled to the street nearby. As my dog went to fetch the ball, a speeding car ran over my puppy and I could hear it crying in pain. I rushed to the spot and found my pup covered in blood. I rushed him to the hospital immediately but it was too late and he was bleeding profusely and succumbed to injuries. I was very upset and grief-stricken by this incident. In due course of time, I recovered from my loss, but that incident is fresh in my memories and I still love my dog and miss him dearly.

   (Students can write this answer as per their personal experiences.)

3. **Do you keep a diary? Given below under 'A' are some terms we use to describe a written record of personal experience. Can you match them with their descriptions under 'B'? (You may look up the terms in a dictionary if you wish.)**

A	B
(i) Journal	A book with a separate space or page for each day, in which you write down your thoughts and feelings or what has happened on that day
(ii) Diary	A full record of a journey, a period of time, or an event, written every day
(iii) Log	A record of a person's own life and experiences (usually, a famous person)
(iv) Memoir(s)	A written record of events with times and dates, usually official

   Answer:

A	B
(i) Journal	A full record of a journey, a period of time, or an event, written every day
(ii) Diary	A book with a separate space or page for each day, in which you write down your thoughts and feelings or what has happened on that day
(iii) Log	A written record of events with times and dates, usually official
(iv) Memoirs	A record of a person's own life and experiences (usually, a famous person)

4. Here are a few sentences which have idiomatic expressions. Can you say what each means? (You might want to consult a dictionary first.)
   (i) Our entire class is *quaking in its boots*. _____
   (ii) Until then, we keep telling each other *not to lose heart*. _____
   (iii) Mr Keesing was annoyed with me *for ages* because I talked so much. _____
   (iv) Mr Keesing was trying to play a joke on me with this ridiculous subject, but I'd make sure *the joke was on him*. _____

   Answer:
   (i) Our entire class is *quaking in its boots*. – **shaking with fear and nervousness.**
   (ii) Until then, we keep telling each other *not to lose heart*. – **not to lose hope or expectation**
   (iii) Mr. Keesing was annoyed with me *for ages* because I talked so much. – **for a long time**
   (iv) Mr. Keesing was trying to play a joke on me with this ridiculous subject, but I'd make sure *the joke was on him*. – **he was outwitted by her.**

5. Combine the two sentences to make a single meaningful sentence using word hints given in the brackets.
   (a) This is the bus. It goes to Agra (which/that)
   (b) I would like to buy a shirt. The shirt is in the shop window (which/that)
   (c) You must break your fast at a particular time. You see the moon in the sky (when)
   (d) Find a word. It begins with better? (which/that)
   (e) Now find a person. His or her name begins with letter? (whose)

   Answer:
   (a) This is the bus which goes to Agra
   (b) I would like to buy the shirt that is in the shop window
   (c) You must break your fast when you see the moon in the sky
   (d) Find a word which begins with letter?
   (e) Now find a person whose name begins with letter?

6. Here are thirty adjectives describing human qualities. Discuss them with your partner and put them in the two-word webs (given below) according to whether you think they show positive or negative qualities. You can consult a dictionary if you are not sure of the meanings of some of the words. You may also add to the list the positive or negative 'pair' of a given word.

   kind, sarcastic, courteous, arrogant, insipid, timid, placid, cruel, haughty, proud, zealous, intrepid, sensitive, compassionate, introverted, stolid, cheerful, contented, thoughtless, vain, friendly, unforgiving, fashionable, generous, talented, lonely, determined, creative, miserable, complacent

   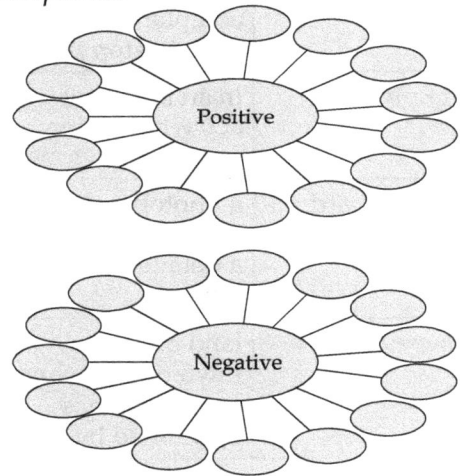

   Answer:

Some Thoughtful Questions

7. Colours are used to describe feelings, moods and emotions. Match the following 'colour expressions' with a suggested paraphrase.

(i) the Monday morning *blues*	feel embarrassed/ angry/ashamed
(ii) go *red* in the face	feel very sick, as if about to vomit
(iii) look *green*	sadness or depression after a weekend of fun
(iv) the *red* carpet	the sign or permission to begin an action
(v) *blue*-blooded	a sign of surrender or acceptance of defeat; a wish to stop fighting
(vi) a *green* belt	in an unlawful act; while doing something wrong
(vii) a *black*guard	a photographic print of building plans; a detailed plan or scheme
(viii) a *grey* area	land around a town or city where construction is prohibited by law
(ix) a *white* flag	an area of a subject or a situation where matters are not very clear
(x) a *blue*print	a dishonest person with no sense of right or wrong
(xi) *red*-handed	a special welcome
(xii) the *green* light	– of noble birth or from a royal family

Answer:

(i) the Monday morning *blues*	sadness or depression after a weekend of fun
(ii) go *red* in the face	feel embarrassed/ angry/ashamed
(iii) look *green*	feel very sick, as if about to vomit
(iv) the *red* carpet	a special welcome
(v) *blue*-blooded	of noble birth or from a royal family
(vi) a *green* belt	land around a town or city where construction is prohibited by law
(vii) a *black*guard	a dishonest person with no sense of right or wrong
(viii) a *grey* area	an area of a subject or a situation where matters are not very clear
(ix) a *white* flag	a sign of surrender or acceptance of defeat; a wish to stop fighting
(x) a *blue*print	a photographic print of building plans; a detailed plan or scheme
(xi) *red*-handed	in an unlawful act; while doing something wrong
(xii) the *green* light	– the sign or permission to begin an action

8. Look at these words: upkeep, downpour, undergo, dropout, walk-in. They are built up from a verb (keep, pour, go, drop, walk) and an adverb or a particle (up, down, under, out, in).

Use these words appropriately in the sentences below. You may consult a dictionary.

(i) A heavy _____ has been forecast due to low pressure in the Bay of Bengal.

(ii) Rakesh will _____ major surgery tomorrow morning.

(iii) My brother is responsible for the _____ of our family property.
(iv) The _____ rate for this accountancy course is very high.
(v) She went to the Enterprise Company to attend a _____ interview.

Answer:
(i) A heavy **downpour** has been forecast due to low pressure in the Bay of Bengal.
(ii) Rakesh will **undergo** major surgery tomorrow morning.
(iii) My brother is responsible for the **upkeep** of our family property.
(iv) The **dropout** rate for this accountancy course is very high.
(v) She went to the Enterprise Company to attend a **walk-in** interview.

9. **Now fill in the blanks in the sentences given below by combining the verb given in brackets with one of the words from the box as appropriate.**
Over, by, throughout, up, down
(i) The Army attempted unsuccessfully to _____ the Government. (throw)
(ii) Scientists are on the brink of a major _____ in cancer research. (break)
(iii) The State Government plans to build a _____ for Bhubaneswar to speed up traffic on the main highway. (pass)
(iv) Gautama's _____ on life changed when he realised that the world is full of sorrow. (look)
(v) Rakesh seemed unusually _____ after the game. (cast)

Answer:
(i) The Army attempted unsuccessfully to **overthrow** the Government.
(ii) Scientists are on the brink of a major **breakthrough** in cancer research.
(iii) The State Government plans to build a **bypass** for Bhubaneswar to speed up traffic on the main highway. (pass)
(iv) Gautama's **outlook** on life changed when he realised that the world is full of sorrow.
(v) Rakesh seemed unusually **downcast** after the game.

10. **Given below are some nouns, and a set of modifiers (in the box). Combine the nouns and modifiers to make as many appropriate phrases as you can. (Hint: The nouns and modifiers are all from the texts in this book.)**

temple	girls	triangle	dresses
person	thoughts	boys	roar
gifts	scream	farewell	expression
time	subject	landscape	handkerchief
crossing	flight	chatterbox	profession
physique	coffee	view	Celebration

college	rough	hundred	stone	ordinary
love	uncomfortable	white	slang	slack
bare	railroad	tremendous	family	marriage
plump	invigorating	panoramic	heartbreaking	birthday
incorrigible	ridiculous	loud	first	three

Answer:

1.	Temple	White temple, Stone temple
2.	Gifts	Ordinary gift, birthday gift.
3.	Time	First time, family time, college time, rough time
4.	Crossing	Railroad crossing, first crossing
5.	Physique	Plump physique, ordinary physique
6.	Girls	Plump girls, college girls
7.	Thoughts	Uncomfortable thoughts, ridiculous thoughts, ordinary thoughts, good thoughts, invigorating thoughts, heartbreaking
8.	Scream	Loud scream, heartbreaking scream
9.	Subject	Ordinary subject, college subject
10.	Flight	First flight, ordinary flight, rough flight, uncomfortable flight
11.	Coffee	Black coffee, ordinary coffee, invigorating coffee
12.	Farewell	College farewell, heartbreaking farewell
13.	Landscape	Rough landscape, bare landscape
14.	Chatterbox	Incorrigible chatterbox, ridiculous chatterbox
15.	View	Panoramic view, ordinary view, tremendous view
16.	Dresses	Ordinary dresses, birthday dresses, marriage dresses, hundred dresses
17.	Handkerchief	White handkerchief, clean handkerchief, ordinary handkerchief
18.	Profession	Family profession, first profession, ordinary profession
19.	Celebration	Birthday celebration, tremendous celebration, family celebration
20.	Roar	Loud roar, tremendous roar

Subjective Section

1. Fill in the blanks with the right information.
   (i) Adverbs modify:
   (a) _____
   (b) _____
   (c) _____
   (d) _____
   (ii) They answer questions like:
   (a) _____
   (b) _____
   (c) _____
   (d) _____
   (e) _____
   (f) _____
   (iii) Identifying adverbs can be tricky. Many adverbs end in -ly. Provide 5 examples.
   _____
   _____
   _____
   _____
   _____
   (iv) However, this is not an exact method of identifying adverbs. Some common adverbs do not end in -ly. Provide 5 examples.
   _____
   _____
   _____
   _____
   _____
   (v) Some words that end in -ly are not necessarily adverbs. Provide 5 examples.
   _____
   _____
   _____
   _____
   _____

   The only way to be sure a word is an adverb is by looking at its function within the sentence.

   Answer:
   1. (i) (a) verbs, (b) adjectives, (c) other adverbs, (d) whole sentences

      (ii) (a) how? (b) when? (c) where? (d) why? (e) in what order? (f) how often?

      (iii) happily, sharply, cheerfully, loudly, swiftly

      (iv) everywhere, never, fast, much, rather

      (v) friendly, lively, rally, lonely, sickly

2. Look at the picture given below and fill in the blanks with the correct prepositions based on it.

A female employee is sitting _____ a chair with her coat hanging _____ it _____ her. She is typing on the keyboard with her elbows resting _____ the desk. Her desk is full _____ stationery.

Another female staff is standing diagonally _____ the front cubicles and talking to someone in _____ of her. Except her, all the people visible in the photo are busy looking _____ their computer screens. There's a picture _____ the world map and different times zones _____ the wall.

Answer:
2. on, over, behind, at, of, across, front, at, of, on

3. Read the body of a letter below and choose the correct word in its correct form for each gap to make collocations.

I'm sorry for (A) _____ (have/take/be) such a long time to write back. I've been so busy at work lately. I've also not been studying very hard and my English exam is next month! To (B) _____ (tell/say/speak) you the truth, I'm getting a bit nervous and will have to (C) _____ (work/make/do) some revision! The good news is I'm going on holiday with my parents before the exam, so if I (D) _____ (get/win/take) the chance I'm going to try to (E) _____ (make/give/do) an effort and work on my English. Anyway, the reason I'm writing is to ask you if you would like to come to India. I know you haven't been here before and we could (F) _____ (make/go/do) sightseeing. Let me know what you think.

Answer:
3. A: taking (time), B: tell (the truth), C: do (revision), D: get (the chance), E: make (an effort), F: go (sightseeing)

4. Fill in the blanks by using the appropriate part of speech of the words provided within the brackets. Mention the part of speech you have used in the sentence.
   (a) Take whichever you like. It's your _____ (choose). [Part of speech used: _____]
   (b) Their _____ (refuse) came as a big surprise. [Part of speech used: _____]
   (c) They offer free _____ (deliver) to this area. [Part of speech used: _____]
   (d) The _____ (rob) took place at around midnight. [Part of speech used: _____]
   (e) They are _____ (disappoint) as they couldn't get bookings for the show. [Part of speech used: _____]

Answer:
4. (a) choice, Noun (b) refusal, Noun (c) delivery, Noun (d) robbery, Noun (e) disappointed, Verb

5. Describe Transitive and Intransitive verbs with examples. Can a verb be used as both transitive and intransitive?

Answer:
5. Transitive verbs are action verbs that have an object to receive that action. Examples: I baked some cookies, I rode the bicycle, etc. Both the verbs in the above sentences are transitive because there are objects receiving the action of the verbs.

Intransitive verbs are action verbs but unlike transitive verbs, they do not have an object receiving the action. Examples: I laughed, I cried.

Many verbs can be used both as transitive and intransitive. Example: I sang a song.

6. Write a paragraph, making sure you use all of the following conjunctions: and, for, yet, so, although, because, since

Answer:
6. Sam and Peter are studying very hard since the beginning of the month for their exams. Although they've been studying regularly throughout the year, yet they are not fully prepared. So, they are putting in more effort now because they both want to get good scores.

7. Punctuate the following sentences:
   (a) He bought the groceries eggs butter jam sugar and pot noodles.
   (b) She read the book it was an adventure story.
   (c) These were the reasons for his odd behaviour fear of the dark fear of confined spaces fear of spiders and way too much caffeine that morning.

   Answer:
   7. (a) He bought the groceries: eggs, butter, jam, sugar and pot noodles.
   (b) She read the book; it was an adventure story.
   (c) These were the reasons for his odd behavior: fear of the dark, fear of confined spaces, fear of spiders and way too much caffeine that morning.

8. Write, in your words, what happens to the Subject in
   (a) active voice?   (b) passive voice?

   Answer:
   8. In active voice, the subject performs the action denoted by the verb. In passive voice, the object of an active sentence appears as the subject of a sentence and the subject of an active sentence becomes the object.

9. Rewrite the passage into past tense:

   I am happy and elated, whereas you are miserable and melancholy. They are brave and courageous; however she is timid and frightened. Everyone has different feelings – sometimes good; sometimes bad. We are all just humans, after all.

   Answer:
   9. I was happy and elated, whereas you were miserable and melancholy. They were brave and courageous; however she was timid and frightened. Everyone had different feelings – sometimes good; sometimes bad. We are all just humans, after all.

10. Rewrite the passage into present tense:

    Keith will be going to pick up his two children from school. They will be going to Alton Towers with their mum. She will buy the tickets from a website on the Internet. It will be cool! The children will want to go on the Storm Force 10 and the Apocalypse rides, which are amongst the scariest. You will be jealous to see them enjoying so much.

    Answer:
    10. Keith goes to pick up his two children from school. They go to Alton Towers with their mum. She buys the tickets from a website on the Internet. It is cool! The children want to go on the Storm Force 10 and the Apocalypse rides, which are amongst the scariest. You are jealous to see them enjoying so much.

11. Rewrite the sentences using 'if':
    (a) You dive into this river and you will hurt yourself.
    (b) The sun shines and the children will play outside.
    (c) Richard will walk to school in case he misses the bus.
    (d) Emily will buy the cola in case you pack the picnic basket.
    (e) I will rent a boat in case I am in Venice.

    Answer:
    11. (a) If you dive into this river, you will hurt yourself.
    (b) If the sun shines, the children will play outside.
    (c) Richard will walk to school if he misses the bus.
    (d) Emily will buy the cola if you pack the picnic basket.
    (e) I will rent a boat if I am in Venice.

12. Underline all the phrasal verbs in the following passage:

    When Amy woke up this morning, she discovered that her toddler had thrown up in her crib last night. She, therefore, cleaned her bedding up before she chowed down on breakfast. While she was tucking into her food, however, her daughter started acting up. She just suddenly broke down and threw a tantrum on the kitchen floor. After falling apart for

only a few minutes, the tantrum blew over and her daughter calmed down. Amy then finished eating and logged onto her computer. But, before she could access the Internet, the computer blew up. Amy looked the phone number up, called for technical help, and told the IT technician off. She only eased up when the tech threatened to put her on hold.

Answer:

12. When Amy woke up this morning, she discovered that her toddler had <u>thrown up</u> in her crib last night. She, therefore, cleaned her bedding up before she <u>chowed down</u> on breakfast. While she was tucking into her food, however, her daughter started <u>acting up</u>. She just suddenly <u>broke down</u> and <u>threw a tantrum</u> on the kitchen floor. After falling apart for only a few minutes, the tantrum blew over and her daughter calmed down. Amy then finished eating and logged onto her computer. But, before she could access the Internet, the computer <u>blew up</u>. Amy <u>looked</u> the phone number <u>up</u>, called for technical help, and <u>told</u> the IT technician <u>off</u>. She only <u>eased up</u> when the tech threatened to put her on hold.

13. Write down the meaning of the following phrasal verbs and use them in sentences of your own:
    (a) call on somebody   (b) break down
    (c) check out   (d) drop out
    (e) figure something out

    Answer:

13. (a) call on somebody: (i) visit somebody. We called on you last night but you weren't home. (ii) ask for an answer. The professor called on me for question 1.

    (b) break down: (i) stop functioning (machine). Our car broke down on the highway due to snowstorm. (ii) get upset. The woman broke down when the police told her that her son had died.

    (c) check out: (i) leave a hotel. You have to check out of the hotel before 11:00 AM. (ii) check out somebody/something look at. Check out the crazy hair on that guy!

    (d) drop out: quit a class, school etc. I dropped out of Science because it was too difficult.

    (e) figure something out: understand, find the answer. I need to figure out how to fit the piano and the bookshelf in this room.

14. What are the modal verbs to express necessity or requirement? Make your own sentences using them.

    Answer:

14. The modal verbs to express necessity or requirement are as follows.

    Must: You must have a passport to cross the border.

    Have to: Elisabeth has to apply for her visa by March 10th.

    Need to: I need to drop by his room to pick up a book.

15. Use the following idioms in sentences of your own.
    (a) Beat around the bush
    (b) Cry over split milk
    (c) Devil's advocate
    (d) Hit the nail on the head
    (e) Speak of the devil

    Answer:

15. (a) Beat around the bush: If you want to ask me, just ask; don't beat around the bush.

    (b) Cry over split milk: I know you didn't mean to break my phone, so there's no use in crying over spilt milk now.

    (c) Devil's advocate: Mary offered to play devil's advocate and argue against our case so that we would find out any flaws in it.

    (d) Hit the nail on the head: Mike hit the nail on the head when he said most people can use a computer without knowing how it works.

(e) Speak of the devil: Did you hear what happened to Anna yesterday - oh, speak of the devil, here she is.

16. Use the following homonyms in sentences of your own to bring out the differences in meaning.
    (a) (i) ad (ii) add
    (b) (i) break (ii) brake
    (c) (i) nose (ii) knows
    (d) (i) maid (ii) made
    (e) (i) led (ii) lead

    Answer:
    16. (a) (i) ad: They are running an ad campaign for this product.
    (ii) add: Add 2 spoons of sugar to my tea.
    (b) (i) break: Don't break the glass.
    (ii) brake: The car's brake is not working properly.
    (c) (i) nose: My nose has become so cold due to the chilly weather.
    (ii) knows: She knows about that incident in details.
    (d) (i) maid: She works as a maid.
    (ii) made: He has made this table.
    (e) (i) led: She led the team in the match.
    (ii) lead: Lead is a metal.

17. Explain the difference between countable and uncountable nouns with examples.

    Answer:
    17. Countable and Uncountable nouns. Countable nouns are those that can be enumerated or counted. Examples include desk, tree, and chair. On the other hand, Uncountable nouns are mass nouns, which do not normally occur in the plural form. They often refer to abstractions and carry a collective meaning. Examples include love, honesty, luggage, and water.

18. Define these one-words:
    (a) Dotage
    (b) Incorrigible
    (c) Archaeology
    (d) Intellectual
    (e) Oligarchy

    Answer:
    18. (a) Dotage: Extreme old age when a man behaves like a fool
    (b) Incorrigible: That which cannot be corrected
    (c) Archaeology: The study of ancient societies
    (d) Intellectual: A person of good understanding knowledge and reasoning power
    (e) Oligarchy: State in which the few govern the many

19. Identify the misspellings and re-write the passage with correct ones.

    It is hardly possiblle for human biengs to be practikal al the time. Often, there emosional side surfaces and they end up decieving there own personalyties to the ekstent of revaeling dangrous truths about themselvs. Evn the most acomplished people of the world, inspite of aquiring fame and waelth end up showing there emosional side at times. Basicaly, we are al very vulnareble and alow our hart to take over our mind more than reqiured.

_____
_____
_____
_____

Answer:

19. It is hardly possible for human beings to be practical all the time. Often, their emotional side surfaces and they end up deceiving their own personalities to the extent of revealing dangerous truths about themselves. Even the most accomplished people of the world, inspite of acquiring fame and wealth end up showing their emotional side at times. Basically, we are all very vulnerable and allow our heart to take over our mind more than required.

20. You are the Cultural Secretary of your school. You have been asked to inform students of Class IX to Class XII about an inter-school painting contest. Draft a notice in not more than 50 words for the students' Notice board will all necessary details. Put the notice in box.

Answer:
20.

{Your School's Name, City}
Notice

{Today's Date}

OPPORTUNITY FOR BUDDING PAINTERS

An Inter-School Painting Competition will be held {a future date} at Town Hall. An audition will be held to select 10 students to represent the school for the competition.

Date of Audition: {a future date}
Time: 11 am
Venue: School auditorium
Eligibility: Class IX to XII
Last date to give names: {a future date}
{Your Name},
Cultural Secretary

---

21. Complete the passage with suitable articles. If you feel that certain blanks don't need any articles, leave them blank.

I am from Winchester, Hampshire. Winchester is _____ city in _____ United Kingdom. I live in _____ town called _____ Taunton which is on _____ River Tone. I live in _____ house in _____ quiet street in the countryside. _____ street is called "Hudson Street" and _____ house is old - more than 100 years old! I am _____ English lecturer at _____ college near _____ centre of _____ town. I like _____ books, music and taking _____ photographs. I usually have _____ lunch at college. I usually go _____ home by _____ car. We have all kinds of food in _____ England. I like _____ Polish food very much. Sometimes, I go to _____ Polish restaurant in Bath. _____ restaurant is called "Magda's". _____ Polish food is delicious!

Answer:
21. I am from Winchester, Hampshire. Winchester is a city in the United

Kingdom. I live in a town called Taunton which is on the River Tone. I live in a house in a quiet street in the countryside. The street is called 'Hudson Street' and the house is old - more than 100 years old! I am an English lecturer at a college near the centre of the town. I like books, music and taking photographs. I usually have lunch at college. I usually go home by car. We have all kinds of food in England. I like Polish food very much. Sometimes, I go to a Polish restaurant in Bath. The restaurant is called 'Magda's'. Polish food is delicious!

22. Fill in the blanks with the appropriate words in the following cloze passage.

    IQ tests were at one ___(i)___ very popular. An IQ test is supposed to measure thinking ability. 'I' stands for intelligence and 'Q' for quotient. An IQ is therefore ___(ii)___ in numerals.

    Many psychologists used to believe that everyone has a fixed ___(iii)___ of intelligence and that it could be measured in a single test. Alfred Binet designed a set of tests which was given to French children in 1905. The questions were based on what the students were taught and their ___(iv)___ were supposed to reflect how well they could use words and numbers, follow directions and ___(v)___ problems in a common-sense way. Binet thought these ___(vi)___ were useful in separating the intelligent from the dull ones. Later, he decided to do more. He wanted to find out how ___(vii)___ a child was. "If nine-year-old Felicia was smart, was she as smart as a ten-year-old or an eleven-year-old?" The answer was given in a number now known as IQ.

    IQ tests were conducted to test the intelligence of children in schools. However, it was later found that some ___(viii)___ who did well in an arithmetic test did poorly on the word questions. The question of how they were to be classified arose. It became clear that intelligence is not a trait like having brown eyes and dark hair. There are ___(ix)___ ways of being smart. Many schools no longer give IQ tests. Instead, children are given many different tests to find their ___(x)___ and weaknesses. They are then helped to develop their strengths and get over their weaknesses.

    Answer:

    22. (i) time (ii) written (iii) amount (iv) answers (v) solve (vi) tests (vii) smart (viii) children (ix) many (x) strengths

23. Fill in the blanks below to complete the telephonic conversation:

    Sara: I am so excited to hear that you are in Paris. Where have you put up?

    Mary: _____

    Sara: Oh! That's terrible. I will still manage to meet you somehow. Tell me what time your meeting will get over tomorrow.

    Mary: _____

    Sara: Don't worry! I will manage it somehow. See you at the hotel at 5 o'clock tomorrow!

    Answer:

    23. Mary: I have put up at the Hyatt Regency, but I am hardly staying there. My entire day is spent in meetings.
        Mary: I am not sure. But tomorrow I plan to go back to the hotel by 5 pm.

24. Fill in the blanks below to complete the telephonic conversation:

    Peter: I am getting late. Can I call you tomorrow?

    Lucy: _____

    Peter: I really think the discussion can wait. I have to rush now for an important meeting.

    Lucy: _____

Peter: I am sorry but I have to hang up now.

Answer:

24. Lucy: No, I want to discuss about that issue right now.
    Lucy: It's very important for me.

25. Fill in the blanks below to complete the conversation:

    Alec: _____

    John: What a surprise. I haven't seen you in a long time. How have you been, Alec?

    Alec: _____

    John: I finally have some free time. I just finished taking a big examination, and I'm so relieved that I'm done with it.

Answer:

25. Alec: Hey John, how have you been?
    Alec: I'm doing very well. How about you?

I. Complete the following sentences with the appropriate forms of the given verbs.

1. Every day I (go) to school in a bus but today I (go) by car because the bus operators are on strike.
2. "Baichung Bhutia (pass) the ball to Bannerjee ; Bannerjee (take) a shot at the goal but it (be) way above the goal post. The Indians (attack) much more now …"
3. I (think) you (make) a mistake by signing this contract.
4. The doctor (say) mother (respond) to the treatment well.
5. Farzana (be) not well. She (not come) to school today.

Answers:

1. go, am going
2. passes, takes, is, attack
3. think, are making
4. said, responded/says, is responding
5. is, hasn't come

II. Complete the following sentences correctly by using the simple past or past perfect forms of the given verbs.

1. We _____ already _____ (reach) home when Irfan _____ (say) that he _____ (forget) his books at school.
2. Wendy _____ (wake up) late, then she _____ (miss) her school bus, so by the time she (reach) school, it _____ already _____ (start).
3. I _____ (visit) my town again ten years after I _____ (leave) it and (find) _____ that it _____ completely _____ (change).
4. When Feroze and Mehr _____ (meet) for the first time, they (not like) each other but now they are married.

Answer:

1. had, reached, said, had forgotten
2. woke up, missed, reached, had, started
3. visited, had left, found, had, changed
4. met, had not liked

3. Read the following conversation carefully and complete the following passage by filling in the blank spaces appropriately. Do not add any new information. Write the answers in your answer sheet against the correct blank number.

Patient : Doctor, I have a terrible toothache.
Doctor : Well, sit down. I need to examine your teeth. Please open your mouth wide.
Patient : Is there any serious problem, doctor ?

The patient told the doctor (a) _____.
The doctor told him to sit down as (b) _____. He also requested the patient (c) _____. The patient then enquired (d) _____.

Answers:

(a) that he had a terrible toothache
(b) he needed to examine his teeth
(c) to open his mouth wide
(d) if there was any serious problem

IV. Read the following sentences. Each of them contains one error. Correct the error:

1. One of my friends have gone to Canada.

2. Every one of the managers have applied for leave today in protest against the management.
3. Neither of the boxers were able to score a decisive victory:
4. Tobacco and alcohol is injurious to health.
5. He and I was at Patna University together.
6. Oil and water does not mix.
7. Age and experience bring wisdom to man.
8. Slow and steady win the race.
9. Bread and Butter are what the poor want.
10. My uncle and guardian want me to start my own business,
11. The Collector and District Magistrate are away.
12. The notable patriot and orator are no more.
13. The industrialist and the politician has been invited to the function.
14. Neither Raju nor Sheela have come first in the race.
15. No scholarship or reward were given to the student who stood first in the examination.

Answers:
1. One of my friends has gone to Canada.
2. Every one of the managers has applied for leave today in protest against the management.
3. Neither of the boxers was able to score a decisive victory.
4. Tobacco and alcohol are injurious to health.
5. He and I were at Patna University together.
6. Oil and water do not mix.
7. Age and experience brings wisdom to man.
8. Slow and steady wins the race.
9. Bread and Butter is what the poor want.
10. My uncle and guardian wants me to start my own business.
11. The Collector and District Magistrate is away.
12. The notable patriot and orator is no more.
13. The industrialist and the politician have been invited to the function.
14. Neither Raju nor Sheela has come first in the race.
15. No scholarship or reward was given to the student who stood first in the examination.

V. Fill in the blanks using the correct form of the words given in the box below.

When the teacher caught the boy _____ in the examination, he stood there _____ and _____, _____ the loud admonition of the teacher, the headmaster rushed in. The boy started to cry _____ that he would be expelled from the school. _____ the situation very quickly, the headmaster asked the boy to follow him to his room.

Answer:
cheating, trembling, quivering Hearing, fearing, Assessing

VI. Rewrite the sentences using an infinitive instead of the underlined clause.

Example : Hillary was the first man who climbed Mt. Everest.

Hillary was the first man to climb Mt. Everest.

1. Shah found <u>that ₹ 20,000 of the sales money was</u> missing from the box.
2. The Court declared <u>that the officer was guilty</u> of gross negligence.
3. Evidence showed <u>that the document was a fabrication</u>.
4. The court warned the representatives <u>that they should not tamper</u> with the evidence.
5. The minister was annoyed <u>when he learnt that</u> he had lost the elections.

Subjective Section

6. You would be silly _if you dyed your hair green_.

Answer:
1. Shah found ₹ 20,000 of the sales money missing from the box.
2. The Court declared the officer to be guilty of gross negligence.
3. Evidence showed the document to be fabricated.
4. The Court warned the representatives not to tamper with the evidence.
5. The minister was annoyed to learn that he had lost the elections.
6. You would be silly to dye your hair green.

VII. Correct the following sentences :
1. Her actions make my blood to boil.
2. They are counting on me playing for their team.
3. He is thinking to write his autobiography.
4. I am hopeful to secure full marks in the Mathematics paper.
5. We were prevented to enter the classroom.
6. You had better to send your application by fax.

Answer:
1. Her actions make my blood boil.
2. They are counting on my playing for their team.
3. He is thinking of writing his autobiography.
4. I am hopeful of securing full marks in the Mathematics paper.
5. We were prevented from entering the classroom.
6. You had better send your application by fax.

VIII. Read the following sentences and punctuate them, using commas where necessary.
1. Tushar who is my best friend is studying in Cornell University, USA.
2. Konark where we are going for our next excursion is famous for its sun temple.
3. Mr. Misra who was in the US has started his own business in New Delhi.
4. Yesterday I met Saina Nehwal who is a famous badminton player.
5. Popeye likes to eat lots of spinach which contains iron.

Answer:
1. Tushar, who is my best friend, is studying in Cornell University, USA.
2. Konark, where we are going for our next excursion, is famous for its sun temple.
3. Mr. Misra, who was in the US, has started his own business in New Delhi.
4. Yesterday I met Saina Nehwal who is a famous badminton player.
5. Popeye likes to eat lots of spinach which, contains iron.

IX. Write a second sentence in each pair, using the clues and a suitable connector.
1. Harbhajan scored a half century in the first Quarter Finals of the World Cup Cricket Match against the West Indies, (five wickets)
2. Rohini is a good singer, (dancer)
3. Deforestation leads to drought, (global warming)
4. Wildlife sanctuaries in India are home to elephants, tigers and rhinos, (preserve endangered species)

Answers:
1. Harbhajan scored a half century in the first Quarter Finals of the World Cup Cricket Match against the West Indies. Furthermore, he got five wickets.

2. Rohini is a good singer. In addition, she is a good dancer.
3. Deforestation leads to drought. Moreover, it leads to global warming.
4. Wildlife sanctuaries in India are home to elephants, tigers and rhinos. Furthermore, these preserve endangered species.

X. **Combine the following pairs of sentences by changing the adjective to a noun.**

Question 1. He was honest. The Principal commended him at the assembly.

Ans. The Principal commended his honesty at the assembly.

Question 2. Rajesh is a very amiable person. It has endeared him to his colleagues.

Ans. Rajesh's amiability has endeared him to his colleagues.

Question 3. The actor was famous. It got him many endorsements.

Ans. The actor's fame got him many endorsements.

Question 4. The young businessman was extravagant. It led to his downfall.

Ans. The extravagance of the young businessman led to his downfall.

Question 5. James was silent during the enquiry. It did not help the police in bringing the culprit to book.

Ans. James's silence during the enquiry did not help the police in bringing the culprit to book.

XI. **Read the following sentences carefully and circle the reporting verbs. Write the ways in which each reporting verb adds to the meaning of its arrangement.**

1. "When I was in school, I used to skip a few classes, especially Moral Science because of the bookish manner in which it was taught," confessed the retired IAS Officer.
2. Saurav's friends protested that he should have been included in the school badminton team, on the basis of his fine performance in the inter-house matches.
3. "Make a circle, make a circle !" Mira shouted, firmly pulling and pushing the children till a kind of vague circle was formed.
4. The music teacher warned the children against getting carried away and getting out of tune.
5. "Father, you must tell me what you meant exactly when you said that I was the same as every other teenager," Varun insisted.
6. "Oh God ! She is coming again," the children whispered to each other, when they saw Mrs. Sharma striding towards their classroom for the third time that day.

Answers:

1. 'Confessed' to be circled is the reporting verb used in the sentence. It reveals the mood of the speaker as he admits his weakness of skipping the class which was contrary to rules.
2. 'protested' is to be circled in the reporting verb used in the sentence. The verb shows Saurav's friends' mood.
3. 'shouted' is to be circled in the reporting verb in the sentence. 'Shouted' shows Mira's mood ie, irritable manner.
4. 'warned' is to be circled in the reporting verb in the sentence. It reflects music teacher's manner of speaking to the children ie, threatening manner.
5. 'insisted' is to be circled in the reporting verb in the sentence. This verb shows Varan's emphatic manner.
6. 'whispered' is to be circled in the reporting verb in the sentence. This verb shows children's tone and manner i.e. afraid and disliking.

XII. Rewrite the following in reported speech:
(a) Sheela to Rashmi: "You can come and stay at my place if you're ever in Delhi".
(b) Anand to Renu : "I don't know what Gayathri is doing these days. She hasn't visited us for ages".
(c) Teacher to Students : "We shall go on a field trip to study water pollution".

Answer:
(a) Sheela told Rashmi that she could come and stay at her place if she was ever in Delhi.
(b) Anand told Renu that he didn't know what Gayathri was doing those days as she had not visited them for ages.
(c) The teacher informed the students that they would go on a field trip to study water pollution.

XIII. Rewrite the following in indirect speech:
(a) He said, "Who has moved into the neighbouring house?"
(b) He said, "What have you bought for Deepawali?"
(c) He said to me, "Why didn't you wear your new dress for the party?"
(d) "Is anyone there ?" he asked.
(e) "Shall I wait for the doctor or come again tomorrow?" she asked the receptionist.

Answer:
(a) He asked who had moved into the neighbouring house.
(b) He asked her what she had bought for Deepawali.
(c) He asked me why I had not worn my new dress for the party.
(d) He enquired if anyone was there.
(e) She asked the receptionist if she would wait for the doctor or come again the following day.

XIV. Correct the following sentences.
(a) It is essential that we discuss about your proposal before reaching any decision.
(b) The class fell silent as the teacher entered into the classroom.
(c) I have been living here since four years.
(d) The tournament will be held between Monday to Friday.
(e) Rani closely resembles to her maternal aunt.
(f) As the train was approaching to the station, someone pulled the chain and brought it to a halt.
(g) Connectors are also called as discourse markers.

Study sentences (a), (b), (e), (f) and (g). What conclusion can you draw from these examples about the correct use of prepositions? Rewrite sentences if, needed.

Answers:
(a) It is essential that we discuss your proposal before reaching any decision.
(b) The class fell silent as the teacher entered the classroom.
(c) I have been living here for four years.
(d) The tournament will be held from Monday to Friday.
(e) Rani closely resembles her maternal aunt.
(f) As the train was approaching the station, someone pulled the chain and brought it to a halt.
(g) Connectors are also called discourse markers.

In sentences (a), (b), (e), (f) and (g), prepositions are not required. The verbs used in them do not need prepositions.

XV. Fill in the blanks with suitable determiners.
(i) _____ books are missing from the library. (Any, Some)
(ii) She has not solved _____ sums. (many, any)
(iii) This book is mine but _____ is yours. (that, any)
(iv) _____ boys have done their work. (That, These)

(v) He didn't make _____ progress. (much, many)
(vi) He has forgotten _____ of the details. (some, many)
(vii) The District Magistrate visited _____ flood affected area. (every, either)
(viii) _____ villa is this? (Whose, What)
(ix) He is the _____ boy who has joined this gym. (first, whose)
(x) I met her _____ week. (this, those)

Answer:
(i) Some
(ii) many
(iii) that
(iv) These
(v) much
(vi) some
(vii) every
(viii) Whose
(ix) first
(x) this

Model Test Paper 1

Direction (1-2): Choose the most suitable word/phrase for each blank.

1. I cannot make the cake now as I have _____ of milk.
   (a) Run into   (b) Run away
   (c) Run by   (d) Run out

2. With lot of struggle, the firefighters were able to _____ the fire.
   (a) Put off   (b) Put in
   (c) Put out   (d) Put away

3. Choose the correct spelling.
   (a) Milennium   (b) Millenium
   (c) Millennium   (d) Millennum

4. Select the correct phrase.
   (a) Beating the bush
   (b) Beating around bushes
   (c) Beating the bushes around
   (d) Beating around the bush

Direction (5-6): Fill in the blanks with suitable option.

5. It's raining heavily outside, so _____
   (a) party must be missed
   (b) we will have to miss the party
   (c) we miss a party
   (d) miss the party

6. There's a _____ the river, so you can easily go to the other side.
   (a) bridge on
   (b) bridge across
   (c) bridge over
   (d) bridge upon

Direction (7-9): Read the passage given below and answer the questions that follow.

Twenty years ago, kids in school had never even heard of the internet. Now, I'll bet you can't find a single person in your school who hasn't at least heard of it. In fact, many of us use it on a regular basis and even have access to it from our homes! The 'net' in internet really stands for network. A network is two or more computers connected together so that information can be shared, or sent from one computer to another. The internet is a vast resource for all types of information. You may enjoy using it to do research for a school project, downloading your favorite songs or communicating with friends and family. Information is accessed through web pages that companies, organizations and individuals create and post. It's kind of like a giant bulletin board that the whole world uses! But, since anyone can put anything on the internet, you also have to be careful and use your best judgement and a little common sense.

Just because you read something on a piece of paper that someone sticks on a bulletin board doesn't mean it's good information, or even correct, for that matter. So you have to be sure that whoever posted the information knows what they're talking about, especially if you're doing research! But what if you're just emailing people? You still have to be very careful. If you've never met the person that you're communicating with online, you could be on dangerous ground! You should never give out any personal information to someone you don't know, not even your name! And just like you can't believe the information on every website out there, you can't rely on what strangers you 'meet' on the internet tell you either. Just like you could make up things about yourself to tell someone, someone else could do the same to you!

7. According to the passage, a network means:
   (a) a spiral web on which lot of computers are linked
   (b) multiple computers connected together to share information
   (c) computers connected to the internet
   (d) information sharing on any two devices

8. All the information available on internet
   (a) is safe and reliable
   (b) is as correct as all information put on bulletin boards
   (c) should be used carefully and with our best judgement
   (d) can be trusted like all the emails sent to us

9. The main focus of the passage is on
   (a) keeping caution while using internet
   (b) companies and organizations accessing internet for information
   (c) making new friendships on the internet with strangers
   (d) the use of internet to do research for school projects, downloading songs and communicating with friends and family

Direction (10-12): Choose the most suitable sentence to complete the paragraph.

10. Housewife (upon looking at two beggars at her doorstep): "So you are begging in two's now?"
    Beggar: "No, only for today. _____
    (a) I am scared to beg alone.
    (b) We get double the alms at each house if we beg together.
    (c) I'm going on a holiday and, therefore, have got my replacement.
    (d) We are partners.

11. Lisa: What have you got inside that bag?
    Jack: It's a vacuum cleaner.
    Lisa: _____
    (a) I am so happy as this is an expensive gift.
    (b) I am so glad as it's going to help me clean up the house faster.
    (c) I will never use it
    (d) Can you pack it back again?

12. **Sentence 1:** Your abdominals, commonly called abs, consist of several muscle groups, all located in the mid-section, just below your chest to your pubic bone.
    Sentence 2: _____
    Sentence 3: The upper, middle and lower abs start near the middle of your sternum and runs vertically to the lower part of the pelvis; they are responsible for flexing the vertebral column or helping you curl your trunk as you would when doing crunches or sitting up in bed.
    (a) These include: rectus abdominis, which is made up of upper, middle, and lower abs; transverse abdominis; and the obliques.
    (b) The internal obliques are located beneath the external obliques; they also help you twist.
    (c) In addition, most low-back pain is attributed to weak abdominals.
    (d) The flat bench abdominal leg pull ins target your abdominal muscles (rectus abdominis) and provide minor tension to your hip flexors.

Direction (13-14): Choose the best word to complete the sentence.

13. I have been waiting for you _____ 7 pm and now it is _____ late for us to go out.
    (a) from, to   (b) since, too
    (c) at, very   (d) till, so

14. My team has played very well today, so we hope _____
    (a) winning the prize
    (b) to win the prize
    (c) for the prize winning
    (d) to win prize

Model Test Paper 2

Direction (1-2) : Choose the most suitable word/phrase for each blank.

1. I had not met her for a long time, but today suddenly I _____ her at the shopping mall.
   - (a) Ran into
   - (b) Ran over
   - (c) Ran by
   - (d) Ran up

2. That shop is really expensive. They always try to _____ the customer.
   - (a) Rip off
   - (b) Rip up
   - (c) Rip away
   - (d) Rip apart

3. Choose the correct spelling.
   - (a) Supercede
   - (b) Superceed
   - (c) Supersede
   - (d) Superseed

4. Select the correct phrase.
   - (a) Cry over split milk
   - (b) Cry and spill milk
   - (c) Cry over split water
   - (d) Cry over milk

Direction (5-6) : Fill in the blanks with suitable option.

5. I am not able to take any more printouts _____
   - (a) the printer broke down
   - (b) printer breaks down
   - (c) as the printer has broken down
   - (d) broken down printer it is

6. I've already started from my office and should reach your place _____
   - (a) by 6 pm
   - (b) on 6 pm
   - (c) at 6 pm
   - (d) after 6 pm

7. Read the sentences given below and find the error.
   - (a) Although Denise
   - (b) had some doubts,
   - (c) she found the courses very useful
   - (d) No error

Direction (8-10) : Read the passage given below and answer the questions that follow.

It happened over 300 years ago in Holland. Anton van Leeuwenhoek (AN-tun van LAY-vun-hook) had a new microscope that he had made. One day he looked through it at a drop of lake water. What he saw surprised him.

The water was alive with what Leeuwenhoek called "wee beasties." The microscope made tiny organisms look 200 times larger than life size. Leeuwenhoek was one of the first scientists to see living things that were that small. His work was a giant step for science.

Today, microscopes are much stronger. An electron microscope can make tiny organisms look 200,000 times life size. A few electron microscopes can see individual atoms. Pictures can be made to show the objects or organisms much bigger. The pictures add greatly to what we know about tiny objects and organisms. Microscopes have come a long way in 300 years!

8. Leeuwenhoek was surprised to see
   - (a) living things with the microscope
   - (b) he had taken a giant step in science
   - (c) such small living things for the first time
   - (d) tiny organisms 200 times

9. Electron microscopes are much advanced because
   - (a) they can see tiny organisms
   - (b) they can see individual atoms
   - (c) they help us to make pictures
   - (d) they help us see the smallest of objects and organisms, and know about them

10. The main focus of the passage is on
    - (a) microscopes and how they are made
    - (b) Anton van Leeuwenhoek
    - (c) how the discovery of microscope has helped us know about the tiny objects and organisms.
    - (d) how we can make pictures based on the images microscopes see.

Direction (11-13): Choose the most suitable sentence to complete the paragraph.

11. Interviewer: What is three times seven?

    Ron: Twenty-two.

    Interviewer: It's twenty-one. We will still offer you the job as _____
    (a) you have the courage to give a wrong answer.
    (b) you are the closest to the actual answer.
    (c) we like your answer.
    (d) your clothes are very nice.

12. Don: What was that clicking sound?

    Jane: _____

    Lisa: Oh! I didn't see you pressing your car remote-control device.
    (a) I don't know!
    (b) Do you really need to know everything?
    (c) It was just the doors unlocking!
    (d) Oops! Did you hear a sound?

13. **Sentence 1:** Even though kettlebell training has been around for a long time, it seems that the popularity of this type of training is at an all time high..

    Sentence 2: _____

    Sentence 3: Kettlebells are used to perform ballistic exercises that combine cardiovascular, strength and flexibility training.

    (a) We have created a huge database of kettlebell exercises with photos and instructional tips to use them effectively!
    (b) A kettlebell is a cast iron weight that looks a little like a cannonball or a bowling ball with a handle attached to it.
    (c) Position the kettlebell on the ground between your feet. Explode up while raising the kettlebell to the top position.
    (d) Keep reading about an exercise you should probably already be doing.

Direction (14-15): Choose the best word to complete the sentence.

14. I don't like walking alone _____ nights as I am _____ scared of the dark.
    (a) throughout, to   (b) over, too
    (c) at, very   (d) in, so

15. The student refused _____ although the teacher insisted again and again.
    (a) answer question
    (b) to question answer
    (c) to answer the question
    (d) answering question

Answer Keys

Scan the QR Code to see the Hints and Solutions

Access Content Online on Dropbox: https://www.dropbox.com/scl/fi/x1il8nzpuzwm1qyz8yycu/NSO-01-Science-Olympiad-Hints-and-Solutions.pdf?rlkey=kzkx1753ie7dfs4rlkt3yo4pa&dl=0

SECTION 1: WORD AND STRUCTURE KNOWLEDGE

1. NOUN

Answer Key

I

1. Common	2. Common	3. Proper	4. Common	5. Proper
6. Proper	7. Common	8. Proper	9. Proper	10. Common

II

1. Uncountable	2. Uncountable	3. Countable	4. Uncountable	5. Countable
6. Countable	7. Uncountable	8. Countable	9. Countable	10. Uncountable

HOTS

1. permission	2. belief	3. improvement	4. information	5. happiness

2. ADJECTIVE

Answer Key

I

1. Heavy – adjective of quality	2. Several – indefinite numeral adjective
3. Faithful – adjective of quality; its – possessive adjective	4. Every – distributive numeral adjective; his – possessive adjective
5. Few – indefinite numeral adjective	6. Neither – distributive numeral adjective
7. Which – interrogative adjective	8. Long – adjective of quality; cold – adjective of quality
9. Every – distributive numeral adjective	10. Several – indefinite numeral adjective

II				
1. prettier	2. Nice	3. most intelligent	4. well	5. biggest
6. big	7. bigger	8. most interesting	9. smarter	10. shorter

HOTS

1. careful	2. fluent	3. complete	4. serious	5. sudden

3. ARTICLES AND PREPOSITIONS

Answer Key

I									
1. an	2. a	3. the	4. a	5. a	6. an	7. the	8. the	9. an	10. the

II									
1. The	2. No article	3. No article	4. an	5. No article	6. No article, a	7. an, The	8. a	9. a, The	10. the

III									
1. (c)	2. (a)	3. (a)	4. (c)	5. (b)	6. (c)	7. (a)	8. (c)	9. (b)	10. (a)
11. (b)	12. (c)	13. (b)	14. (c)	15. (a)	16. (c)	17. (b)	18. (a)	19. (a)	20. (c)
21. (c)	22. (b)	23. (d)	24. (a)	25. (b)	26. (c)	27. (b)	28. (d)	29. (b)	30. (a)
31. (b)	32. (a)	33. (a)	34. (b)	35. (a)	36. (b)	37. (c)	38. (a)	39. (c)	40. (a)
41. (a)	42. (c)	43. (d)	44. (c)	45. (a)	46. (b)	47. (a)	48. (d)	49. (a)	50. (b)
51. (c)	52. (d)	53. (a)	54. (d)	55. (c)	56. (a)	57. (b)	58. (a)	59. (c)	60. (b)
61. (a)	62. (d)	63. (b)	64. (a)	65. (b)	66. (d)	67. (b)	68. (c)	69. (d)	70. (c)
71. (d)	72. (a)	73. (d)	74. (c)	75. (b)	76. (a)	77. (c)	78. (b)	79. (c)	80. (a)

HOTS

I

| 1. the, the | 2. an | 3. a | 4. a | 5. The |

II

| 1. on | 2. since | 3. in | 4. to | 5. with |

4. VERBS, ADVERBS, PHRASAL VERBS AND MODALS

Answer Key

I

1. does is a finite verb	2. doing is a non-finite verb
3. are is a finite verb	4. speaks is a finite verb
5. has is a finite verb	6. been is a non-finite verb
7. tried is a finite verb	8. laugh is a non-finite verb
9. Finding is a non-finite verb	10. cleaned is a non-finite verb

II

1. going – Gerund	2. to study – Infinitive
3. telling – Gerund	4. to speak – Infinitive
5. to help – Infinitive	6. to come – Infinitive
7. Hearing – participle, qualifying the pronoun we	8. Watching – gerund, object of the preposition by
9. Standing – participle, qualifying the noun clown	10. Asking – gerund, subject of is; answering – gerund

III

1. easily	2. badly	3. out	4. aggressively	5. immediately
6. highly	7. nearly	8. often	9. extremely	10. frightened

11. disappointed	12. relaxed	13. ashamed	14. interested	15. often go
16. never smokes	17. I rarely	18. usually do	19. hardly ever gets	20. has already finished
21. I will definitely	22. don't really	23. always went	24. I seldom have	25. probably won't
26. I have never been	27. do I do			

IV				
1. Yesterday	2. fast	3. repeatedly	4. loudly	5. never
6. everywhere	7. soon	8. formally		

V				
1. (a)	2. (d)	3. (d)	4. (a)	5. (c)
6. (c)	7. (a)	8. (c)	9. (a)	10. (c)

VI									
1. (b)	2. (a)	3. (d)	4. (c)	5. (b)	6. (d)	7. (b)	8. (c)	9. (d)	10. (b)

VII									
1. (a)	2. (c)	3. (a)	4. (c)	5. (a)	6. (b)	7. (b)	8. (c)	9. (d)	10. (b)

VIII									
1. (d)	2. (c)	3. (b)	4. (d)	5. (d)	6. (b)	7. (d)	8. (b)	9. (a)	10. (c)

IX				
1. Could	2. Could	3. won't be able	4. Can	5. Will, be able to

X				
1. might	2. may	3. May	4. might	5. may

XI					
1. shouldn't	2. should	3. should	4. ought	5. Should	6. shouldn't

XII						
1. have to	2. must	3. must not	4. has to	5. don't have	6. need to	7. don't need to

Answer Keys

XIII						
1. Will	2. would	3. won't	4. would	5. would	6. will	
XIV						
1. (a)	2. (c)	3. (c)	4. (b)	5. (b)	6. (a)	7. (c)	8. (c)
XV									
1. (b)	2. (a)	3. (c)	4. (c)	5. (c)	6. (b)	7. (b)	8. (a)	9. (d)	10. (b)
11. (c)	12. (d)	13. (d)	14. (d)	15. (b)	16. (c)	17. (b)	18. (a)	19. (c)	20. (b)

HOTS

I				
1. quickly	2. terribly	3. continuously	4. happily	5. specially
II				
1. cheer up	2. split up	3. catch up with	4. sort out	5. turn up

5. CONJUNCTIONS

Answer Key

I									
1. (c)	2. (b)	3. (a)	4. (b)	5. (b)	6. (a)	7. (a)	8. (a)	9. (a)	10. (a)

II	
1. If – subordinating conjunction	2. After – subordinating conjunction
3. Till – subordinating conjunction	4. And – coordinating conjunction
5. Unless – subordinating conjunction	6. Before – subordinating conjunction
7. For – coordinating conjunction	8. Since – subordinating conjunction
9. Lest – subordinating conjunction	10. If – subordinating conjunction
11. Because – subordinating conjunction	12. Than – subordinating conjunction
13. When – subordinating conjunction	14. Till – subordinating conjunction
15. Whether – subordinating conjunction	

	HOTS			
1. Although	2. When	3. so	4. but	5. where

6. PUNCTUATIONS

Answer Key	
I	
1. After a hard day at the office, I like to relax with a large gin.	2. The recipe needed jam, flour, sugar, fruit, eggs, ketchup and baking powder.
3. "Look at this," he whispered.	4. Paulina, his wife of many years, had decided to go and live in Greece.
5. As the sun began to sink over the sea, Karen got ready to go out.	6. She was intelligent, not especially practical.
7. The thief was wearing impractical high heels, so she could not run fast.	8. We go to Blackpool for the cuisine, not the weather.
9. "I advise you," said the teacher, "not to cross me again today."	10. Steven, his head still spinning, walked out of the office for the last time.

II

1. b, c	2. a, b	3. b, c	4. a, d	5. c

III

1. (d)	2. (a)	3. (a)	4. (b)	5. (d)	6. (c)	7. (d)	8. (c)	9. (c)	10. (a)

IV

1. We had a great time in France – the kids really enjoyed it.	2. Some people work best in the mornings; others do better in the evenings.
3. What are you doing next weekend?	4. Mother had to go into hospital: she had heart problems.
5. Did you understand why I was upset?	6. It is a fine idea; let us hope that it is going to work.
7. We will be arriving on Monday morning – at least, I think so.	8. A textbook can be a 'wall' between teacher and class.

HOTS				
1. (b)	2. (b)	3. (b)	4. (d)	5. (c)

7. TENSES

Answer Key

I

1. (a)	2. (c)	3. (d)	4. (b)	5. (a)	6. (c)	7. (a)	8. (b)	9. (a)	10. (b)
11. (a)	12. (a)	13. (a)	14. (b)	15. (a)	16. (b)	17. (d)	18. (c)	19. (a)	20. (a)
21. (b)	22. (b)	23. (a)	24. (c)	25. (d)	26. (d)	27. (b)	28. (d)	29. (d)	30. (a)
31. (d)	32. (b)	33. (d)	34. (a)	35. (d)					

II

1. (b)	2. (d)	3. (b)	4. (d)	5. (c)	6. (c)	7. (d)	8. (b)	9. (d)	10. (a)
11. (c)	12. (c)								

HOTS									
1. (b)	2. (a)	3. (b)	4. (d)	5. (a)	6. (c)	7. (a)	8. (d)	9. (b)	10. (c)

8. CONDITIONALS

Answer Key

I

1. (c)	2. (a)	3. (d)	4. (c)	5. (c)	6. (c)	7. (a)	8. (a)	9. (c)	10. (a)

II

1. (a)	2. (b)	3. (d)	4. (a)	5. (b)	6. (a)	7. (b)	8. (b)	9. (c)	10. (a)

III

1. (a)	2. (a)	3. (a)	4. (b)	5. (a)	6. (c)	7. (c)	8. (a)	9. (a)	10. (b)

IV										
1. (c)	2. (a)	3. (b)	4. (d)	5. (a)	6. (d)	7. (a)	8. (b)	9. (c)	

V										
1. (b)	2. (a)	3. (c)	4. (b)	5. (b)	6. (c)	7. (c)	8. (d)	9. (d)	10. (d)
11. (a)	12. (d)	13. (a)	14. (c)	15. (a)	16. (a)	17. (b)	18. (c)	19. (c)	20. (b)

VI

1. If I go to Leipzig, I'll visit the zoo.
2. If it didn't rain, we'd be in the garden.
3. If you had worn a lighter jacket, the car driver would have seen you earlier.
4. We would have watched TV tonight if Peter hadn't bought the theatre tickets.
5. She wouldn't have had two laptops if she had not signed the contract.
6. If I was/were a millionaire, I would live in Beverly Hills.
7. You would save energy if you switched off the lights more often.
8. If we had read the book, we would have understood the film.
9. My sister could score better on the test if the teacher explained the grammar once more.
10. They might have arrived on time if they hadn't missed the train.
11. If it rains, the boys won't play hockey.
12. If he grew his own vegetables, he wouldn't have to buy them.
13. Jim would see whisky distilleries if he travelled to Scotland.
14. Would you go out more often if you didn't have to do so much in the house?
15. She wouldn't have yawned the whole day if she hadn't stayed up late last night.
16. If you wait a minute, I'll come with you.
17. If we arrived at 10, we would miss Tyler's presentation.
18. We would have helped John if we'd known about his problems.
19. If they had used new batteries, their camera would have worked correctly.
20. If I went anywhere, it would be New Zealand.

HOTS

1.	Shikha is in her farm-house. During her morning walk one day, she narrowly escapes being bitten by a snake. What do you think would happen if she was bitten by a snake?	If Shikha was bitten by a snake, she could have died.
2.	I have misplaced the book Ajay gave me on my birthday. I must find it. If I lost the book, how would Ajay feel?	Ajay would feel bad, I could not find the book that he gave me on my birthday.
3.	Mira might win an air-ticket to Europe. She has been dreaming of going to England. Where do you think you would go if you won an air-ticket?	If I won an air ticket, I would go for a trip to Australia.
4.	Delhi Textile Mill is planning to close down its factory. As a consequence, many workers would lose their jobs. The Workers' Union wants it to stay open and says to the management:	If Delhi Textile Mill is closed down, many workers would lose their jobs.
5.	Your friend Mani parks his scooter in the lane outside: You fear that it will be stolen one day if he continues to park it there. So you ask him:	What would you do if your scooter is stolen from lane outside?

9. VOICE AND NARRATION

Answer Key

I

1. (b)	2. (b)	3. (b)	4. (b)	5. (a)	6. (b)	7. (c)	8. (b)	9. (a)	10. (a)
11. (c)	12. (c)								

II

1. will be sent	2. was told	3. was not paid	4. are often asked	5. is cut
6. will be asked	7. are taught	8. was phoned	9. were eaten up	10. will be answered

III

1. (a)	2. (d)	3. (e)	4. (b)	5. (c)	6. (b)	7. (a)	8. (e)	9. (c)	10. (b)

HOTS				
1. (b)	2. (a)	3. (c)	4. (a)	5. (d)

10. SPELLINGS, ANALOGY AND COLLOCATIONS

Answer Key

I				
1. truly	2. severely	3. completely	4. sincerely	5. arguing
6. argued	7. coming	8. writing	9. judging	10. careful.

II				
1. ceiling	2. receiving	3. weird	4. piece	5. believe
6. their	7. Neither	8. neighbors	9. weighs	10. freight

III				
1. tried	2. cried	3. theories	4. betrayed	5. studying
6. Loneliness	7. flies	8. relied	9. apologies	10. pitiful

IV				
1. cemetery	2. quantities	3. benefit	4. privilege	5. unpleasant
6. separate	7. independent	8. excellent	9. categories	10. irrelevant

V				
1. shining	2. controlled	3. beginning	4. poured	5. forgetting
6. admitted	7. sweating	8. occurred	9. hopping	10. referred

VI				
1. guarantee	2. surprised	3. probably	4. realize	5. Describe
6. until	7. recommended	8. aspirin	9. athletic	10. temperature

VII				
1. acquired	2. basically	3. environment	4. disappear	5. business
6. similar	7. finally	8. disappointed	9. laboratory	10. government

				VIII					
1. (b)	2. (b)	3. (c)	4. (d)	5. (d)	6. (b)	7. (b)	8. (c)	9. (b)	10. (c)
11. (a)	12. (b)	13. (a)	14. (c)	15. (a)	16. (a)	17. (b)	18. (d)	19. (c)	20. (c)
21. (a)	22. (b)	23. (b)	24. (a)	25. (b)	26. (d)	27. (b)	28. (d)	29. (a)	30. (a)
31. (c)	32. (d)	33. (a)	34. (a)	35. (d)					
				IX					
1. (a)	2. (b)	3. (d)	4. (c)	5. (b)	6. (c)	7. (d)	8. (a)	9. (c)	10. (d)
11. (b)	12. (c)	13. (c)	14. (c)	15. (a)	16. (b)	17. (c)	18. (a)	19. (d)	20. (a)

HOTS

1. (d)	2. (d)	3. (d)	4. (c)	5. (c)

11. SYNONYMS, ANTONYMS, HOMONYMS AND HOMOPHONES

Answer Key

				I					
1. (a)	2. (d)	3. (c)	4. (c)	5. (a)	6. (c)	7. (d)	8. (a)	9. (d)	10. (a)
11. (d)	12. (d)	13. (a)	14. (d)	15. (c)	16. (c)	17. (a)	18. (d)	19. (b)	20. (a)
21. (c)	22. (c)	23. (a)	24. (d)	25. (d)	26. (b)	27. (a)	28. (b)	29. (d)	30. (a)
31. (c)	32. (d)	33. (c)	34. (c)	35. (a)					
				II					
1. (d)	2. (b)	3. (c)	4. (d)	5. (a)	6. (a)	7. (c)	8. (c)	9. (b)	10. (d)
11. (b)	12. (c)	13. (d)	14. (b)	15. (a)	16. (d)	17. (b)	18. (c)	19. (a)	20. (b)
21. (b)	22. (d)	23. (a)	24. (a)	25. (c)	26. (b)	27. (d)	28. (c)	29. (b)	30. (a)
31. (a)	32. (d)	33. (a)	34. (b)	35. (b)	36. (c)	37. (a)	38. (d)	39. (c)	40. (d)

III									
1. (a)	2. (b)	3. (a)	4. (b)	5. (b)	6. (a)	7. (a)	8. (a)	9. (a)	10. (a)
11. (a)	12. (b)	13. (b)	14. (b)	15. (b)					

IV									
1. (a)	2. (a)	3. (a)	4. (b)	5. (b)	6. (a)	7. (a)	8. (b)	9. (b)	10. (b)
11. (a)	12. (a)	13. (b)	14. (b)	15. (b)					

V				
1. their	2. too	3. right	4. him	5. aisle
6. due	7. blew	8. bear	9. reigning	10. Eight

VI				
1. to	2. pair	3. sent	4. bored	5. their
6. wear	7. rain	8. road	9. band	10. toes
11. aisle	12. pain	13. principal	14. sell	15. past
16. knows	17. four	18. break	19. paws	20. He'll

HOTS

1. Attract	2. Applaud	3. Artificial	4. Monologue	

5. What looks like a convenient shortcut may prove to be very inconvenient in the long run.
6. No one wants to listen to an ignorant man but everybody listens to a wise man.
7. Gold in an expensive metal while iron is cheap.
8. My application was accepted but his was rejected.
9. The teacher tried to make the student confident but he still looked very diffident.
10. He failed to qualify in the first two attempts but succeeded in the third one.

Answer Keys

12. ONE WORD

Answer Key

I

1. (c)	2. (b)	3. (c)	4. (d)	5. (a)	6. (c)	7. (d)	8. (c)	9. (a)	10. (c)
11. (b)	12. (d)	13. (b)	14. (b)	15. (d)	16. (a)	17. (a)	18. (b)	19. (c)	20. (a)
21. (b)	22. (a)	23. (d)	24. (b)	25. (c)	26. (a)	27. (d)	28. (c)	29. (b)	30. (a)
31. (b)	32. (d)	33. (b)	34. (d)	35. (c)	36. (c)	37. (a)	38. (a)	39. (d)	40. (b)
41. (b)	42. (a)	43. (b)	44. (c)	45. (d)	46. (a)	47. (c)	48. (c)	49. (d)	50. (b)
51. (d)	52. (a)	53. (c)	54. (b)	55. (a)	56. (c)	57. (d)	58. (c)	59. (b)	60. (d)
61. (b)	62. (b)	63. (a)	64. (a)	65. (a)	66. (c)	67. (b)	68. (d)	69. (d)	70. (a)

HOTS

1. (b)	2. (d)	3. (b)	4. (c)	5. (a)	6. (d)	7. (c)	8. (a)	9. (b)	10. (c)
11. (c)	12. (b)	13. (a)	14. (a)	15. (b)	16. (c)	17. (d)	18. (b)	19. (c)	20. (c)
21. (a)	22. (d)	23. (b)	24. (b)	25. (d)					

13. IDIOMS

Answer Key

I

1. (c)	2. (b)	3. (b)	4. (d)	5. (a)	6. (b)	7. (b)	8. (b)	9. (b)	10. (c)
11. (c)	12. (a)	13. (a)							

II

1. (c)	2. (d)	3. (b)	4. (a)	5. (c)	6. (b)	7. (d)	8. (a)	9. (d)

III

1. (a)	2. (c)	3. (a)	4. (a)	5. (d)	6. (b)	7. (d)	8. (d)

HOTS

| 1. (c) | 2. (d) | 3. (a) | 4. (b) | 5. (a) |

14. QUESTION TAGS

Answer Key

I

1. It is not very hot today, is it?	2. They haven't paid their dues, have they?
3. That is your book, isn't it?	4. The sun does not shine at night, does it?
5. He studies very well, doesn't he?	6. These shirts are very expensive, aren't they?
7. Raju works hard, doesn't he?	8. Earth goes round the sun, doesn't it?
9. Children rush about, don't they?	10. You received the parcel in the morning, didn't you?

II

| 1. (b) | 2. (c) | 3. (d) | 4. (a) | 5. (c) |

HOTS

1. (d)	2. (c)	3. (d)	4. (b)	5. (d)	6. (b)	7. (b)	8. (d)	9. (b)	10. (b)
11. (a)	12. (b)	13. (b)	14. (a)	15. (b)					

SECTION 2: READING COMPREHENSION

COMPREHENSION

Answer Key

Exercise 1.	1. (a)	2. (c)	3. (d)	4. (b)	5. (b)
Exercise 2.	1. (c)	2. (d)	3. (c)	4. (b)	5. (b)
Exercise 3.	1. (a)	2. (d)	3. (c)	4. (d)	5. (b)
Exercise 4.	1. (d)	2. (b)	3. (c)	4. (c)	5. (c)
Exercise 5.	1. (a)	2. (b)	3. (d)	4. (b)	5. (a)
Exercise 6.	1. (d)	2. (b)	3. (c)	4. (a)	5. (a)

MODEL TEST PAPER – 1

Answer Key

1. (d)	2. (c)	3. (c)	4. (d)	5. (b)	6. (c)	7. (b)	8. (c)	9. (a)	10. (c)
11. (c)	12. (a)	13. (b)	14. (b)						

MODEL TEST PAPER – 2

Answer Key

1. (a)	2. (a)	3. (c)	4. (a)	5. (c)	6. (a)	7. (c)	8. (d)	9. (b)	10. (c)
11. (a)	12. (c)	13. (b)	14. (c)	15. (c)					

Appendix

There are different organizations that conduct these examinations and covering all of them is not needed as the focus should be to understand the main type of exams conducted. They are similar for these organizations with the difference being the change in name of the exam.

By Science Olympiad Foundation (SOF)		
S. No.	Name of Exam	Grade
1.	National Science Olympiad (NSO)	Class 1-10
2.	National Cyber Olympiad (NCO)	Class 1-10
3.	International Mathematics Olympiad (IMO)	Class 1-10
4.	International English Olympiad (IEO)	Class 1-10
5.	International Commerce Olympiad (ICO)	Class 1-10
6.	International General Knowledge Olympiad (IGKO)	Class 1-10
7.	International Social Studies Olympiad (ISSO)	Class 1-10

By Indian Talent Olympiad (ITO)		
S. No.	Name of Exam	Grade
1.	International Science Olympiad (ISO)	Class 1-12
2.	International Math Olympiad (IMO)	Class 1-12
3.	English International Olympiad (EIO)	Class 1-12
4.	General Knowledge International Olympiad (GKIO)	Class 1-12
5.	International Computer Olympiad (ICO)	Class 1-12
6.	International Drawing Olympiad (IDO)	Class 1-12
7.	National Essay Olympiad (NESO)	Class 1-12
8.	National Social Studies Olympiad (NSSO)	Class 1-12

By EduHeal Foundation		
S. No.	Name of Exam	Grade
1.	Eduheal International Cyber Olympiad (ICO)	Class 1-12
2.	Eduheal International English Olympiad (IEO)	Class 1-12
3.	National Interactive Math Olympiad (NIMO)	Class 1-12
4.	National Interactive Science Olympiad (NISO)	Class 1-12
5.	International General Knowledge Olympiad (IGO)	Class 1-12
6.	National Space Science Olympiad (NSSO)	Class 1-12

\multicolumn{3}{c}{**By Humming Bird Education**}		
S. No.	Name of Exam	Grade
1.	Humming Bird Commerce Competency Olympiad (HCC)	Class 1-12
2.	Humming Bird Cyber Olympiad (HCO)	Class 1-12
3.	Humming Bird English Olympiad (HEO)	Class 1-12
4.	Humming Bird General Knowledge Olympiad (HGO)	Class 1-12
5.	Humming Bird Hindi Olympiad (HHO)	Class 1-12
6.	Humming Bird Mathematics Olympiad (HMO)	Class 1-12
7.	Humming Bird Science Olympiad (HSO)	Class 1-12
8.	Humming Bird Aptitude and Reasoning Olympiad (ARO)	Class 1-12
9.	Humming Bird Spelling Competition (Spell BEE)	Class 1-12
10.	Humming Bird Language Olympiad	Class 1-12

\multicolumn{3}{c}{**By International Assessments for Indian Schools (IAIS) (MacMillan and EEA Collaboration)**}		
S. No.	Name of Exam	Grade
1.	IAIS Maths Olympiad	Class 3-12
2.	IAIS ScienceOlympiad	Class 3-12
3.	IAIS English Olympiad	Class 3-12
4.	IAIS Digital Technologies Olympiad	Class 3-12

\multicolumn{3}{c}{**By SilverZone Foundation**}		
S. No.	Name of Exam	Grade
1.	International Informatics Olympiad	Class 1-12
2.	International Olympiad of Mathematics	Class 1-12
3.	International Olympiad of Science	Class 1-12

\multicolumn{3}{c}{**By Unified Council**}		
S. No.	Name of Exam	Grade
1.	Unified Council Cyber Exam	Class 1-12
2.	Unified International English Olympiad.	Class 1-12
3.	Unified International Mathematics Olympiad (UIMO)	Class 1-12

\multicolumn{3}{c}{**By Unicus**}		
S. No.	Name of Exam	Grade
1.	Unicus Non-Routine Mathematics Olympiad (UNRMO)	Class 1-11
2.	Unicus Mathematics Olympiad (UMO)	Class 1-11
3.	Unicus Science Olympiad (USO)	Class 1-11

4.	Unicus English Olympiad (UEO)	Class 1-11
5.	Unicus Cyber Olympiad (UCO)	Class 1-11
6.	Unicus General knowledge Olympiad (UGKO)	Class 1-11
7.	Unicus Critical Thinking Olympiad (UCTO)	Class 1-11
By CREST (Online Mode)		
S. No.	Name of Exam	Grade
1.	Mathematics (CMO)	Classes KG-10
2.	Science (CSO)	Classes KG-10
3.	English (CEO)	Classes KG-10
4.	Computer (CCO)	Classes 1-10
5.	Reasoning (CRO)	Classes 1-10
6.	Spell Bee Summer (CSB)	Classes 1-8
7.	Spell Bee Winter (CSBW)	Classes 1-8
8.	Mental Maths (MMO)	Classes 1-12
9.	Green Warrior Olympiad (GWO)	Classes 1-12

How To Apply?

Anyone willing to participate in the Olympiad exam can follow these steps to apply for the exam:

- Log in to the official website of the conducting organization.
- Find the Registration Option to register
- Fill up the details such as Student Name, Parent Name, School Name, Class, Postal Address, E-mail Address, Password, etc.
- Select the subjects you want to apply for. Pay the necessary registration fees and you are done.
- You will receive necessary details on your email id.

There are no minimum marks required by the Olympiad conducting organizations to apply for the exam.

Awards

Based on the organization rules, students as well as schools participating in these exams are awarded with several recognitions based on the marks they score.

www.ingramcontent.com/pod-product-compliance
Lightning Source LLC
Chambersburg PA
CBHW062128160426
43191CB00013B/2235